WOMAN'S OWN

Book of
Fund Raising

WOMAN'S OWN

Book of
Fund Raising

COLLINS

First published in 1986 by
William Collins Sons & Co Ltd
London . Glasgow . Sydney
Auckland . Toronto . Johannesburg

Editor: Kati Nicholl
Art Editor: Petsa Kaffens

Contributors
Cookery: Trisha Davies
Home Makes: Deborah Evans
Knitting: Elizabeth Rideaux
Legal: Erica Allen

Illustrations: Maggie Sayer
Diagrams: Maggie Sayer, John
  Saunders and Jeremy Firth

Woman's own book of fund raising
1. Fund raising – Great Britain
361.7'0941   HV41

ISBN 0 00 412110 4

Typeset by V & M Graphics
Printed and bound by
William Collins, Glasgow

Contents

Introduction

On a plaque inside the vital bone marrow unit at London's Westminster Children's Hospital are inscribed words that fill everyone at *Woman's Own* with pride. And not just the staff – the readers too. The magnificent *Woman's Own* readers who raised nearly £1½ million to ensure the survival of this life-saving unit. And because of them the unit hasn't just survived – it's been expanded by ten beds. And that means hundreds more children are being given a fighting chance.

£1½ million is an awesome amount – and a sum, as far as we know, that no other magazine in the world has ever raised. Iris Burton, then Editor of *Woman's Own*, was the instigator and the driving force behind the appeal. People asked her at the time what made her think it could be done and, she says now, 'I had a sort of an answer – albeit only a gut feeling – that the generosity, ingenuity and energy that characterised our readers would *make* it work.

'And I was right. Within a week of the launch of our appeal, the offers of help rolled in – and so did the money. A few pence to thousands of pounds, a child's pocket money and an old lady's legacy – it just poured in. And most of it from women – and men and children – who had never raised a penny in their lives before. It seemed to me that throughout that year there wasn't a single street in Britain that didn't have a *Woman's Own* Fund Raiser organising coffee mornings, jumble sales, dinner and dances, sponsored walks, bazaars!'

It's their stories that inspired this book. Because along the way we all, staff and readers alike, learned a great deal about fund raising – and that's what we want to share with you.

It doesn't matter what your good cause is, whether you want to raise a few hundred or a few thousand pounds. In this book you'll find all the ideas and advice you'll need to reach your goal as we reached ours. And those words on the plaque? 'The creation of the Westminster Children's Hospital Bone Marrow Transplant Unit was largely made possible by *Woman's Own Magazine* and the generosity of its readers with the support of the Save The Children Fund.'

Kati Nichol

1
Ways to do it

If you've bought this book, then you have probably decided that you would like to raise money for a good cause – whether it's for one of the big registered charities or for a special local need like, for instance, the P.T.A., the scouts, even a costly operation for a sick child. Congratulations! But ... how successful can you expect to be? What this book sets out to show is that it is not only possible to raise a good deal of money – it can also be enormous fun. But both the success and the enjoyment depend on careful planning.

There are two ways to go about it. You can raise money as an individual and send it off to your charity or you can organise a group of people with a similar interest and pool your resources. Essentially, this book is aimed at group activities – but any individual can take ideas from it and apply them. Just remember that the money you raise has to go where you say it will and there are certain legal requirements if you want to do something big like running, for example, a jumble sale, a fête or a dinner dance. (See the chapter on Fund Raising and the Law, page 30.) And, believe us, there is a vast variety of ways to raise anything from a few pounds to a few thousand pounds. *Woman's Own* readers did just that in little over a year when they contributed £1.5 million for a new bone marrow unit at Westminster Children's Hospital in London. How they did it, in groups or individually, has provided many of the ideas you will find in the following pages. We hope they will inspire you in your efforts.

SETTING UP A COMMITTEE

You will see that, although there are lots of ways of raising money through individual efforts, the most effective fund raising is definitely a group activity. And a group means a committee. Don't be scared off by the formal sound of it. Setting up a committee really is the most sensible way of distributing the work load and getting things done. It can meet around the kitchen table – or more grandly in the local hall – but essentially it will make life a lot easier for everyone and get you to your goal more quickly.

The usual set up is: a Chairperson; a Secretary to take care of the minutes of the meetings and write letters; a Treasurer to handle the finances; two organisers of events. Five is a good number because you can never have a 'hung' group! You can then co-opt people who have specialist knowledge or expertise in the areas you require (seriously, no one person is great at everything!). By all means have a larger committee if you want it – but the more voices you have, generally speaking, the more chance of dissension.

Your first decision must be the target figure – how much money you want to raise. And if your objective is to support a number of causes or charities you must also decide what proportion you want to give to each (no point in coming to blows over who gets what once you've raised the money).

Ideally, your Treasurer should have a book-keeping background – retired accountants can often be persuaded to give their services for a good cause. But someone 'good at figures' and fairly precise can usually be found among most groups. For it is essential that the proper books are kept from the outset – money raised, money spent, expenses etc.

Registered charities (see page 46) must have clearly written rules about accounts and funds, but it's not a bad idea for all groups to establish similar rules so that there can be no financial misunderstandings. One of the Treasurer's tasks is to look after any money collected. If your fund raising is to be a long term affair, then he or she will have to arrange to deposit the bulk of the money taken in a place where it will gather interest – a Building Society or bank deposit account, or a short-term investment scheme. A current account should also be opened so that there is easily-available working capital to use when you are organising events. At least one other person in the group must have access to this account in case of illness or un-availability of the Treasurer.

Your committee's Secretary will be responsible for confirming booking arrangements, writing to companies for donations (see page 44), writing thank you letters, etc. He or she should be able to write exciting, informative but succinct letters and keep minutes of meetings fully, with notes of precisely who has agreed to do what. He or she should also be responsible for drawing up a mailing list of all possible contacts for donations, noting who actually did donate and keeping in touch with them when any function is being organised.

Your organisers should be enthusiastic and energetic, prepared to give their time unstintingly and know at the planning stage how much available time they have. It's no good saying at the critical point that they are too busy.

Most important of all, the Chairperson must be able to do everyone's job at the drop of a hat (emergencies always occur) and be able to command everyone's attention with a firm word.

The people you co-opt must be clear about what they're doing, when they have to do it and be certain that they can do it. And while the Chairperson or Secretary can find out the legal requirements for any event you decide to hold, if you can co-opt someone with a legal background to do such checking, so much the better.

Try to hold your committee meetings on a regular basis each week, fortnight or month. As your planned event approaches you may find you need an extra meeting or two to finalise all the details.

Right, let's presume you have your basic committee, you know what you're raising money for, and you have decided what your target figure is. What can you do to raise money?

PLANNING

Once you've decided what to do, you must decide who is going to do what and how much time they have to do it in. Everyone should have written instructions and a check list (see our recommended check list on page 173) of what they're doing (and notes of what everyone else is doing to avoid duplication) so that nothing gets forgotten.

And you must make your fund-raising events suitable to the talent you have available. It's no good having a Craft Stall if none of you can knit, sew or work in wood. It is much better to stick to what you know and do it well. Be aware, too, of how much time you have available to work on projects – some projects, as you'll see, are more time-consuming than others.

If you plan to hold regular fund-raising events where you'll be catering, it's well worth obtaining a cash and carry card. Buying in bulk obviously saves you money and time. Some cash and carry stores are for trade customers only and these are usually the cheapest stores. However, if you apply for a card on your official notepaper, you may be given one for your group's use.

PUBLICITY

If your Secretary has the time, he or she can probably handle the publicity. If not, do appoint a publicity officer whose duty it is to write enticing posters and to contact the press. In any fund-raising project the help of a local newspaper, TV or radio station can't be underestimated. Because the more people who know about your event before it takes place, the higher the attendance will be. Photographs and a story afterwards can lead to donations from those who couldn't make it. Most local newspapers have sections where you can advertise your craft fair/jumble sale etc. at no charge.

Your local library will have all the information you need on useful addresses and telephone numbers and your publicity officer ought to make contact with an individual reporter with whom she can build up a relationship. And if you're running a competition, invite the Editor of the local newspaper, or a TV or radio personality to be one of the judges. Perhaps you have a celebrity living locally who would be willing to help.

PROGRAMMES

These can provide an extra means of making money at any event. You may have to pay a local printer to print the programme of events at whatever function you are running, or he may donate his services free. In any case, the basis of the programme is what's happening and when – for example, if it's a fête you list the events as follows:

2.00 pm: Beautiful Baby Competition
2.30 pm: Dancing Display
3.00 pm: Parachute Jump
3.30 pm: Marching Bands Competition

You then approach local businesses and sell them advertising space in the pages around the list of events and, in the programme, you can also give thanks to anyone who has donated goods or services to the event.

Use the programme, also, to give information about your group, its aims and efforts, and include an address to write to for those interested in helping you.

SPONSORSHIP

Many large companies set aside part of their budget each year for charity. Obviously, the later in the year you contact them the less money they will have available, so if possible write early for Christmas donations, such as turkeys. Approach them either through someone who works for them locally or write direct to the Promotions or Marketing Director (a phone call will give you a name to write to – the personal approach is best!). Keep your letter brief and to the point. Say *why* you are raising money, *what* you intend doing (a raffle at a fair, a tombola at a dance, for instance), *how many* people will be at the function, what publicity you expect and how their company's name will be displayed (if you are producing a programme or list of donations). Being blunt, the name of the game is to promote the company, not simply to give to a good cause. However, some companies sometimes don't want to be identified. If you have ever raised money before, tell them how much you raised, and how you did it and send press cuttings if you have them.

What you're looking for is either a financial contribution or a material contribution – items that will make attractive prizes in a raffle or tombola, for example. Because people who go to fêtes and fairs are looking for bargains and the chance to win something for next-to-nothing. Go for cameras, television sets, music centres, expensive soft toys, holidays (travel firms can be a good source of prizes), theatre tickets, glassware, china, cutlery, electrical goods and so on. Things that people will *want*. If you are doing your own catering for a barbecue, dinner and dance etc., try to get some of the food donated – sausages, cheese, meats. It all helps to cut your costs!

Here are suggestions for different ways of raising money. **Now select your idea!**

JUMBLE SALES

These are always good fund raisers and, after paying for the hire of the hall and whatever advertising you've done, all the money you take is profit. Check the legal section on page 39 for regulations concerning jumble sales and also see our comments on planning on page 11.

You'll need a hall – a local church or school hall – and you can get a list of the ones which are available for hire from the reference section of your local library. Go round and have a look at them and decide which one is best – it's got to be easy to get to and be big enough for people to walk round easily to see the goods.

As Saturday is the most popular day for holding jumble sales (and if you plan to hold yours then) you may find you have to wait some weeks before the hall is free. In the summer, however, you could consider holding the sale early in the evening, during the week.

Check that the day you've chosen doesn't clash with any big local function or holiday and be sure that all your organisers/helpers are available during the week before to collect jumble and are free on the day itself to run stalls.

Type up leaflets asking for jumble, giving the day, time and venue of the jumble sale also, and pop them through the letterboxes of local houses. Give a day you will be collecting in that particular street, or phone numbers to ring so that you can collect jumble from them, or state a day when they can bring their jumble direct to you. It's a good idea for someone's garage to be used as the collection point for the jumble. You can also advertise for jumble in the local newspaper.

You must, of course, advertise the event itself. You can make up your own posters and display them locally in shops, the library, town hall, etc., and your leaflets asking for jumble will have been an advert in themselves. Make sure it's clear where the sale is being held and at what time, and what the charitable cause is.

Sort out and clearly label the jumble before you take it to the hall – you may only have the morning before the sale to set things up. And be stringent about what you actually choose to sell – jumble doesn't mean rubbish. If some of the clothing is in very good condition, have a 'Nearly New' stall where you can charge that bit more.

Display the goods according to type – women's summer wear, men's winter wear, children's clothes, baby clothes, bric-a-brac, and so on.

Most jumble sales ask for a small admission charge of, say, 10p, and you'll need someone on the door of the hall to collect this.

Pin large, clear notices on the wall behind each stall so that customers can aim for the stall they're interested in. And remember, each stall holder will need a cash float with plenty of small change and a secure place to keep the money.

Have a stall selling refreshments. Most halls have kitchens where you can make tea and coffee. Check the hot water urn and put it on in good time! Make small cakes, biscuits and nibbles to serve with the tea and coffee and offer soft drinks as well. You could also have a stall near the refreshment area selling well-wrapped home-made cakes and biscuits (see Cook It To Sell on pages 49–107 for things to make).

You won't sell everything – so, if you plan to hold regular jumble sales and have storage facilities, sort out, from jumble left over, any that can be sold next time. Otherwise make an arrangement with a local used clothes dealer before the sale to come and take everything that's left when the sale closes. The hall's owners won't want your jumble remains! And make sure you leave the hall clean and tidy – you may want to use it again one day.

SUMMER FAIR

Hire a field for this one! Again, schools and churches are your best bet but check your local library – and maybe one of your friends has a very large garden they wouldn't mind lending.

Essentials

Do read the legal section on page 41 and do have a First Aid Post. Check out the British Red Cross Society or St. John's Ambulance Brigade in the Yellow Pages or local telephone directory and ask them for assistance (remember you'll need to make a donation) and check whether or not they supply their own tent and bed. Consult your local police about car parking facilities.

Remember that you'll be spending a good bit of money to get the fair operating – you may have to hire tables and chairs for the stalls and tea tent – so you must charge sensible prices on all the items you sell in order to make a profit. Don't forget a float for each stall!

Publicity is vital! Advertise the fair well in advance of the day with posters, leaflets to schools and shops, and place an advert in the local paper if necessary. Contact your local radio station, TV station, newspaper. They're always looking for neighbour-hood news and might give you a free mention if they have a 'what's going on this weekend' spot.

Decide what stalls and games you're going to have and how many people you'll need to run them. It's a good idea to go for variety but do place items for sale in groups. Have a look at the Spring/Summer recipes on page 51 and the Anytime recipes on page 82 for things to make for your food stalls and refreshment tent. See page 175 at the end of the book for a list of addresses of where to hire things like inflatables, candy floss machines, stalls, games, tents, etc.

Stalls should be attractively laid out and clearly advertised – two poles, firmly stuck in the ground or tied to table legs, with a banner (made from an old white sheet) strung between saying, in large letters, what's on sale is all that's needed.

Select from – or choose all of – the following:

Craft stall: knitted/crochet items; macramé; patchwork; needlepoint, etc.

Fashion stall: jewellery; new clothes (try local shops for donations); accessories (see Make It To Sell on page 119 for ideas of things to make).

Cake stall: just check out Cook It To Sell for everything you need! But on this stall you could also have a 'Guess the Weight of the Cake' competition. Have entry forms ready and at least three pens on long bits of string attached to the table. For a small fee entrants write down their guess and their names and addresses. If

they win, they get the cake and you can announce the winner at the end of the day.

Baby stall: doting grandparents can't resist home-made baby things, so devote one stall solely to sewn and knitted items for baby. There are some lovely ideas for robes, bags and mats on page 138 if you can sew. But don't forget to price goods properly – check what local shops are charging for mass-produced items and don't ever sell your goods for less than they've cost to make.

Book and record stall: collect second-hand books well in advance from everyone you know and lay them out by category – romance, crime, children's, and so on. The same with records. Charge according to condition.

Tombola: approach your local shop-keepers for donations to this. All the items have a number and you sell identically numbered raffle tickets to win them. But you can sell twice or even three times as many tickets as there are prizes but you must remember to sell only one ticket of each numbered prize.

Food stall: jams, preserves pâtés, sweets, breads, home-made wine, vinegars and so on. You'll find all the recipes you need in Cook It To Sell on page 49. Cover your stall with a clean white tablecloth and decorate the table with fresh flowers to give it appeal. Label all the goods clearly, listing the contents, date made, how long they will keep, whether they can be frozen, and the price. See page 34 for rules and regulations about food.

Tea tent: no fair is complete without a tea tent! As far as possible, collect donations of cakes and buns (people baking for the cake stall could do some extra) and if there's a friendly biscuit or cake factory in the neighbourhood, approach the manager nicely and ask for a contribution (see page 44 for advice on requesting donations). And you can always ask the local baker, too. But you will have to purchase tea, coffee, soft drinks, milk, sugar, bread, margarine and fillings for sandwiches. You'll need paper cups, plastic spoons, paper napkins, paper plates, a hot water urn, ice to pack the soft drinks in (if possible) and most of all you'll need a good team of sandwich-makers!

Remember to charge a fair price to cover the cost of the materials you've bought and the hire of any catering materials you might need, as well as allowing a profit margin for the charity.

Bric-a-brac stall: small items like old jewellery, pretty ornaments, knick-knacks.

White elephant stall: assorted anythings of the larger sort!

Toy stall: used toys, home-made and knitted toys (see Make It To Sell on page 109).

Plant stall: cuttings, houseplants, bedding plants and so on (see page 163 for ideas). You could also include items like bags of pot pourri (see page 166) and dried flowers (page 165).

Good as new stall: divide into men's, women's and children's (try to have three tables) and display the garments as attractively as you can so that they look new. Price them sensibly.

SIDE SHOWS

If you're organising a fête with stalls selling items, don't forget to organise side shows as well. You may be able to hire equipment from local organisations like the Round Table or the church, or check The Showman's Directory (Stephen & Jean Lance Publications) at your local library. This lists every type of equipment needed for fairs and gives suppliers and hirers – there's also a section on entertainers. You'll need attractive prizes –

but most visitors will have a go at the side shows just for fun, and as a way of supporting the charity rather than in any serious attempt to win the prize. Here are some ideas which do not need specially built equipment.

Treasure Trove
Your customers have to find the winning square under which the treasure trove is buried!

Draw out a map on a large sheet of paper. The map can represent a 'Treasure Island' with beaches, jungle, mountain and rocks, or it could be based on your own town or village. Make the map about 60 cm x 120 cm (2 ft x 4 ft). Draw a grid of lines 2.5 cm (1 inch) apart over the map. This will give you over 1,000 squares – you could reduce the number for example by covering only the land with the grid. On the back of the map, mark with a soft crayon the winning square, ensuring that there is no sign of the mark on the right side of the map. (Alternatively, label the squares by numbering each row in one direction and assigning a letter to each line in the other direction. Decide on the winning square and put the combination into a sealed envelope.)

Mount the map on a piece of soft board. Take as many cocktail sticks as there are squares on the paper and make a flag out of paper for each one and stick it on with adhesive tape (or alternatively, use ready-pasted or self-adhesive envelope labels). Charge a fee per turn according to the costs involved in producing your map. Each customer writes his name (and phone number if necessary) on a flag, and sticks it in a square (only one flag per square). At the end of the fair the winner is announced and awarded the prize which, hopefully, a local trader will have donated.

Bottle stalls
Ask local shops for donations of bottles of

food and drink and organise a 'bottle bank' whereby supporters can donate a bottle to the stall at weekly meetings.

Approach local guide and scout groups, put up notices at evening classes and schools in the area. You'll soon build up a good selection of bottles. Another idea is to collect empty bottles, then buy in bulk to fill them: bath salts, herbs, muesli made up from cereal and nuts from local health food stores. Or make vats of jam and chutney to fill them. (See page 62 for recipes and page 34 for regulations concerning food preparation.)

Stick one half of a raffle ticket on each bottle and arrange them on the stall. Keep back a supply of bottles and tickets to fill the tables as people win their prizes. Put the best bottles in the middle at the back, raised up on boxes, and hope that the first customers don't win them! The other halves of the raffle tickets are then placed in a drawstring bag. Customers pay a good price and draw out a ticket. Everyone gets a prize, so people don't mind paying quite high stakes.

Test of strength

Test your customers' strength and co-ordination with a hammer and nail competition. Set a long block of wood, at least 10 cm (4 inches) square, on to a bench, clamping it firmly in place. You will also need a medium weight hammer and a large supply of 5 cm (2 inch) nails.

Knock each nail 14 mm (½ inch) into the wood, so everyone has an equal chance. Charge each customer per go. The aim is to knock the nail home in as few blows of the hammer as possible (misses count as blows!) To attract as many customers as possible, divide entrants into several categories: men, women, under 15s, under 10s. Note down names of high (or low) scorers. If there are several entrants tying for first prize at the end of the day, hold a

'hammer off' with a lighter hammer and longer nails.

Holiday snaps

Use a Polaroid camera to take snaps of visitors to the fair. Remember that Polaroid film is expensive, so you'll probably have to charge quite substantially per print to show much profit. You can also make the snaps more fun by painting seaside postcard characters, or cartoon characters, on to a piece of plywood. Then cut out ovals for the faces so that customers can put their heads through, while you take a photo.

Tests of judgement

A quick way to raise money at fêtes and fairs is to ask people to use their judgement at guessing games. You'll need an exercise book (or printed sheets) to write down names and guesses. You can sit at a stall, but better still wander around the event in pairs (one to take the money and note the guess, another to carry the item). If you approach people directly they'll find it difficult to refuse to have a go.

This is a good way to keep people at the event all afternoon – but tell them at what time the winner will be announced, and take down their name and address if they are not staying until the 'prize-giving'.

Some ideas for guessing games:
Guess the length of a ball of string
Guess the number of sweets in a jar
Guess the number of (or value of) coins in a piggy bank
Guess the number of stitches on a piece of knitting (make up a panel or scarf using a random selection of stitches, and changing to different needle sizes using a mixture of textured yarns)
Guess the weight of the cake (see page 14)
Guess the number of coffee beans in a large sealed plastic bag
Guess the number of sequins on a Pearly Queen's outfit (or on a ball gown)

COMPETITIONS

Arrange a seating area, and hold competitions so that people can sit and be entertained in between making their purchases.

Fancy dress: charge an entrance fee. Give prizes in two or three age categories. Suggest a theme for the competition to suit the theme of your fair, for example, circus characters, hallowe'en characters, even pop songs.

Exercise bike races: borrow a set of exercise bikes from a local gym. Charge an entrance fee and see who can pedal the fastest in 30 seconds. The winner of each heat can go in to a final.

Dog shows: you don't have to belong to a kennel club to hold a show. Local children can bring along their pets and a panel of judges selects the most obedient or best groomed. (You don't have to limit the competition to dogs – why not a cat obedience competition?)

Baby shows: select a panel of judges – the owner of a local childrens' clothes shop, a midwife or matron from the maternity hospital – and ask them to pick out the best baby or toddler at the fête: criteria for judging should include looks, behaviour, general development (how old they were when they said their first words/took their first steps). Again, charge a reasonable entry fee. Perhaps the owner of the local childrens' clothes shop could donate the prizes. Make satin sashes for the winners to wear.

Glamorous granny/knobbly knees/ beauty contests: organise these along the same lines as the baby show.

INDOOR GAMES

Spin A Number: for this you need a large board on which you draw a circle and divide it into ten parts, writing on each a number from one to ten. You'll need an arrow that spins in the centre of the board. On each game, sell all ten parts and while one person spins the arrow, the other collects the money (charge per go) and drums up custom. Prizes can be bottles of cider (not for younger winners!) or a can of soft drinks or chocolate bars. Display the variety of prizes with the winning numbers but keep the bulk of the prizes under the table – it lessens the chance of accidents.

Pick An Egg: you'll need a table, a box about 6 cm (2½ inches) deep, a dozen hard-boiled eggs (in their shells), two dozen used eggshells and sand to half-fill the box. (You can make up more than one box if you expect a lot of people.) Put the sand in the box, write the prize on the bottom of the whole eggs, bury the half eggshells so that they look like whole eggs and bury the whole eggs among them. Entrants pay a small entrance fee and try to pick a whole egg. If successful, they win the prize written on their egg. Try to get all the prizes donated by local shops.

Computers: if you can persuade a local shop to lend you a couple of computers, screens and software games, you'll make a fortune from children attending the bazaar. If you undertake to display a placard saying who's loaned the computers, and where they can be bought, most shops will go for the publicity value. Check whether you'll need extension leads and extra plugs if there aren't many electric points at your venue. Charge for, say, three minutes a go with no child having more than six minutes at a time unless there's no one waiting. You'll have to make sure there's a responsible adult present throughout to take charge and load the games if the child doesn't know how to.

CHRISTMAS BAZAAR

A fair indoors! Check out your local halls

at the library, choose the one that's most convenient, book it well in advance of the day you've planned to hold the bazaar and publicise it with posters, leaflets through doors, adverts in the local paper (see page 11). Check the legal section on page 39 for licences, insurance, etc.

Decorate the hall if you can with a Christmas tree, holly, green and red balloons, red and green bunting.

Decide what you're going to sell, who's going to make what, how many helpers you'll need on the day and also for collecting goods and decorating the hall and for setting up the stalls. Don't forget your cash float for each stall!

As well as tea, coffee and sandwiches, serve mince pies on your refreshment stall to give a Christmas flavour, and perhaps you could persuade someone to do roast chestnuts on a barbecue outside.

Have a look at the Autumn/Winter recipe ideas on page 62 for edible goods to make and sell; and also have plenty of items like covered coat hangers (page 135) and make-up bags (page 128) because they make ideal gifts that people will want to buy.

Have a Tombola stall (you'll need lots of prizes) and also run a raffle. Persuade a local shopkeeper to donate a super soft toy, a Christmas hamper, a turkey, or whatever as the prize. If you can get more than one prize, so much the better. And advertise them on your publicity leaflets.

CAR BOOT SALES

These are increasingly popular as a way of getting rid of items you no longer want. But they're also a useful way to raise funds for charity.

You can run one yourself – you'll need to hire a field or a car park or school playground to do so – and you'll have to check with your local police about licences, safety factors and so on. Check how many cars and tables your area will hold and if your group can't use all the space, advertise for other groups or individuals to buy space at your event and charge them for their pitch. Or you can hire space from some other organisation (if it's for charity, the fee is often waived) which has space to fill.

Make sure everyone knows that the goods on your stall are for sale for a charity, or the local P.T.A. or church roof fund, etc. Pin up a large poster, and ask friends and family for their unwanted goods.

You'll need a table to display your goods, clearly-marked pricing labels – and a cash float to get started.

GARAGE SALE

This is easy to run as an individual and is a good way to dispose of large unwanted items *and* benefit your favourite charity at the same time.

If you ask you might find your neighbours have the odd wardrobe or old iron bedstead they've been promising to take to the dump but haven't. So ask around and when you know approximately what you have to sell, put an advert in the local paper saying where and when the sale will take place. Decide what the lowest price is that you will accept for each item and allow customers to make you an offer – what's junk to you is a treasure to them so you may get a surprise at how much they're willing to pay!

PARTY SALES

You can buy anything from make-up to pottery, jewellery to fashion clothes at home these days, not just Tupperware! Check your Yellow Pages to find out who's selling what and ask your friends, too. Then contact the representative and ask if she/he would be willing to give 10% of the profit to your charity if you hold a party in your house for the sale of goods to your friends. (See the legal section on page 36.) Decide how many people your house will hold comfortably and hand out that number of invitations (friends can give to friends if you don't know enough people personally). Hand round coffee and tea, or wine and nibbles while people view (you could make a small charge to cover the cost of refreshments). The representative brings the goods, takes the orders, delivers the items, and gives you 10% of the profit for your charity.

COFFEE MORNINGS

These are a great way to get started on the fund-raising bandwagon. You invite a small group of friends and relations to coffee-and-cake and make a small charge. Increase your takings by doing a bring-and-buy sale at the same time – children's toys, clothes, jewellery, whatever the group's main interest is – or run a raffle. One *Woman's Own* reader, Sheila Lovie, raised the fantastic sum of £1,895 for charity by doing six hours of sponsored patchwork cushion making. She then held a coffee morning to raffle the cushions. 60 adults and 40 children came! Now, you wouldn't normally expect to make anything like that sum, but what you do make can either be sent direct to the charity or used to fund a larger project – a jumble sale or bazaar. Check out the legal section on page 36 for advice on insurance, etc.

CHEESE AND WINE PARTIES

These serve much the same function as coffee mornings and can be great fun as well as being worthwhile. If you ask enough people you could probably run a small tombola to give added interest. Make sure you know how many people are coming. If you ask friends to ask friends, tell them to let you know how many have accepted *before* you buy the wine and cheese. Getting payment in advance from those coming is also a good idea! Ask your local wine merchant to let you have the wine on sale or return and see if he'll loan you glasses free, or buy plastic ones from a cash and carry. Check the legal section (page 36) for advice on licences, insurance and so on.

DINNER AND DANCE

You'll need a fair amount of cash up-front to hold a dinner and dance because you'll either have to hire a hall, or a marquee (summer only!), or a restaurant with a dance floor. If the owners of your venue are agreeable, there's no reason why you can't tackle the catering yourself, providing you plan well ahead and serve a basically cold buffet with one hot dish and rice, potatoes, or pasta dish. Check out the kitchen facilities at the venue and the time you can start using them. Get everyone to make their own special dish and make sure that you've got enough variety – one savoury dish to three puddings doesn't make for a satisfying meal!

If you're holding your dance in a restaurant, the owners will often be happy to cater for you. Negotiate a price per head and be clear what this includes – always confirm in writing.

Alternatively, have the function catered for privately. Check your Yellow Pages for local caterers and ask for sample menus and prices – then get names of people who've used them in the recent past and find out how good they are.

See if you can hire a group or band (back to the Yellow Pages!) and do the same sort of checking. Confirm how many of them there will be and whether or not their fee will include food and drinks. Perhaps offer supper and one free drink – free drinks all night for a band of six can be expensive!

If you are supplying your own wine, etc., try to buy on a sale or return basis and look for free glass loan. If the owners of the venue are selling the drinks, try to negotiate a reduction in their normal bar prices – pin up a notice saying 'Messrs Bloggs have kindly agreed to reduce their bar prices in aid of...'

Book your hall, marquee or restaurant well ahead of time and plan the evening down to the very last detail. Are you going to have a cabaret? If so, what? Many entertainers will give their services free or at a much-reduced rate for charity, or you might persuade the local dancing school to put on a display (children always go down well at functions).

And you must have a raffle, or a tombola, or both. Try and persuade a local business to give you something really special (Jackie Berger, who organised a dinner and dance to raise money for the *Woman's Own* Bone Marrow Appeal, managed to get a gold necklace worth £800 out of one jeweller and a ferry crossing for one car and four people out of a travel agent. Her function raised £12,000!).

Make sure that you have plenty of helpers, that everyone knows who's doing what and that you have stand-bys for emergencies. If you can organise older teenagers into a baby-sitting service for the night, that too will add to funds. Approach your local school for volunteers and advertise the service when you advertise the event.

If you have any sort of mailing list send details out well in advance and ask people to send their cheques to you by a certain date. Perhaps give an incentive reduction on pre-paid tickets.

Posters in shop windows telling people where the function is to be held, when and where they can buy tickets and how much they are, must be put up well in advance so that you can finalise the numbers for your catering at least a week before the big night. Advertise in the local paper, and if you're going to run any sort of competition during the evening (a talent or beauty contest) ask the Editor to be a judge. That guarantees you free publicity after the event which might bring in more donations!

Check the legal section on page 38 for advice on insurance, safety, licences and so on, and the list of addresses on page 175 of where to hire marquees and other catering equipment.

FASHION SHOW

Here you really do need expert help! If you have a local department store you can approach the manager and see if they will lend you garments from the store for the function, or even run the show in the store itself. You tell the store manager that the store will be given full credit, which will encourage the audience to go and buy there.

If you decide to organise it yourself, you'll need to hire a hall with a stage and appropriate changing accommodation for your models; and have someone who knows about stage lighting to light it. Approach your local amateur dramatic society (local library should have a list) and see if their lighting person will donate his services.

Go to all your local boutiques and ask if they'll supply garments and promise them plenty of publicity. Choose your models (one of the boutique people might help here) and arrange for someone to provide music. Check the number of electrical points.

You'll need at least two dress rehearsals and lots of helpers to get the models in and out of the clothes. Make sure there's plenty of hanging space and well-lit make-up mirrors.

Serve wine to the audience (price two glasses in with the price of the tickets) and coffee and snacks at the interval (see page 90 for snack ideas). **Don't** serve anything to the models until all the clothes are safely packed away!

Advertise the show well in advance by putting posters in local shops, mailing all your contacts and placing an ad in the local paper. Invite the Woman's Page Editor of the paper to cover the show and contact your local radio and TV stations. Meta McComb of Belfast organised just such a show for the *Woman's Own* Bone Marrow Appeal and raised £2000.

Check the legal section on page 38 for insurance advice, licences and so on.

FILM SHOW

If you're a large group you can probably attract enough people to fill a cinema. Approach your local cinema and see if you can either hire the cinema or whether there's any chance of the management donating it for a Sunday morning (especially for children's shows) or a late night screening. Ideally, you'll want to screen a movie that hasn't been seen in your area and the manager will be able to tell you which film companies to approach to rent the film from. Publicise the event for at least a couple of weeks before and be sure you have enough advance bookings to cover your expenses. Remember, you may have to hire a projectionist, cleaners, cashiers, a confectionery stand person if they are unwilling to donate their services free.

CONCERT

One school of dancing raised £300 by putting on a show for the *Woman's Own* Bone Marrow Appeal and if you're involved in such a school, either as a teacher or parent, it's worth considering this sort of event. You'll need a hall, of course, and plenty of helpers to cope with the costumes and the make-up and it's best if you can do two shows – a matinée and an early evening. Have a refreshment stall in the foyer serving tea, coffee and buns – and a sweet and soft drink stall for juniors.

You can, of course, put on a really big concert by approaching local personalities to do a turn. This will mean hiring a theatre (see Yellow Pages), stagehands, lighting experts, musicians and so on. All of which means a lot of money up-front so you have to be pretty certain you can attract an audience that will pay enough to make it worthwhile. Have a word with your local theatre manager and see what he thinks the possibilities are and whether or not he'd be willing to volunteer his services to help you plan things. If you do decide to go ahead, you'll have to plan well in advance. First check the dates your 'acts' have free and see which ones coincide with a good date to give the concert. It's not worthwhile doing one in mid-summer in an industrial town when most people are off at the seaside, for instance!

You'll need music licences, insurance and so on, so check the legal section on page 40. Also the services of the St. John's Ambulance people (see Yellow Pages). And whatever sort of show you put on, publicise it well beforehand. Send information to your local paper, radio, TV station and advertise heavily with posters in shops and ads in the local paper.

BEETLE DRIVES

You'll need a hall, tables, chairs, cards, pencils, dice for every table, slips of paper to give the winning totals, and a couple of people to walk round ensuring there's no cheating (you'd be amazed!).

The object of the exercise is for groups of four people to play against one another in trying to draw a beetle – one head, one body, six legs, two eyes and two antennae – by throws of the dice. You have to throw a six for the body, a five for the head, four for the eyes, three for the antennae, two for the legs. The winners from each table play against each other until you have one supreme winner who receives ... whatever you've got as the main prize. Those who aren't winners play against each other for fun!

Serve refreshments included in the ticket price – first check out the facilities to determine whether refreshments can be hot or cold – and, if you've had donations from local shops as prizes, run a raffle. Adults and children both get great fun from this.

Publicise the event with posters in local shops and check the legal section on page 36 for Whist Drives.

WHIST DRIVES

Same as Beetle Drives except you play Whist!

BINGO

You can play Bingo for money or prizes but check the legal section on page 37 because the law differs according to which you do.

For Bingo you'll need cards, pencils, numbers in a drum or a hat, a caller and a couple of checkers as well as a hall, tables, chairs and a refreshment stall – Bingo's thirsty work! The object of the exercise is to cross out the numbers on your card as the caller pulls them from the drum or the hat. The first person to complete their card wins.

Charge an entrance fee which includes one game then charge for each game thereafter. You can play as many cards as you like so long as you pay for each one. One local Cubs group reckons to make £80 on a Bingo night, so it's both a profitable and enjoyable way to raise money. Ask local businesses, or people in the group to donate prizes.

TOURNAMENTS

For the *Woman's Own* Bone Marrow Appeal, one group ran a snooker tournament that made £686. The tables were sponsored by local businessmen and you could adapt this idea to lots of sports – tennis, football, squash, cricket and so on. Organise your tournament in conjunction with a local club and charge the audience for admission. Get the entrants to find their own sponsors.

Serve refreshments at the interval (for an outdoor summer tournament, try selling the popcorn made from the recipes on page 99), and at a winter football match try to organise hot dogs, or baked potatoes and hot soup. Publicise the event well ahead of time in shop windows, local papers and so on. Get participants and fund raisers to stick posters in their home and office windows. (Read the relevant legal section on page 41.)

STUNTS

Always fun and always good for publicity in the local paper at least and sometimes, if it's a light day for news, on TV as well. Let your local radio, TV and newspaper know in advance what you're doing, when you're starting, how long you think it's going to take, and where the stunt is going to take place.

The basic idea is to do something funny, entertaining and highly visible. Like pushing a bed a given number of miles with other night-clad members of the group walking along with cans and collecting money from passers-by. Here are some of the ways other people have gone about it:

Steve Driver of Cambridge spent nine days and nights lying in a bath of cold pasta (yuck!) and raised nearly £1,000 for his local hospital.

Army chaplain Father John McMillan played the bagpipes and waterskied at the same time – he raised over £2,500.

Jenny Tootal had herself strapped to the wing of a 1937 Tiger Moth and flew over RAF Hullavington. She raised £1,000 for Gliding for the Disabled.

200 people pulled Concorde five miles round Duxford airfield. Concorde weighs 100 tons and it took them all day – but they raised thousands of pounds for a children's charity.

Sergeant Dave Ford and a seven-man team abseiled down the Post Office Tower [147 metres (484 ft)] and raised £10,000 for the Children's Hospital, Gt. Ormond Street.

However, simpler methods include: laying a mile of pennies (get permission from the police to hold it in a central spot, like a shopping centre and publicise it well so that lots of people come with their pennies); a pancake race; egg-and-spoon race; seeing how many people you can pile into a small car or telephone box.

Always check with local police that it's okay with them if you do your stunt in a public place and make sure that you have plenty of people around with the collecting boxes. See the legal section on page 42 for advice.

SPONSORING

The idea of sponsoring is that you do something and somebody else pays you so much per mile, or per minute, to do it. However, unless you get a fair number of sponsors it isn't worthwhile.

Here are some very successful examples of sponsoring: Debbie Bradley of Gosport raised £50 for the *Woman's Own* Bone Marrow Appeal – by staying silent! She got friends and relatives to back her to stay quiet so she obviously had a lot of sponsors to raise £50. The 4½ to 7 year olds at one school raised over £900, also by staying silent, and the 2nd year pupils at Poynton County High School raised over £800 on a sponsored spelling contest! Not only raising money but learning, too. Mr. Charlewood of Purley, though, must be heading for the record books. He raised an incredible £3,445 by competing in the London Marathon for the *Woman's Own* Bone Marrow Appeal.

Other things that attract sponsors are walks, runs, parachute jumps (get in touch with the British Parachute Association, address on page 175), doing aerobics, dancing, cycling, giving up smoking, slimming, knitting, 'toddles' (Tina Eckent and Anne Railton of Newcastle-on-Tyne organised a spon-sored 'toddle' for mums and children round a local park and raised £153 for the *Woman's Own* Bone Marrow Appeal). In fact, almost anything you can think of will find sponsors!

And everyone can find something to do

regardless of their age.

Decide what you're going to do and then prepare your sponsor forms. They should be quite simple: the name of the charity or appeal at the top, the name and address of the participant and what he or she intends to do. Beneath that, rule off four sections vertically and as many as you can horizontally. The first column is for the name and address of the sponsor, the second is for the amount being sponsored, the third is for the sponsor's signature when the participant goes back for the money, and the fourth column is for the total paid by the sponsor. At the bottom of the form there should be a line that says, 'The above participant swam ..... metres in aid of .... (charity's name). Signed .... Official Steward.'

When you approach your sponsors, give them an idea of how much you're likely to swim, walk or whatever, and where children are concerned don't be surprised if they do three times as much as you think they will. That way the sponsors don't get a shock when you demand their money.

If you're organising a sponsored run, walk or swim, you simply must make the event as safe as possible. Involve an expert and take his or her advice on what you'll need – refreshment points, medical stand-bys, maps of the route for all participants, plenty of stewards, or lifeguards to ensure safety. On a sponsored walk or a run you must keep an accurate checklist of who went out and when – and check them in at the end. Have cars and first-aid attendants on hand to rescue drop-outs in trouble and, if you want to do a street collection, make sure that you have the necessary licence well before the big day (see page 30).

Advertise your event and try to get a celebrity to start it off; contact your local paper, TV and radio station and try to persuade them to send someone along to cover the event. Check out the legal section on page 42 for advice on insurance and safety – it's vital.

CAROL SINGING

Singing round the houses is all very well but it's a pretty slow way of making money unless you can bring people out of their houses with amplified carols from a car-drawn 'sledge' carrying a Santa Claus. It's far better to get permission from the police to sing in a busy shopping thoroughfare, outside Tube or railway stations, or in shopping centres. That way you can have helpers with collection cans persuading the passers-by to part with their money while the singers concentrate on singing.

Children under 16 *must* be accompanied by an adult and if you have a large group of children, you should have at least one adult to every 10 children – you must keep check of where they are. See the legal section on page 30 for further advice. And take along some flasks of hot tea or coffee to comfort cold singers and collectors.

COLLECTIONS

The legal section on page 30 lists all the rules and regulations on this. It's a good way to raise money but you must have permission and you must not let children under 16 collect money if they're not accompanied by an adult. And remember that politeness is everything – be persuasive but don't bully.

If you're collecting in the streets, try to have something going on that interests people and makes them want to give – an exercise bike marathon, display of dancing, street mime or something of the sort, but do remember to get police permission.

If you're collecting in pubs, do ask the landlord's permission first. If it's your local he may be agreeable to your having a raffle in the pub, too – everyone who donates gets a free raffle ticket for a prize to be drawn at, say, half an hour before closing time. The landlord may even donate a bottle as the prize!

AUCTIONS

Hold a mini-auction at home among friends during a coffee morning, or wine and cheese evening – you'll be surprised at how valuable your unwanted trinkets can be to someone else!

At a big function (a dinner and dance, fair etc.), try to persuade local businesses to donate some really good items for auction – china, glassware and so on. Or contact a well-known personality and ask for something personal that you can auction. Valuable pieces of craftwork like patchwork quilts or hand-made dolls' houses can raise a lot of money because they are individual. One *Woman's Own* reader raised £100 for charity while she was in hospital by making a quilt and auctioning it. If someone you know has a talent for making things, ask if they'll donate their time to make something if you supply the money for the materials. But be very certain that your bidding audience will be prepared to pay a large sum.

Number each item to be auctioned clearly and perhaps ask a well-known personality to act as auctioneer, or somebody local who is witty and persuasive. Make sure that the name and address of each successful bidder is written down by a helper at the time of the bid, as well as the number of the item, and the sum to be paid for it. Payment should be made at the *end* of the auction and the goods handed over to the purchaser.

RE-CYCLING

Lots of household items can be sold for re-cycling – paper and cardboard, lead, copper, bottles, wool, cotton, for instance. Check your Yellow Pages for waste-paper and scrap-metal dealers and get in touch with them. Find out how much they're paying and in what form they want the items delivered or collected – newspapers and magazines are usually bundled together, with cardboard bundled separately.

You'll need somewhere to store the materials and, as they may have to be stored for some time, you must ensure that it is both large enough and available for the length of time you are likely to need it.

Let people in your area know what you're doing so that they can deliver to you or, every so often, pop notices through doors telling people you'll be collecting on such-and-such a day (see page 13). This sort of re-cycling is worthwhile with large quantities but do remember that the market fluctuates so make sure that you are aware of current prices.

Check the legal section on page 37 for advice on insurance, etc.

STAMPS

Collections of stamps are always worth selling – but few people know that the Post Office will re-purchase unused stamps on Stamped Addressed Envelopes. Our *Woman's Own* readers agreed that the SAEs from their unsuccessful competition entries could be used in this way and we have raised over £2,000. It's obviously only really practical if you work for a large firm that gets a lot of SAEs. See page 175 for the address.

COMPETITIONS

Balloon race: get a stall in a shopping precinct or at a fête. Hire some cylinders of hydrogen (see page 179) and try to persuade a balloon manufacturer to give you a quantity of balloons. Approach your local stationery shop for postcards and plastic sleeves, either to be donated or paid for with a discount. If you have to buy everything, cost it out before you do, work out how many balloons you'll have to sell to make a profit and decide whether or not it's worthwhile going ahead.

The object of the idea is to sell balloons to people passing by. They then fill in their name and address on a postcard which is stamped and addressed to the secretary of the fund-raising group. The card is then put into a protective plastic sleeve with a message to the finder that there is a reward if they return the card of the winning balloon. And the winning balloon is, of course, the one that travels the furthest distance.

Publicise the event beforehand, persuade a local business to donate a worthwhile prize and announce a date after which no cards will be accepted. Charge a sensible amount to enter – children love this sort of thing – and handle the hydrogen with caution. Always make sure someone is in charge of it while others attend to the filling in of cards and taking the money.

Tin pyramid: your local supermarket manager is the person you want to sweet talk about this! Because you want floor space for three to four weeks and a worthwhile prize donated by the store. You'll also need at least two people to be on duty to sell entries for a certain amount of time each day. What happens is this: your kindly manager and one of his staff build a pyramid of tins of all sizes; your entrants fill in their name and address on a large sheet of paper (rule it into three columns – one section for names of entrants, one for their addresses, one for their guessed amount) – and guess how many tins they think are in the pyramid. On the appointed day, you get your local paper along (if it's big enough, your local radio or TV station might send a crew along, especially if you can also persuade a personality to present the prize). You then take pyramid apart, counting the tins into trolleys held by your members. You then look down your list of entries and whoever has the nearest figure wins the prize – which could be a hamper of goodies, a one-minute shopping spree, a crate of wine. It all depends on the store's generosity. And depending on that, you could have more than one prize.

Guess the value: supermarket again. You persuade them to donate a hamper of food and wine and entrants have to guess the value. The nearest guess wins the hamper.

Advertise by posters and hand out leaflets outside the store. Again, try to persuade a local personality, TV station or local paper to attend before you approach the store – the suggestion of all that good publicity could just do the trick! See page 39 for legal advice.

THEATRE BOOKINGS

If you take block bookings you can get the seats cheaper. But if everyone pays the full price the difference can go to the charity.

WEEKEND BREAKS

Hotels often advertise bargain weekend breaks and, again, block bookings will reduce any cut-price rate still further. Charge your group the original cut-price rate and give the rest to your charity.

BOTTLE SAVING

You may find your local publican amenable to placing an outsize empty bottle on the bar counter for customers to put their change into.

SINGLE STALLS

If you can't tackle a whole fair or bazaar, take a stall at someone else's. Check early on what's available. Local summer fairs are good for this sort of thing, and although they'll usually charge a pitch fee, it's rarely very much.

PARTIES

You can arrange all sorts of parties at home with a theme – Valentine, Midsummer, Hallowe'en, Guy Fawkes, Christmas, Fancy Dress, etc. Decide how many people your house or garden will hold and invite accordingly. Plan to run a raffle and the price of the ticket can be the entrance fee. Price it sensibly so that you cover the cost of food, wine and prizes and make a good profit. Check the legal section on page 36 on holding events at home for advice on licences, insurance and so on.

DISCOS

You'll probably need a hall for this and unless someone you know has an effective music centre and a strobe light, you should plan on hiring a DJ and all his equipment for the evening. Yellow Pages will give you the information you need but check the legal section (page 38) to keep within the law. The basic organisation is the same as for a dinner and dance on page 19. If the disco is for teenagers, you'll need discreet adult supervision and a couple of 'bouncers' to get rid of undesirable rowdies. It is, of course, illegal to serve alcohol to anyone under 18, so stick to soft drinks and have hamburgers and hot dogs for sale as well as crisps and nibbles. Make the entrance price reasonable and advertise before the event in local shops, schools and the local newspaper.

SELLING YOUR WARES

It's worth taking plenty of time to set up stalls at fêtes and bazaars. Cover each table with a suitable cloth, and cut letters out of coloured paper to pin to the front of the cloth to indicate what is on sale – 'PLANTS', 'GARDEN STALL', 'BABY CLOTHES' and so on. Better still, if you have a sturdy table (rather than a trestle table) lash two upright poles to the legs and string a sign between the tops of the uprights so that it can be seen over people's heads. It's also a good idea to create different levels on the stall by standing boxes along the back of the table. Wrap them in coloured paper (use remnants of wallpaper) and you'll be able to make a more interesting display. Choose the cloth and paper to suit the items on sale – a green cloth or groundsheet for a garden stall, children's wallpaper for a toy stall.

If you have several examples of one particular item, the way you display them can be very important. Arrange book marks on a pile of books. Slip pictures cut from magazines into the photo frame you are hoping to sell (or put your own snap into one as a display sample) and make sure that you have plenty of labels to price the items for sale.

Once you have decided on the range of stalls (if you are organising the whole affair), appoint a stall-holder to be in charge of each stall who will co-ordinate collecting items for sale and pricing them.

At a fête or bazaar, make sure each stall has a reasonable cash float and make arrangements for a night safe at your bank to deposit your takings at the end of the day.

Don't forget to arrange for cleaners to clean up at the end of your function – you must leave your hall in good condition. And make arrangements for any left-overs to be picked up and stored.

It is important to wrap and display as attractively as possible the items you have made – you've got to entice customers to your stall, and make it easy for them to carry away their purchases once they've bought them. Choose materials carefully: clean, fresh colours are prettier and more eye-catching than dull beiges and browns. And it's worth investing in a few metres of ribbon to add the finishing touch to your packaging.

Here are some suggestions for different ways to present your goods:

● Sweets and biscuits can be packed into plastic bags: 12 oz (350 g) bags of sweets and 8 oz (225 g) bags of biscuits are attractive sizes to choose – and not too pricey for the customer.

● Make packaging more attractive with colourful paper or ribbon bows and neatly written labels describing the contents.

● Collect boxes from gifts and wrap them with coloured wrapping paper, or cut down empty cereal boxes to make card trays for sweets – cover the top with cling film and decorate with ribbon.

● Invest in packs of paper cups for sweets and individual cakes: choose plain white cups, but lay them on trays lined with coloured tissue paper to make them more attractive (you can use the polystyrene trays on which you buy your meat, for example, but do wash them thoroughly).

● Cut 20 cm (7½ inch) squares of coloured paper and roll into cones, held in place with sticky tape, to slip ready-wrapped sweets into.

● For Easter, look out for cheap mugs or egg cups on market stalls in which to stand home-made Easter Eggs, held in place with cling film tied with a colourful bow. But don't forget to include the cost of these when working out your selling price!

● For Christmas, package sweets so that they can be hung on trees: tie bundles up in squares of net (the sort used for underskirts). Tie individually wrapped sweets with glittery yarn and sell several tied together in a bundle ready to hang on trees.

● Make jams, chutneys and marmalades more attractive by designing your own labels to stick on the jars: use felt-tip pens in bright colours to draw simple patterns and write the name of the product and the date it was made on the label. Small cards or labels with serving suggestions and storage times are also a good idea.

● Circles of fabric, cut with pinking shears, slightly larger than the top of the jar and tied on with ribbon over the cellophane cover give jams a 'country' look.

● To make your quantities go as far as possible, collect small jars – the sort used for sauces and mustards are ideal – package them prettily, and customers can buy them to serve on breakfast and tea-trays.

● Cakes can be tricky for you and the eventual buyer to transport: if there is no decoration on the top, stand the cake on a plain white paper plate and wrap it in cling film.

● For cakes with decorated tops, make protective, open-topped boxes by cutting down cereal packets. Paint the packets, or cover them with plain coloured paper if the cake is a very special one. Cover the top of the box with cling film.

● Craft items need protection – they often get handled by over-inquisitive cust-omers, so a supply of clear plastic bags is useful.

● If you have 'mass-produced' a particular item (like baby changing mats or tissue box covers), display your best effort, complete with accessories (baby talc, disposable nappies, for example), but package other samples without the expensive extras to keep costs down.

● Don't forget to decorate the hall where you hold a craft fair, as well as the items you are selling: choose a suitable theme, such as bunnies for an Easter event, holly at Christmas, and use the same motif for your advertising posters. Bunches of balloons make one of the easiest, boldest decorations at any type of event. Hang them outside your venue as well so that they can be seen from the street – and don't forget to use them to hide ugly features in halls.

● Use artificial grass or green crêpe paper to cover the plant stall table.

● Clean white tablecloths should be laid on food stalls.

● Check out prices at other fairs and bazaars and price your goods accordingly. Don't forget that you need to make a reasonable profit, so work out carefully how much your goods have cost to make.

● Label goods clearly, with hints on care of fabric etc. Use brightly coloured felt-tip pens for pricing, and on food items state clearly how soon they should be eaten and if they can be frozen or not.

2
Fund raising and the Law

GENERAL RULES OF CHARITY FUND RAISING

To protect the public and voluntary groups themselves from exploitation, there are strict rules and regulations governing almost every aspect of fund raising.

House-to-house and street collections

These must be authorised by the local licensing authority – the police or local authority. An application must detail the location of the proposed collection, its dates, method and purpose, and the promoter's name.

Permission can be refused on any of several counts – for instance, if campaign expenses are thought to be too high or the collectors are considered unfit (eg., have criminal records or are under 16), or are likely to be disorderly, or are thought to be taking too high a payment for their work. The Charity has a duty to provide full details of the proposed campaign and failure to do this or to return the properly completed application form are also reasons to dismiss the request for permission.

If your application is turned down (reasons will be provided) you can appeal to the Home Secretary within 14 days.

It's worth remembering that a prime reason for turning down these applications is that there are too many charities wanting to run campaigns at a particular time, so it's worth putting in a request as much as a year ahead.

Collectors should wear a badge and carry a certificate or letter of authority from the organisers.

The Charity Commissioners (see addresses on page 175) issue an annual report describing their work and detailing any recent test cases that might have a bearing on charitable activities. And it's certainly worthwhile boning up on this kind of advice before embarking on any new or particularly adventurous fund-raising campaign. Meanwhile, here are some rules of thumb:

● Any funds raised in the name of a particular charity or fund must go there – you can't make a collection on behalf of the RSPCA and then decide it would be more appropriate to donate the cash to Guide Dogs for the Blind. It's a breach of civil law to mislead donors in this way.

● Fund raising groups must abide by the rules and regulations of the parent charity. Although some organisations are content to give their fund-raising sub-divisions a free hand, they must be cautious and vigilant about upholding the charity's most precious asset – its good name.

● Cash-raising campaigns must be organised according to the law. For instance:

If a campaign is being organised on a national level, the Charity may be able to acquire an exemption form applying in numerous areas for the required permission via a single application to the Home Office. However, these are by no means automatically granted.

Lotteries

These are another common form of fund raising and they can range from a basic raffle with small gifts as prizes, to large scale public lotteries with substantial cash sums to be won. This is how the law deals with the three types:

1. Small lottery: usually a raffle held as a side attraction at a bigger event. Expenses covering the cost of raffle tickets and the cost of prizes up to £50 are allowed, but *all* the remaining proceeds must go to the charity. *No cash prizes are permitted, and no tickets can be refunded.* The sale of tickets, draw and declaration of winners must take place during the main event.

2. Private lottery: this is when tickets are sold only to people in a specific group; the tickets must be printed and bear the price and the name and address of the promoters.

It should be stated that sale of tickets is restricted to members of the group and that the prize will go only to the winner. The lottery mustn't be advertised, except on the premises of the charity or their promoter. Apart from allowable expenses – e.g. the cost of tickets – all proceeds must go to the charity or in prizes. Tickets may not be posted.

3. Public Lottery: can be organised only by a registered charity or some other organisation that fulfils certain public criteria – 'the society's lottery'. Promoters must be drawn from the organising group and approved by its' officers, but cannot be paid for their services. The lottery organisers must register with their local authority and give them a breakdown of expenditure and proceeds after the event. If the value of tickets to be sold is more than £10,000, or the largest prize worth more than £2,000, the lottery must be registered with the Gaming Board.

Again all proceeds, apart from the permitted expenses of ticket costs and prizes, must go to charity.

The tickets must bear full details of price, name and address of the promoter, the charity and date of the draw. No-one under 16 can buy or sell the tickets and all the lottery costs must come from the proceeds, not the parent charity.

OTHER CASH RAISING CONSIDERATIONS

If you're involved in fund raising, you must consider your legal and financial obligations to members of the public who give you support. Not only do you have to think in terms of their safety and well being, you should also bear in mind the risks to yourself or your project if things go wrong and rebound on you. Here are some guidelines:

PUBLIC LIABILITY INSURANCE

This is worth considering if you're organising an event that involves any members of the public; it covers all eventualities from someone at a charity football match kicking a ball through a car windscreen, to a visitor to your fête tripping over and breaking a leg. If, for some reason, you do get sued, a settlement could cost you a fortune so it's vital to insure yourself, or your organisation, for at least £500,000 – more if there are a lot of people involved in the

activity. Shop around for the best insurance quotation.

PLUVIUS INSURANCE

Something to think about if you're planning an outdoor event absolutely dependent on good weather – it means that you can insure against loss of takings if you're rained off. The only snag is that you must take out your policy at least 14 days before the event so that local rainfall can be measured and the premium estimated accordingly. In a summer like 1985, it can work out pretty pricey and pluvius insurance is something to worry about only if you're prepared to see a hefty slice of whatever you make going to an insurance company. However, you need not insure the whole event – you can settle for the half hour when your star guest is due to parachute out of the skies! Again, shop around for the best quote.

THEFT

At any fund-raising event, there's likely to be loose cash around and that means there's a risk of theft. You can insure against theft or loss of money, cheques, postal orders etc., and your cover will normally extend to the place of the event, the premises from which you operate and the homes of people involved in the fund raising.

FIRE AND DAMAGE

Many public premises available for hire for functions will be covered by safety regulations – particularly relating to fire prevention – and it goes without saying that you must abide by the rules. However, the general safety situation may be a little ambiguous over small village halls, Scout huts, etc., and obviously where private homes are being used for charity events. The most sensible precaution is to consult the fire officer at your local fire station and also to seek the advice of police before you start organising the function.

When you hire facilities on a short-term basis – for instance, a one-night dinner and dance at your village hall – you may find that any damage caused by your guests isn't covered by existing insurance on the premises. You should either ask your insurers to extend your public liability insurance to cover this, or, if the building is owned by a local authority or major organisation, persuade them to take on this responsibility as part of the hire contract. Make sure you keep your guests within the limited number, or insurance cover could be null and void. Also, it's worth taking out 'consequential insurance' if you could be held responsible for any loss of revenue caused by damage to the premises.

ALL RISKS

It's worth having this insurance to cover any equipment you might use for a function – stereo equipment for dances and discos, glasses, crockery and cooking utensils that might get stolen or broken.

CELEBRITY INSURANCE

Appearance insurance will cover you if any celebrity fails to turn up – a good precaution if your event is heavily dependent on their pulling power. If you're asking a celebrity to do anything out of the ordinary – a sponsored parachute jump, for instance, check whether they themselves have adequate personal insurance cover for this kind of event and arrange any extra if necessary.

ROLL-A-DICE

Sometimes a charity will approach, say, a local garage to offer a new car as a prize in a dice game where the winner rolls, for example, six sixes in a row.

Local businesses may willingly donate such a prize as the likelihood of someone winning is so remote – but, just in case a player does hit the jackpot, the charity can take out insurance enabling them to pay for the prize. The premium cost is determined by the value of the prize.

SPECIAL EVENTS INSURANCE

If you're holding an event not covered by your usual public liability insurance – a show or exhibition, for instance, where valuable items are on loan, you can get an extension of existing cover or a special policy designed to take in all the extras. This may well involve an extra premium.

ENTERTAINMENT LICENCES

If you're planning to charge an entrance fee to any event, you'll need a public entertainments licence. The local authority will need 28 days notice prior to the event and the licence can either be yearly or occasional.

The form is in several sections which are sent off to the police and fire departments and passed on to the council's own planning and environmental departments. If there are no objections the licence should be granted without complication. Terms can vary according to the authority. Fees are fixed by the District Council. At the time of going to press the fee for an occasional licence for one night is £12. An entertainments licence for one year might be as follows:

```
   0 –  250 people – £60
 251 –  500 people – £75
 501 –  750 people – £90
 751 – 1000 people – £115
1001 – 1500 people – £140
1501 –  upwards    – £170
```

The figures shown are from Birmingham.

LIQUOR LICENCES

Permission is needed from local magistrates if you are selling liquor anywhere, at any time and in any place. You can't get round it by saying the price of a glass of wine is included in the entrance ticket – it is still considered to be selling alcohol.

GAMING APPROVAL

There's no need to get official approval for small-time public gaming – such as a tombola, a whist drive, etc. – so long as there are no cash prizes. Cash prizes are allowed only in private gaming, where tickets are sold only among members of a group (see full details of lotteries laws, page 31).

MUSIC LICENCE

Any musical performance is liable for a royalties levy payable to the Performing Rights Society on behalf of the composers of any pieces played – but the PRS will usually waive their charge if the performance is for a cause aimed at 'the relief of human suffering'. The best way is of course to stage performances in premises already holding a Performing Rights Society Licence. Check if you're eligible for the waiver (the licence for a single performance at the time of going to press is around £8, plus VAT) – by contacting the PRS licensing manager (address on page 175).

NOISE AND NUISANCE

If you're staging an event that's likely to be noisy and disruptive and may upset neighbours, it's worth contacting your local Environmental Health Department for guidance – or you may find you're at risk of prosecution for nuisance.

USE OF PREMISES

If you're hiring premises for an event, it's worth checking that the type of event or entertainment you're planning is actually permitted there – for instance, there might be restrictions on holding a charity strip show in a church hall!

It's also a good idea to find out whether the premises are covered for any of the necessary licences – music, drink, entertainment etc., and to what time. You or the owners of the premises may need to apply for an extension of the licence.

FOOD HYGIENE

Rules governing food prepared for charitable purposes are rather complex and also open to interpretation. Environmental Health Officers responsible for enforcing them may react in different ways according to the area and the event involved, so it's always worth checking your position before you go ahead with any function involving sale or preparation of food. The rule of thumb does seem to be that over-stretched Health Departments are likely to turn a blind eye to the occasional fund-raising venture like a cake stall at the annual village fête, so long as reasonable care and awareness is shown in food preparation, storage and serving. However, they are likely to become much tougher if there's any element of regular trading involved, or an extremely obvious public risk – for instance, a hamburger stall being operated next to public lavatories at a charity function. In these cases, there's a strong case for enforcement of Food Hygiene regulations and you could be in legal hot water. It also makes sense to take out insurance to cover any negligence suits if you do have the misfortune to cause food poisoning.

If you're planning to sell or serve food at a charity function, it's as well to take note of the guidelines followed by the National Federation of Women's Institutes (our thanks to them for this information):

Preparation: even if you're not forced to abide by the letter of Food Hygiene laws, it makes sense to ensure that any kitchen area in which you are working is as clean and safe as possible. It should:

- be clear of pets, washing and cleaning implements.
- have clean, uncluttered and scrubbable work surfaces.
- have separate pot washing and hand washing facilities.

And you should:

- have clean overalls and cover your hair.
- be clean and healthy (no smoking!) – don't prepare food for consumption by anyone other than your family if you've a cold or flu, or other infectious illnesses.

You should also avoid preparing risky foods like shellfish, and bear in mind that savouries such as quiche, or anything containing meat and fish, are potentially hazardous – a survey revealed that 35 per cent of ground beef samples from butchers contained salmonella organisms, so it's vital to ensure such products are properly cooked.

Storage: the WI cardinal rule is never to freeze and thaw any of the products they make and sell – there are just too many risks involved; a primary problem is that customers may take produce home and re-freeze it, which constitutes a real danger as far as food poisoning is concerned. Instead, they ensure that all food is sold fresh, but that it is kept very cool from the time it is cooked. All products must be kept covered.

Serving: obviously, no-one serving food should be smoking and there should be adequate washing facilities on hand. Any food sold for future use – eg., hams, cakes, pies etc., should be carefully packaged and covered to prevent contamination. Food sold for consumption on the spot should be served in an hygienic environment and kept cool until it's ready either to be heated or served cold. Raw meat for use at a barbecue, for instance, should be kept refrigerated, and separate from other foods, until it is ready to be cooked.

LEGAL CHECK LIST FOR YOUR FUNCTIONS

Here's a run-down on general rules to bear in mind for whatever function you're staging. It is useful to use this check list when you are organising any charity fund raising event.

EVENTS AT HOME

Coffee Morning/Party Sales

Entertainments licence: only needed if you're charging an entrance fee.

Insurance: it's worth consulting your home insurers, just in case cover doesn't extend to your guests – imagine getting sued for negligence if you spill boiling coffee on someone! You may have to pay a small premium on top.

Safety: unless you're having a huge number of guests, your usual precautions and awareness should be enough. If you're inviting lots of people, do seek advice from your local fire officer and consult police if visitors are likely to cause any traffic or parking congestion.

Food hygiene: make sure all refreshments are prepared, stored and served in hygienic conditions, and that your insurance covers any mishaps.

Whist Drive

Insurance: home insurance should cover visitors, but consult brokers if you're having a large number of people in – an extra premium may be necessary.

Safety: normal precautions should be adequate as long as the number of people is fairly limited.

Food hygiene: make sure all refreshments are prepared, stored and served in hygienic conditions, and that your insurance covers any mishaps.

Cheese and Wine Party

Entertainments licence: necessary if you're charging an entrance fee.

Liquor licence: must get magistrates' permission to sell drink, even if it's included in the ticket price.

Insurance: home insurance should be adequate, but consult brokers just in case you need to pay a nominal premium on top to cover visitors.

Safety: usual precautions, but get advice from fire brigade and police if you're anticipating a crowd.

Food hygiene: any large-scale catering needs guidance from your local Environmental Health Department. However, very basic canapés or snacks should be all right as long as you stick to sensible guidelines – prepare, store and serve the food hygienically; avoid freezing prepared food and don't use risky ingredients like shellfish, pork, etc.

Musical Evening

Entertainments licence: necessary if you're charging an entrance fee.

Liquor licence: necessary if you're selling alcohol, or including it in the price of the ticket.

Music licence: contact the Performing Rights Society to check whether it's necessary – depending on your fund-raising cause, they may waive their royalties charge.

Insurance: whether you need more than your existing home insurance depends on the size of your audience – check whether public liability cover is necessary. If the event is dependent on the appearance of a star performer, consider a non-appearance insurance.

Safety: if you're expecting more than a few guests, check your position with your fire officer and local police.

Food hygiene: make sure all refreshments are prepared, stored and served hygienically and that your insurance covers mishaps.

Garden Fêtes

Entertainments licence: necessary if you're charging an entrance fee.

Liquor licence: necessary if you're selling alcohol in any way.

Music licence: might be necessary if there's any musical performance planned.

Insurance: public liability insurance of at least £500,000 is important; it's also worth considering theft, all risks, special events, roll-a-dice and pluvius cover, depending on the type of event and whether or not its dependent on good weather for success.

Safety: contact your local fire officer and police in advance and ask for their advice on fire risks, traffic problems, parking etc. Where the general public are invited, it's worth siting some notices around the place to encourage people to be responsible for their own property.

Food hygiene: it's worth seeking advice from the Environmental Health Department if you're planning any food extravaganza; otherwise, ensure that you take the greatest care in the preparation, storage and serving of all food sold or provided.

Exhibitions/Craft Demonstrations

Entertainments licence: necessary if you're charging an entrance fee.

Insurance: make sure your guests are adequately covered by your home insurance, and be prepared to pay a small extra public liability premium on top if they're not. Take out non-appearance insurance if your demonstration is being presented by a crowd-pulling personality. Special events insurance is worthwhile if you're responsible for any valuable exhibits or equipment.
Safety: for a limited number of people, normal precautions should be adequate.

Bingo for Prizes

Entertainments licence: you'll need this if you're charging an entrance fee.

Insurance: home insurance should cover a limited number of visitors. If in doubt consult your insurance company. If your prizes have any value, it's worth taking out theft, loss or damage insurance.

Safety: normal precautions should suffice as long as numbers are limited.

Bingo for Money

Gaming licence: where money is offered as a prize, you'll need to contact your local magistrates court.

Insurance: check that your home insurance is adequate cover for visitors and make sure you're also covered for theft or loss of money.

Safety: normal precautions should suffice where there's a limited number of guests.

Collection of Waste/Re-cycling Goods

Insurance: if you're collecting large quantities of, say, old newspapers, stamps, tin foil or bottles, and will be storing them in your home, make sure you're covered for both loss and damage under your home insurance policy.

If not, take extra cover. Additionally, they may constitute a safety risk in themselves, so make sure they're stored according to the terms of your insurance.

Safety: since storage may well be risky, do seek advice from charity organisers who are regularly involved in this kind of operation, plus your fire officer or local safety officer at the police station. Also, your insurers may be able to offer guidelines.

EVENTS IN HIRED PREMISES

Dinner and Dance

Entertainments licence: necessary where an entrance fee is charged. (Check with owner of the premises whether the building already has one.)

Liquor licence: necessary unless the premises already have one. An extension may be required.

Music licence: will be necessary for any music performed – again, check whether the premises are already covered.

Insurance: check what cover the building has and arrange for any extra necessary – for instance, public liability, all risks and theft, consequential cover, etc.

Safety: make sure that the event you're planning complies with activities allowed in the premises. Check and make sure you understand the fire and safety regulations laid down for the building and, if they're not sufficient, get guidance from your local fire officer and police. Ensure that guests are limited to the number covered by insurance. Notices around the premises will remind guests to be responsible for their belongings.

Food hygiene: any large-scale catering should get the approval of the Environmental Health Department. It's vital to follow EH guidelines.

Disco

Entertainments licence: necessary where an entrance fee is charged but check whether the premises already have one if you're hiring.

Liquor licence: necessary where alcoholic drinks are sold or served as part of the entrance package. An extension may be necessary.

Music licence: check with the Performing Rights Society whether it's needed, or whether the premises are already covered.

Insurance: public liability, theft, consequential liability cover etc.

Safety: check that the building is authorised for the event you're planning and make sure that you comply with fire and safety regulations laid down for the premises. If they seem inadequate, contact your fire officer and police for advice. It's worth informing them anyway of such an event.

Food hygiene: any large-scale catering should have guidance from the local Environmental Health Department.

If only very basic food is on sale – filled rolls, sandwiches etc. – make sure that it is prepared, stored and served in hygienic surroundings and sold well wrapped.

Charity Fashion Show

Entertainments licence: necessary if you're selling entrance tickets.

Liquor licence: even if you're providing just a glass of wine included in the ticket price, you'll need local magistrates' approval.

Music licence: this may be necessary – check with the Performing Rights Society and also find out if the premises are already licensed.

Insurance: check what cover the building already has and arrange for any extra insurance necessary – for instance, cover for clothes and jewellery being modelled. Other important considerations are public liability, theft and consequential cover.

Safety: make sure that the event complies with activities allowed on the premises. Check on, and make sure you understand, the fire and safety regulations laid down for the building and, if they seem sketchy, get guidance from local fire officer and police. Ensure that the number of guests is within the limits of your insurance cover. Notices should encourage guests to take care of their belongings.

Food hygiene: any large-scale catering needs guidance from your local Environmental Health Department; if you're merely serving crisps and peanuts, make sure that they are put in clean bowls, and kept in hygienic surroundings.

Jumble Sale, Bazaar, Bring and Buy Sale, Auction etc.

Entertainments licence: necessary if you're charging an entrance fee.

Liquor licence: will be required if you're serving alcohol.

Insurance: check what cover the building already has and make arrangements if more is needed – for instance, public liability, theft, consequential cover etc.

Safety: make sure that the event complies with activities allowed on the premises. Check on, and make sure you understand the fire and safety regulations. If they seem sketchy, get guidance from your local fire officer and police. If there are any limitations on the number of people allowed on the premises at any one time – this may be a stipulation of the terms of insurance – make sure you stick to them.

Food hygiene: if any snacks or coffee are served, obviously they must be prepared, stored and served in an hygienic environment – if in doubt, ask for guidance from your Environmental Health Department. If you're selling home produce – cakes, jams, pies etc. – make sure they've been prepared in clean surroundings and, preferably, have not been frozen before sale in case customers re-freeze them (see page 34). All food sold should be hygenically wrapped.

Sponsored Event (e.g. Singing or Dancing Marathon)

Entertainments licence: needed if you're charging an entrance fee.

Liquor licence: necessary if you're selling alcohol to spectators.

Insurance: check what cover the premises already have and arrange for any extra cover required. Public liability, theft and consequential cover could be considerations.

Safety: make sure that the activity you're planning is allowed on the premises and make sure that you comply with any fire and safety regulations already laid down – if they're sketchy, a sensible precaution is to contact your local fire officer and police. Check with your local Environmental Health Department that you won't be causing any nuisance with noise. Depending on your event consider having a St. John's Ambulance person in attendance.

Music licence: contact the Performing Rights Society, and check whether the premises are already licensed.

Food hygiene: if the sponsored event itself involves food (for instance an oyster-eating marathon!) make sure it's hygienically prepared, stored and served and that you have adequate public liability cover in case things go wrong. Any food served or sold to spectators should meet the same high standards.

Competitions, Contests

Entertainments licence: necessary if you're charging an entrance fee.

Liquor licence: important if alcohol is served, even if included in the price of the entrance ticket.

Music licence: consult the Performing Rights Society and check whether the premises are already licensed.

Insurance: check what cover the premises already have and make arrangements for any extra insurance required – for instance, public liability, consequential insurance, theft etc.

Safety: check fire and safety regulations covering the building but take the precaution of seeking advice from local fire officer and police if these guidelines seem inadequate.

If there are any limitations on the number of people allowed inside the premises at any one time, make sure that they're adhered to. Notices should encourage guests to take care of their property.

Food hygiene: seek advice from the local Environmental Health Department if you're planning any large-scale catering, otherwise make sure that any snacks or refreshments provided are prepared, stored and served in hygienic surroundings.

Exhibitions

Entertainments licence: needed if you're charging an entrance fee.

Insurance: check what cover already exists for the premises, then arrange for any extra insurance needed. For instance, special events cover for the exhibits, consequential cover if the building is somehow damaged to the point where it affects future use, and therefore future revenue made from the premises.

Safety: check the fire and safety regulations on the building and, if in doubt, seek advice from your local fire officer or the police station's safety officer. Make sure that you comply with any

specified limitations on the number of people to be inside the building at any one time.

Concert, Musical Entertainment, Variety Show

Entertainments licence: necessary if you're charging an entrance fee.

Liquor licence: important if you're serving alcohol, even if it's part of the ticket price.

Music licence: you will need to pay a fee to the Performing Rights Society unless they give you a special exemption – for example, if your event is being staged to 'relieve human suffering'. Do contact the PRS to check your position – it could be that the premises already have an annual music licence, so no extra payment may be necessary.

Insurance: check what cover the premises already have, and arrange any extra insurance necessary. This could range from public liability, theft and consequential cover to insurance against loss or damage to any props and costumes used in the event. Also, if you're lucky enough to persuade a celebrity to participate, check what cover they have against accident or injury and arrange extra if necessary. Additionally, if your celebrity is likely to be a big draw for the event, take out non-appearance cover just in case he/she doesn't turn up.

Safety: make sure the activity you're planning is allowed on the premises and ensure that you comply with any fire and safety regulations laid down for the building.

If in doubt, seek advice from the local fire officer and the police safety officer. Do make sure that you observe any limitations on the number of people allowed inside the premises at any one time – this could affect your insurance cover. Notices prominently displayed around the premises should encourage guests to take care of their property. If there's any likelihood of noise and nuisance, check your position with your local Environmental Health Department.

Food hygiene: any large-scale catering should be supervised by Environmental Health Officers – do seek their advice beforehand. Otherwise, make sure that any refreshments provided are prepared, stored and served in hygienic surroundings.

OUTDOOR EVENTS

Jumble Sale, Bring and Buy, Garden Party, Fair etc.

Entertainments licence: necessary if you're charging an entrance fee.

Liquor licence: important if any alcohol is served, even as part of the ticket price.

Music licence: a side-attraction of, say, a pop group or band will need a licence from the Performing Rights Society. Depending on the charitable cause, you may be eligible for an exemption from paying this licence fee. Consult the PRS. Also seek guidance from the local Environmental Health Department if you're likely to make prolonged or loud noise with the music.

Insurance: if your event is very much dependent for success on good weather, you might consider pluvius insurance – as long as it is not too costly. Otherwise, check what cover the ground you're using already has – the insurance cover for the village green may well be different from that of a local sports ground, farmer's field or a stately home. If necessary, arrange for extra insurance cover – public liability, consequential, special events, etc.

Safety: check whether there are any regulations governing use of the ground you're using and make sure you stick to them. However, if they don't provide guidelines dealing with an event such as the one you're planning, contact your local police, fire officer and Environmental Health Department for advice on everything from traffic control and parking, to coping with crowds. Notices should encourage guests to take care of their property.

Food hygiene: any large-scale catering should have guidance from the local Environmental Health Department. Otherwise, snacks, refreshments and any home produce sold should be prepared, stored and served in hygienic surroundings.

All home produce – jams, cakes, pies etc. – on sale should be wrapped and, ideally, should not be frozen before sale as customers may make the mistake of re-freezing it, which could cause food poisoning. (See page 34.)

Sponsored Event (e.g. Marathon, Football Match)

Entertainments licence: necessary if people are charged an entrance fee to watch.

Insurance: it's important to have public liability cover and any peripheral insurance necessary for side-events like exhibits on show to promote the event, and non-appearance cover on any celebrities who may jeopardise the success of the event by failing to turn up. Pluvius cover may be worthwhile if you've any investment at stake – for instance, the cost of hiring a marquee which doesn't get used if the event's a washout.

Safety: if participants are going to be running round the streets as part of the event, it's vital that you take advice from police and seek guidance on your proposed route. In fact, it's vital to get advice from police, fire officers and the local Environmental Health Department on *any* event where you're expecting a large number of people.

It's also important to consult whatever association governs a particular sport or activity to check whether there are any special requirements to be fulfilled – for instance, refreshments and medical aid available at regular intervals for marathon runners, veterinary help on hand where animals are involved in the event.

Food hygiene: any refreshments served should be prepared, stored and served hygienically.

Street Parade

Entertainments licence: you'll need this if you're charging an entrance fee to view any part of the display. Obviously you can't enforce charges on the public highway.

Street Collection: if you have teams of collectors circulating through the crowds, aiming to raise money for charity via the event, you'll have to abide by the strict rulings governing street collections and get approval from the local licensing authority – usually the police (details on page 30).

Insurance: you'll need public liability insurance and check that any vehicles you use are adequately insured. Additionally, you should take out special events cover for any exhibits, costumes and decorations used.

Safety: it's vital to have the co-operation of the local police; contact them early on with details of your plans for approval. Be prepared to accept any advice they offer and make sure you don't ignore any

guidelines – it could affect your insurance cover. You will need them on hand anyway if you're affecting traffic or pedestrian flow. You should also get them and fire officers to check over your floats for safety.

Street Party

Entertainments licence: necessary if you're charging an entrance fee to the event.

Liquor licence: necessary if you're selling alcohol.

Street collection: you'll need approval of the local licensing authority if you're planning to collect money from members of the public in the street.

Insurance: public liability cover is important, and it's wise to take out insurance cover for any equipment hired or borrowed, if it doesn't exist already. Pluvius cover could be considered if there's a substantial financial stake at risk with bad weather.

Safety: it's vital to take advice from the police – you can't expect to just close down any street at any time; you'll need their approval and assistance. It's also worth speaking to your local fire officer and Environmental Health Department, particularly where food is involved.

Food hygiene: any large-scale catering will definitely need guidance from the Environmental Health Department. If you're merely preparing food in your own home, then taking it into the street outside for consumption by friends and neighbours, just make sure that the whole process is hygienically carried out (see page 34).

Barbecue

Entertainments licence: necessary if you're charging an entrance fee.

Liquor licence: necessary for any alcohol served, even if included in the price of the ticket.

Music licence: check with the Performing Rights Society whether you'll need to pay their fee, or whether you're exempt. Check with the local Environmental Health Department if you are allowed to play music out of doors there without causing a nuisance.

Insurance: check what cover the land you're using already has and arrange whatever extra insurance is necessary. Public liability is important and you should have cover for any equipment borrowed or hired. Pluvius cover may be worth considering if you stand to lose a lot financially in the event of bad weather.

Safety: fire is obviously the risk here so it makes sense to get advice from the local fire officer. Police and Environmental Health Officers should also be consulted.

Food hygiene: cooking and serving food in such a potentially risky way as on a barbecue really needs guidance from the Environmental Health Department – otherwise you could find they act on the spot to close down the barbecue. You must consider preparation facilities and positioning of your cooking area – not too close to lavatories, for instance, and do ensure that there are adequate washing facilities nearby. Otherwise, all other food served – salads, bread rolls, ready-prepared desserts etc. – should obviously be prepared, stored and served in hygienic conditions (see page 34).

PROFESSIONAL FUND RAISERS

It's possible – and often advisable – to hire professional, non-charitable workers to organise a fund-raising campaign. The advantage is that they are usually skilled and experienced in fund-raising work, but the charity or organisation making use of them should bear the following points in mind:

Charges for professional services

Many reputable fund raisers will charge only a set fee for time and services involved and not for a proportion of the money raised, which is generally the most satisfactory arrangement. It is also important to establish how the fees should be paid – in a lump sum, or divided into periodical payments? Agree these details in writing to avoid disputes later.

The service provided and staff involved

Be clear exactly what you can expect from the fund raiser, how donations will be collected and expenses deducted. It's also important to have a clear idea of how many volunteers or charity workers will be needed to assist, and for how long. Again, agree in writing.

Letting the public know

It's important that the public should know when fund raisers are being paid for their services. When seeking funds professional fund raisers should not imply that they are on the staff of the charity – they should always explain that a proportion of funds raised will be going on their fee.

OTHER CASH-RAISING METHODS

Making money at street level – via public collections and campaigns – is only one aspect of fund raising. Obviously, the bigger the charity or fund-raising drive, the more varied its options. But even the most unsophisticated group of volunteers may be eligible for official grants and donations:

Government Grants

Although central government grants to charity and voluntary organisations are an important source of income, local authorities are major contributors at grass roots level so it's well worth investigating your eligibility for cash from either source.

Money may well be available towards the running costs of a charity scheme, especially if the government department would prefer the voluntary organisation to undertake the work rather than make its' own arrangements.

Both central and local government have discretionary powers to fund voluntary schemes, so long as they're in the public interest. However, the amount of cash awarded often depends on governmental cash flow – sometimes there is more money available than at other times.

Before approaching the relevant local authority or Civil Service department, the organisation should have a clear case to support its request for funds.

Business

A large proportion of charity and voluntary service funds comes from business and industry. Giant corporations may well make large cash donations, while smaller firms may prefer to help with offers of equipment or services. Well-known chain stores and big banks are major contributors.

Whether you're approaching a large or small company, a personal contact is a useful start on which to base your initial approach. Your patrons or trustees may be able to come up with some names. Large organisations usually have staff to deal specifically with the question of charitable donations, while it makes sense to approach smaller companies directly through their Chairmen or Managing Directors.

In planning your approach, it may well be worth primarily contacting organisations with an interest or sympathy towards your campaign. For instance, sports goods manufacturers may perhaps be slightly more motivated in making a donation towards funding a new sports and leisure centre. Also, you should home in on a small number of firms with your application, then spread your net wider as time goes on.

Be specific about your request; don't be afraid to state exactly the amount you need and be prepared to detail how you plan to use the cash. You'll generally gain more respect and credibility if your appeal is clear, frank and concise – no-one wants to plough through pages of well-meant but woolly explanation. Those considering your request will be interested to know your track record in previous fund-raising efforts and may also be keen to know how their organisation could benefit from association with your efforts. But remember that not all companies want public recognition of their efforts.

If your initial appeal fails, don't be afraid to contact the same corporation at a later date – it could be that they had just allocated all available funds at that time.

Trusts

This is a method where private individuals and businesses can set up charitable endowment schemes which enable them to benefit from generous tax exemptions.

Charitable trusts must be set up for one or more of the four aims given on page 47 under a trust deed establishing their criteria. They are an enormous source of funds for charities, producing income derived from their capital. Anyone looking for a trust likely to make a donation to their particular cause should consult the Directory of Grant Making Trusts which lists more than 2,400 trusts in the UK.

Covenant

This is a very straightforward method of getting a tax refund.

A covenant is a legal agreement where donors, either as individuals or on a collective basis, promise a specified sum to a charity so the tax they have already paid can be reclaimed by that charity. In other words, if you donate £100 a year, the charity will get £100 *plus* the tax you have paid.

However, the tax will be refunded only as long as the donor adheres to the rules; for a start the covenant has to run for at least three years and a donor can't profit from the covenant. Forms are available from the charities you want to benefit.

Legacies

Legacies are an important source of funds to charities, especially those involved in the care of animals.

However, it's vital that any bequests made in a will are legally beyond dispute; they should be clearly worded and the charity should be accurately named, otherwise there could be wrangles over the intended destination of the money; cash could end up being divided between several charities with a similar title or, in extreme cases, the courts could end up deciding where it should go.

There may be restrictions in the will on how a bequest is spent by a charity – these

can only be overturned by the Charity Commission if it is thought that the conditions are unreasonable or unlawful.

There are several types of bequest:
● Lump sum payments
● 'Residuary' – where the charity receives the remainder of an estate once other bequests have been disbursed
● 'Reversionary' – where someone arranges for their estate to pass on to the charity after, say, the death of their spouse

If the husband or wife dies before the testator, the money automatically goes to the charity.

A charity is free to advertise for legacies and this is a very straightforward route to attract new funds.

Trading

Although charities cannot operate a money-spinning business as their main aim, many set up subsidiaries which direct their profits back to the parent charity by way of a covenant.

There are numerous methods of trading, from running thrift shops to selling high quality merchandise advertising the charity, ranging from Christmas cards to china, clothing and crafts.

A charity's trading activities are generally taxable, although there are exemptions and some loopholes (such as covenants) to help their cause. If a charity trades in taxable goods and services, and its turnover exceeds the VAT threshold – currently £19,500 a year – the charity must acknowledge its liability to be registered as a VAT trader.

Events like charity jumble sales are tax exempt – as long as they are one-off events and not held, say, every weekend thus competing with other traders and being given public support because of their charitable efforts.

CHARITIES – HOW THEY OPERATE

The prime purpose of fund raising and charity work is to fill the gap between what the State will provide for the sick, the needy and other worthy causes and what we can afford to pay out of our own pockets.

Fund raising is big business. With everyone from the local Brownie pack to massive international organisations like Oxfam competing for untapped public, private and business donations, it has become a sophisticated industry turning over billions of pounds each year.

Few charities and voluntary organisations could survive on what is raised via flag days and street collections. More and more, they are turning to the business sector for support and relying on grants from both central and local government.

It's not just the major fund-raising organisations who find their cash there – funds are available too for small, local community campaigns; but while giant charities can justify paying for professional promoters and staff to plan and organise their cash-generating drives, small voluntary groups must rely far more on their own limited resources and success often depends on the organisational abilities of enthusiastic but inexperienced workers. That's one very good reason why they should bone up very thoroughly on the different fund-raising methods and cash sources available to them.

What's the difference between charity fund raising and non-charity fund raising? It's really the complex question of charitable status; while all charities are voluntary organisations, not all voluntary organisations qualify for charitable status, even when their objectives are beyond reproach and in the community interest.

However, it's always worthwhile pursuing the possibility of charitable status as it provides such huge financial advantages. A non-charitable organisation which invests the proceeds of a money-making campaign is very likely to be liable for at least 30% tax on any income from this.

Why be a Charity?

Although any organisation that achieves charitable status becomes answerable for its aims and activities to the Charity Commissioners (that's in England and Wales; in Scotland it's the Scottish Home and Health Department, and in Northern Ireland the Inland Revenue has controlling powers), there are strong advantages to be weighed against this loss of independence

● *Tax Exemption*
This is the major boon of charitable status – charities are exempt from most forms of direct taxation. This includes Income and Corporation Tax as well as Capital Gains and Capital Transfer taxes. There are numerous other exemptions available, such as stamp duty on transfers of property to charity.

● *Rates Reduction*
Charities are automatically entitled to a 50% rates reduction on their premises – more at the discretion of their particular local authority.

● *Public Image*
The 'Charity' tag undoubtedly inspires public confidence and thus improves fund-raising prospects.

● *Help from Other Charities*
An off-shoot of charitable status is that an organisation is eligible for aid – especially financial – from other charity groups.

How to become a Charity

Not every philanthropically-inspired organisation is automatically eligible for charitable status – there are strict legal requirements to be fulfilled and these are strictly protected. To qualify as a charity an organisation must have one of four defined aims:

1. The Relief of Poverty

This is fairly broad-based; poverty is defined rather more as 'going short' than being destitute and the organisation need be providing aid only to a small minority rather than to a wide section of the community.

2. Advancement of Education

This, of course, is what allows the independent schools system to flourish. Without their charitable status, private schools would be far beyond the financial reach of most parents. However, charity in education extends over a wide area; the only exclusions are where the 'education' is considered too much a general experience – as in the university of life! – or to be politically motivated.

3. Advancement of Religion

This is not restricted to any one religious creed or doctrine; the only limitation is that the group must be founded on the belief in a god – hence the exclusion of spiritualism and free-masonry from this category.

4. Other Purposes Beneficial to the Community

This final category has been created by the courts to broaden the definition of charity to include those that don't fit into the first three sections but nevertheless do provide a valid public service – for instance, animal and bird protection, preservation and improvement of the environment, community care and leisure projects, work aimed at rehabilitating offenders.

There is no set definition of organisations eligible for charitable status within this category, but it's generally necessary to prove that a reasonable section of the community are receiving some benefit from the organisation's activities.

The mechanics of becoming a charity are straightforward, once eligibility is established. Registration is effected through standard forms from the Charity Commission. However, the specific aims of the charity must be laid down in a written document or constitution. As this is legally binding, it's advisable to get a lawyer's advice, though the Charity Commission will provide some guidance to steer applicants clear of the major pitfalls.

Once the aims and objects of the charity have been formally declared in a constitution, they cannot be changed without permission from the Charity Commission.

The trust deed is a common form of charitable constitution (especially where the organisation is managed by a small number of people not answerable to a membership). Other forms of constitutions are listed on the next page.

● *An Unincorporated Association*
This is appropriate where members are actively involved in management of the charity and is ideal for small-budget organisations.

● *Charitable Corporation*
This is recommended, where, for example, staff are to be employed and funds handled on a significant scale. This arrangement is complicated by the legal obligation to conform to the Companies' Act, for instance in relation to presenting annual accounts, passing resolutions and winding up. It's more complicated and costly than the other methods of management.

3
Cook it to sell

What would fêtes and fairs be like without lots of scrumptious foods to buy? In this section you'll find everything from marmalade to toffee apples, mouth-watering terrines to Christmas cake – plus a special section for children, things they can make themselves with minimal supervision to raise money for Cub, Guide or school funds. Whatever time of the year it is, there are plenty of suggestions here from which to choose.

Keeping in mind that you want to price your goods as low as possible and try to make between 50–75% profit, ask local shops for material contributions and get together with friends to swop home grown fruit and vegetables or buy in bulk from cash and carry stores (see page 11).

HYGIENE IS A MUST

Pay careful attention to hygiene when cooking or storing food – it should be made fresh and heated to a centre temperature of 75°C (167°F). Once cooked, cool it quickly to below 10°C (50°F).

Take care to reheat foods quickly to a high temperature for a sufficient time to kill off any harmful bacteria. And don't leave food in a warm place – it is a good medium for bacteria to grow.

Remember to keep raw and cooked foods completely separate, even when preparing food. Ideally, ingredients should be kept in a cool place or in a refrigerator until used.

Items like cooked meats, fresh and synthetic cream, fish etc., must be handled as little as possible and kept covered – and don't forget to empty opened canned foods into bowls. All kitchen equipment, surfaces, etc., *must* be extremely clean and should be washed in hot soapy water, then thoroughly dried.

When preparing food, keep your hair tied back and wear clean, protective clothing. Make sure your hands are scrupulously clean and if you have any cuts make sure they are covered with water-proof dressings. It's advisable if you have a cold or a tummy upset not to prepare or serve food.

Packaging is also important, when dividing up a cake, tea loaf, biscuits and quiches. Slice the food evenly into portions then wrap in a see-through wrapper like cling film, polythene or cellophane bags. Clearly label the item on the pack – give sell-by date, weight when applicable and say how much it costs.

Remember that presentation adds to temptation, see pages 27–9 for ideas!

Do ensure when transporting foods that they are in rigid, sealed containers, either plastic or tin, labelled with details of the contents. Store liquids either in insulated vacuum flasks or clean plastic bottles.

Where specific instructions regarding labelling and storage of food are needed we have added them after each recipe.

Note that all our 'To store' information refers to freshly-made foods. Make sure your label gives the information and, if you've cooked and stored or frozen the items before the sale, state on the information label that they should be eaten at once and, where appropriate, *not* refrozen. If the food is freshly-made, state on the label how to store/how long it will keep frozen.

CONVERSION CHART

The quantities for the recipes are in imperial and metric measurements. Exact conversion from imperial to metric would be difficult to work out, so the metric measures have been rounded off into 25 grams. Use either imperial or metric quantities and do not mix them or interchange them. See table below:

Ounces	Recommended conversion to nearest unit of 25 g
1	25
2	50
3	75
4	100
5	150
6	175
7	200
8	225
9	250
10	275
11	300
12	350
13	375
14	400
15	425
16 (1 lb)	450
17	475
18	500
19	550
20 (1¼ lb)	575

Liquid Measures
Imperial (pints and fluid ounces) and metric (millilitres) have been used in this section. See chart for conversion.

Imperial		Recommended ml
5 fl oz	(¼ pint)	150 ml
10 fl oz	(½ pint)	300 ml
15 fl oz	(¾ pint)	450 ml
20 fl oz	(1 pint)	600 ml
30 fl oz	(1½ pints)	900 ml
45 fl oz	(1¾ pints)	1000 ml (1 litre)

Spoon Measures

All spoon measures are level unless otherwise stated.

teasp. – teaspoon
tbsp.   tablespoon

Oven Temperatures

The table of oven temperatures below gives the oven settings in Gas Mark, Fahrenheit and Celsius Scale.

	Gas Mark	°F	°C
Very cool	1/4	225	110
	1/2	250	120
Cool	1	275	140
	2	300	150
Moderate	3	325	160
	4	350	180
Moderately	5	375	190
hot	6	400	200
Hot	7	425	220
	8	450	230
Very hot	9	475	240

SPRING AND SUMMER

FRUIT PRESERVES

If you have a delicious glut of soft summer fruits like blackberries, strawberries and raspberries, perhaps you would like to make jam but don't have the time to make it conventionally. The following is an ideal method but the jam does not set as firmly as when made in the normal way.

Strawberry

Makes about 3–3½ lb (1½ kg)

1¼ lb (575 g) strawberries

2 lb (1 kg) caster sugar

2 tbsp. lemon juice

½ bottle commercial pectin

Wipe and hull the strawberries, cutting out any bruised or damaged fruit. Crush the fruit in a mixing bowl. Stir in the sugar, lemon juice and pectin well, leave covered for 45 minutes stirring frequently. Spoon into small plastic freezer containers or small sterilized, clean jars leaving ¾ inch (2 cm) headspace to allow for expansion in the freezer. Cover with waxed discs, and lids. Level and leave for 24 hours to settle.

To vary

1 Replace the strawberries with raspberries, tayberries or blackberries.
2 For a raspberry and apple preserve, use 1¼ lb (575 g) raspberries and 8 oz (225 g) peeled, cored and finely-diced eating apples.

To label/store

Label with freezer proof labels and pen. Freeze for up to 1 year. Once open store in a refrigerator and eat within 1–2 weeks.

MICROWAVE PRESERVES

There is no reason why you can't adapt traditional recipes to your microwave oven, but the timing and liquid content are vitally important. Follow the instructions in your manufacturer's booklet.

Summer Marmalade

Makes about 3½ lb (1½ kg)

1 grapefruit

2 large sweet oranges

2 lemons

1 bottle commercial pectin

4 lb (2 kg) sugar

Remove rinds from all the fruit and chop finely. Discard pith, chop flesh and place pips in a muslin bag tied with string. Place all fruit and muslin bag in a large bowl and cover with 2 pints (1 litre) water. Leave for 2–4 hours.

Simmer fruit, bag and water for about 2 hours in preserving pan until rind is tender, or bring to H/15 lb pressure, in a pressure cooker, for 15 minutes. Remove the muslin bag when cool enough to squeeze out excess juice. Add sugar, stirring until dissolved. Stir in the pectin, boil for 1 minute until setting point is reached, then cool and bottle (see page 51).

Apricot Marmalade

Makes about 4½ lb (2¼ kg)

1 lb (450 g) dried apricots

1 lb (450 g) oranges

1 lemon

2½ lb (1.1 kg) preserving sugar

Wash the apricots; place whole pieces in a pan with the juice and finely-chopped flesh of the oranges and lemon and 1½ pints (900 ml) of water. Bring to the boil, simmer gently until fruit is tender. Add the sugar, dissolve and bring to the boil. Boil rapidly until setting point is reached, then bottle as usual.

Rum Pots

This traditional method from Germany of bottling fruit is done in large ceramic pots or tall jars, where no light can get in. You can use one variety of fruit or, to make things really interesting, start at the beginning of the season and keep adding different berries as they become available. Use unblemished fruit, but it doesn't matter if it is soft. This is quite expensive to make and would make a good prize in a raffle but a cheaper rum or brandy can be used if liked. It is certainly worth while.

Hull, stone and wash the fruit, then dry thoroughly. Sprinkle each 1 lb (450 g) of fruit with 8 oz (250 g) sugar, leave to stand for 1 hour, mix and place in jar or container. Pour on amber or dark rum, to a level 1 inch (2.5 cm) above the fruit. Top up with more fruit the same way. When full, make sure the fruit is below the level of the liquid by weighting it down with a saucer if necessary. Then cover tightly and store in a cool dark place.

To label/store

Can be eaten after a few days or leave up to 2 months for a boozy treat. As the fruit is eaten, the Rum Pot can be topped up in the same way with additional fruit. Make a big label saying when additional fruit has been added.

Cherries in Brandy

4 lb (2 kg) plump cherries, stoned

1 lb (450 g) granulated sugar

1 pint (600 ml) water

15 fl oz (450 ml) brandy (cheap cooking one if possible)

Pack the fruit into small bottling jars. Dissolve the sugar in the water and bring to the boil. Add the brandy and leave to cool. Cover the fruit with the syrup and seal.

To vary
Peaches, nectarines
Skin and stone then process as above.

Pineapple
Cut off the skin, then core and dice the fruit, and continue as above.

Clementines
Peel the fruit and leave whole. For an extra special treat use all brandy.

To label/store
Keep the fruit for 2–3 months. Store in a cool, dark place. Make sure you label the jars well, giving details of the date when they were made, contents and the price.

Rose Hip Syrup

This is a syrup that can be made into a refreshing drink. It is also very rich in Vitamin C. Make sure when you gather the rose hips that they are free from insecticides.

1 lb (450 g) rose hips, washed and chopped

3 pints (1.75 litres) boiling water

To each 1 pint (600 ml) of juice add 8–12 oz (225–350 g) sugar

Put the rose hips into an enamel saucepan and add the water. Simmer for 5 minutes and then take off the heat and leave for 15 minutes. Strain through a jelly bag and measure, then add the sugar. Heat together, stirring well, until the sugar has dissolved. Pour the syrup into warmed jars with well-fitting new screw tops leaving ¾ inch (2 cm) space to allow for expansion. Stand bottles and jars in a very deep pan with a rack at the bottom. Loosen screw band half a turn and put in enough water to cover the liquid level in the jars. The water should be heated to simmering point only and kept at that temperature for 30 minutes. Carefully take out the jars, screw down the tops and leave to cool.

To vary
Fruit syrup: damson, blackcurrant, redcurrant raspberry, cherry, strawberry, rhubarb and elderberry. Place 1 lb (450 g) fruit and 5 fl oz (150 ml) water into a basin which has been placed in a pan of simmering water.

Press down the fruit with a potato masher and cook for about 1 hour. Squash the fruit at regular intervals. Strain through a jelly bag. Measure the juice and continue as for Rose Hip Syrup.

To label/store
Label each jar with the quantity, price and storing instructions. Use the syrup once opened within one month. Store in the refrigerator.

WINE MAKING

Beginner's Guide

1 Absolutely everything used in wine-making must be sterilised to prevent airborne yeasts and vinegar fly (the two biggest causes of wine going bad) affecting the wine. The easiest way is to use a manufactured steriliser – Campden tablets – dissolved in a large bowl of hot water.

2 Prepare fresh ingredients as described in the recipe and add water and sugar.

3 Add the yeast and nutrient to the liquid, cover or fit air-lock filled with water and a Campden tablet. Leave to ferment at room temperature for required time. This can vary from about one week to a month or more. Fermentation has finished when bubbles stop coming up through the air-lock.

4 It is sometimes necessary to strain wine through a jelly bag or nylon sieve, if it is made from fresh ingredients.

5 Wine is ready for racking when fermentation has ceased and the sediment has fallen to the bottom of the jar. Syphon off carefully into clean container. The easiest way to do this is to place the full container on a level above the empty container.

6 It is normally advisable, especially with wines made from fresh ingredients, to now add wine finings, re-fit air-lock and leave again until clear. Rack again.

7 After racking, syphon into clean bottles and cork. This you will have a great difficulty doing without a special corker. Cover with plastic tops, label and leave for as long as you can to mature. Naturally the longer the better.

Starter Words For Wine-Makers

Air-lock This is the lock fitted into the neck of the demi-john to prevent infection. It's full of water, in which a Campden tablet has been dissolved.

Concentrate The concentrated juice of white or red wine grapes (with added sugar), which is sold in cans.

Fermenting This happens when the yeast acts upon the sugar content of the wine to create alcohol. You should be able to see occasional bubbles come up through the air-lock during fermentation.

Must The basic ingredients or pulp used to make the wine.

Racking Syphoning the wine off the sediment with a tube, prior to bottling. This is by far the best way to clear wine.

Sterilisation It's essential to sterilise all equipment before making wine to prevent infection. Campden tablets are particularly convenient for this – see the equipment check list.

Wine finings Added to clear a wine. Considered to be the last resort by experienced wine makers as they find it removes flavour.

Yeast The most important ingredient in wine-making. Rather than using baker's or brewer's yeast, buy a wine yeast. It gives a firmer sediment so that racking the wine is easier and it's not so likely to 'give off' flavours to the wine (see 'racking' above).

Yeast nutrient A nitrogenous substance added to activate the yeast. Available from chemists and large department stores.

Equipment

You will need two demi-johns (1 gallon/4.5 litre containers) or one plastic 5 gallon/22.5 litre container, two stoppers to fit, an air-lock, syphon tube, caps and labels, Campden tablets, finings, yeast, yeast nutrient, sugar and a can of grape juice concentrate; or fresh produce, plus any flavourings necessary for the recipe.

Nettle Wine

This wine can be a popular way of ridding the garden of some of the nettles, but do remember to pick with gardening gloves on!

Makes 6 bottles

4 pints (2.25 litres) nettle tops

1 gallon (4.5 litres) cold water

piece fresh root ginger, chopped

2½ lb (1¼ kg) sugar

2 level teasp. yeast

2 level teasp. yeast nutrient

Rinse nettles in cold water. Put in a large saucepan (or preserving pan) with 6 pints (3.6 litres) of the water and ginger. Bring to the boil and simmer for 30 minutes. Strain and make up liquid to 1 gallon (4.5 litres) with cold water.

Stir in sugar, then transfer to a plastic bucket and add yeast and yeast nutrient. Leave, tightly covered, for 2 days. Strain into demi-john using muslin bag or fine nylon sieve and fit air-lock filled with water. Liquid should come to about 1 inch (2.5 cm) below bottom of lock. Top up with extra water if needed. Leave until bubbling quietens – up to 1 week – then syphon into demi-john. Re-fit air-lock and leave 6 weeks or more, until fermentation is complete. Syphon into bottles, cork and label. Store at least 3 weeks.

Tea Wine

Makes 6 bottles

1 gallon (4.5 litres) cold water

4 level tbsp. tea leaves

2½ lb (1¼ kg) sugar

2 level teasp. citric acid

2 level teasp. yeast

2 level teasp. yeast nutrient

Boil 2 pints (1.2 litres) of the water. Pour over tea and stir in sugar. Leave to infuse until cool. Stir in citric acid. Strain into demi-john, add remaining water to make 1 gallon (4.5 litres), yeast and yeast nutrient. Follow Nettle Wine recipe as above.

Dandelion Flower Wine

Makes 6 bottles

6 pints dandelion heads (stalks removed), tightly packed

Juice of 2 oranges

Juice of 1 lemon

¼ oz (5 g) root ginger

1 gallon (4.5 litres) boiling water

1 level teasp. dried yeast

3 lb (1½ kg) granulated sugar

1 lb (450 g) raisins, scalded, drained then chopped

Place washed and cleaned heads in a sterilised bucket with the orange and lemon juice and ginger. Pour on the water and leave for 3 days, stirring several times a day. Cover. Strain off the liquid and discard the heads. Dissolve the yeast in a little warm water with a pinch of the sugar, leave for 5 minutes then add to the liquid along with the sugar. Stir well to dissolve the sugar. Pour into a fermentation jar, add the raisins and seal with a fermentation lock. Leave in a warm place until bubbles have ceased (make sure the fermentation lock is kept filled with water). Syphon the wine, taking care not to suck up any sediment, into sterilised bottles. Cork, cap and label. Store on its side in a cool dark place. Leave for at least 2–3 months.

Wine Making Kits

The big advantage of using a kit is the minimal preparation involved. You start with a can of grape juice concentrate, so you don't need to find the raw ingredients. Also the wine matures much more quickly, so for those who are impatient to taste the results you can drink some types within 2–3 weeks of bottling, which is a good point if you don't have much storage space and want to sell the wine quickly. There's a vast selection available – Muscatel, Sauternes, Rosé and Burgundy are some of the most popular.

Herby Oil

Buy a bottle of best quality olive oil or good vegetable oil. Place several generous sprigs of herbs, like tarragon, chives, or thyme, into the glass bottle, along with a few black peppercorns, 1 clove of garlic or half a shallot. Reseal the bottle. Cap and re-label. Leave for 2–3 weeks before selling, then pour into smaller bottles. Add some sprigs of fresh herbs, seal and stick a pretty label on each bottle giving the contents and date.

This is a great way of brightening up your own salad table or homemade mayonnaise.

Tarragon Vinegar

Makes 1 gallon (4.5 litres)

1 gallon (4.5 litres) malt, white **or** cider vinegar

6 oz (175 g) fresh tarragon stems (with leaves)

4 cloves garlic, peeled and cut in halves

8 bay leaves

Several sprigs of parsley and chives

Empty a little vinegar into pretty, wide-mouthed, glass jars with cork stoppers. Evenly distribute the herbs, garlic, bay leaves, parsley and chives between the jars. Pour in the vinegar and seal. After 2–3 weeks remove the herbs and garlic and reseal, cover and label.

(Place a fresh sprig of tarragon in the vinegar to make the presentation jar look especially attractive.)

Sweet Tomato Chutney

A delicious chutney using lovely summer tomatoes.

Makes about 2 lb (1 kg)

3 lb (1½ kg) ripe tomatoes

1 cucumber

1 green pepper

2 medium onions

1 tbsp. rock salt **or** sea salt

10 oz (275 g) soft brown sugar

1½ pints (900 ml) malt vinegar

1 piece root ginger, bruised

1 clove garlic

2 bay leaves

6 cardamoms

6–8 black peppercorns

6–8 cloves

Chop tomatoes; peel and chop cucumber; de-seed and chop pepper and slice onions. Place in preserving pan or pressure cooker with salt, sugar and vinegar. (Halve vinegar if cooking under pressure.) Place remaining ingredients in a small muslin bag and tie with string. Add to pan and leave to marinate for 24 hours.

Stir well, then simmer gently for 1½ hours or bring to H/15 lb pressure for 10 minutes. Remove lid and boil tomato mixture until thick. Remove muslin bag. Cool and bottle.

To label/store
Label with name and date.
Store for 2–3 weeks in a cool, dry place before using.

TERRINES

The word 'terrine' in French originally meant an earthenware dish, but now it more often refers to the contents of the dish – fish, poultry, meat, cheese, game or vegetables. Do make sure they are sealed well with jelly or fat so they are airtight. If you do this, they will keep for some days in perfect condition stored uncut in the refrigerator and can be sold in chunks or whole. If you plan to sell them on your refreshment stand, terrines must be well chilled before serving, sliced, either with bread or salad.

Normandy Terrine

This tasty terrine has just a hint of spice and a lovely rough texture.

Serves 10–12

1 large onion, peeled

6 oz (150 g) pie veal

6 oz (150 g) belly pork

2 tbsp. freshly chopped parsley

¼–½ teasp. ground mace

2 teasp. powdered gelatine dissolved in 4 teasp. hot water

1 fl oz (30 ml) brandy

Salt and freshly ground black pepper

12 rashers streaky bacon

1 turkey steak, cut in half, or small turkey breast

Preheat oven to Mark 4, 350°F, 180°C. Coarsely mince onion, veal and pork and mix together in a bowl. Mix in the parsley, mace, gelatine, brandy and seasoning. Line sides and base of 2½ pint (1½ litre) terrine with bacon, reserving 4 rashers for the top. Half fill terrine with meat mixture, add turkey, then remaining layer of mixture. Top with remaining bacon. Cover with foil. Bake in a bain-marie or roasting tin half filled with water for 1¼–1¾ hours. Leave to cool before placing in the fridge.

Vegetable and Cream Cheese Terrine

A delicious light terrine.

Serves 12–14

4 tbsp. powdered gelatine dissolved in 3 fl oz (90 ml) white wine or chicken stock, warmed

8 fl oz (240 ml) milk

1½ oz (35 g) butter or margarine

Salt and freshly ground black pepper

¼ teasp. ground nutmeg

4 oz (100 g) plain flour

2 eggs, separated

1½ lb (675 g) cream or curd cheese

5 fl oz (150 ml) whipping cream

2–3 tbsp. lemon juice

6 oz (150g) whole new carrots, scraped and lightly cooked

4 oz (100 g) whole French beans, topped and tailed and cooked

Fresh herbs – tarragon, chives and green peppercorns – to garnish.

Dissolve gelatine and allow to cool. Bring milk and butter to the boil. Take off the heat and, with a balloon whisk or wooden spoon, beat in seasoning and flour. Return to the heat and cook for 1–2 minutes without browning the mixture. Add egg yolks one at a time, beating well. Beat in cheese, then fold in cream and stiffly beaten egg whites. Pour in half gelatine mixture and lemon juice and carefully fold in. Spoon one-third of the mixture into a lightly greased 2–2½ pint (1½ litre) terrine. Add 1 layer of carrots, then more cheese mixture and then a layer of beans. Finally add the last of the cheese mixture and smooth the top with a round bladed knife. Pour remaining gelatine on top and garnish with herbs and peppercorns. Leave to set firm, and chill before transporting or serving.

or loaf tin with the bacon, reserving 4 rashers for the top. Coarsely mince pork, beef and onion. Add pepper, kernels, herbs, brandy, garlic, wine and breadcrumbs. Mix to a moist consistency. Spoon into the prepared terrine, packing down well. Top with remaining bacon. Cover tightly with foil and cook for 1½–2 hours. Leave to cool. Weigh down and leave overnight in fridge to set. Serve cold. Store covered in the fridge for 4–5 days.

Nutty Pork Terrine

This terrine is quite coarse, so if you prefer a smoother version blend the pork and beef in a liquidiser or food processor instead of in a mincer.

Serves 10–12

12 rashers streaky bacon

1 lb (450 g) lean pork

8 oz (225 g) shin of beef

1 onion, peeled

Freshly ground black pepper

2 tbsp. pine kernels

1 tbsp. mixed dried herbs

1 tbsp. brandy (optional)

1 clove garlic, peeled and crushed

1 fl oz (30 ml) red wine

2 oz (50 g) fresh breadcrumbs

Fresh herbs – sage, thyme and parsley – to garnish

Preheat oven to Mark 4, 350°F, 180°C.
    Remove rind from rashers and stretch them with the flat blade of a knife. Line sides and base of a 2½ pint (1½ litre) terrine, soufflé dish

EASTER FUN

Hot Cross Buns

Makes 12 buns

½ oz (15 g) dried yeast

5 tbsp. warm water **or** milk

1 teasp. sugar

12 oz (350 g) strong white flour, sieved

½ teasp. salt

1 teasp. mixed spice

½ teasp. ground nutmeg

¼ teasp. ground cloves

1 oz (25 g) butter

6 oz (175 g) currants

2 oz (50 g) caster sugar

2 oz (50 g) mixed peel

1 egg

5 fl oz (150 ml) milk

For the crosses
2 oz (50 g) flour

4 tbsp. water

For the glaze
4 tbsp. each of water and sugar

Blend the yeast with the warmed liquid and 1 teasp. sugar. Set aside until very frothy and doubled in size. Put the flour, salt, and spices in a warm bowl and rub in the butter. Stir in the currants, sugar, and peel. Add the yeast mixture, egg and up to 5 fl oz (150 ml) of the milk, kneading firmly to give a soft dough. Cover with a cloth and leave in a warm place until doubled in size. Knead again and form into 12 balls. Place on a greased baking tray. Mix the flour and water together to a paste to make the crosses and pipe onto each bun. Leave the buns to double in size. Bake at Mark 7, 425°F, 220°C for 15–18 minutes. Cool. Glaze with the sugar and water boiled together.

Easter Cookies

4 oz (100 g) butter **or** margarine

4 oz (100 g) caster sugar

1 egg

Few drops of vanilla essence

8 oz (225 g) plain flour, sieved

2 teasp. grated lemon rind

Preheat oven to Mark 4, 350°F, 180°C.
   Cream the fat and sugar together until light and fluffy. Beat in the egg. Add a few drops of vanilla essence, then stir in the flour and lemon

rind. Knead lightly. Roll out to ¼ inch (6 mm) thick. Cut into letter shapes or animals. Bake for 15–20 minutes or until light golden brown. When cold, decorate the biscuits with piped coloured glacé icing, and cake decorations. Or decorate with edible food colouring pens (available from kitchen specialists).

Chocolate Easter Eggs

Chocolate eggs can easily be made at home. Leave them as just simple chocolate shells or fill with delicious goodies and decorate extravagantly.

Metal and plastic moulds are available in plenty of different sizes with a great choice of designs. Look for them at kitchen-ware specialists.

To make a simple egg: melt cooking or eating chocolate in a bowl over hot, not boiling, water. Using a pastry brush, coat the inside of the mould two or three times – the more coats, the stronger the finished egg. Leave somewhere cool to set (but not in a fridge or the chocolate will shrink and crack). Tap the mould sharply and the egg should drop out. Handle carefully – fingermarks on chocolate can't be removed, so finger as little as possible.

Seal the egg halves together with piped melted chocolate, then cover the joins with decorative piping. Add other decorations – name, ribbons, sugared flowers or piped icing. One that's easy to make is made from 1 egg white, 1 teasp. lemon juice and a few drops glycerine mixed with enough icing sugar [up to 8 oz (225 g)] to give piping consistency. The eggs can be filled with sweets; or fill with fondant mixture – mix with a little egg white to make the fondant soft and wrap it around some jam, liqueur-soaked fruit or glacé fruit.

See also page 96 for ideas for other chocolate novelties.

Sugar Eggs

Makes about 12 eggs

8 oz (225 g) caster sugar

1 egg white

Put the caster sugar in a bowl, add enough pink food colouring to tint slightly, and bind sugar with egg white. Shape spoonfuls of this mixture between two teaspoons, or roll in your hands, to form eggs. Add more colouring to sugar mixture after each egg is formed to give a range of shades. Leave to dry.

Coloured Eggs

Place eggs in cold water with 2–3 tbsp. vinegar. Add food colouring. Bring to boil and cook 10 minutes. Plunge into cold water immediately.

Hand-painted Eggs

Create your own designs with pens, paints or felt tips. To prevent nasty breakages, though, blow the eggs first! Make a small hole in each end and carefully blow out the contents into a bowl. Wash out shell and dry.

Frosted Petals and Leaves

These add a lovely, pretty touch when decorating Easter eggs, cakes, biscuits, desserts and drinks.

Gather fresh edible petals and leaves like violets, forget-me-nots, rose petals, fruit blossom, mint leaves, etc.

Beat one egg white with 1 teasp. cold water. Carefully dip or paint the petals or leaves with the egg white, making sure they are all covered.

Dredge them with caster sugar, shaking off any excess. Place on a wire try in a warm place, loosely covered. Turn once or twice to prevent sticking.

You can use immediately or store for one month only in an airtight box layered with crumpled tissue, otherwise they start becoming soft.

Chocolate Shapes

Curls are made with a vegetable peeler or knife on the flat base of a bar of chocolate. This is easier if the chocolate has been placed in the refrigerator for an hour before use. For chocolate leaves, paint one side of clean, deep-veined, dry rose leaves with melted chocolate. Cool on waxed paper. Carefully peel away leaf.

AUTUMN AND WINTER

PRESERVES

Guide Lines

1 Use firm fruit and vegetables.

2 If possible use preserving sugar as it gives a clear preserve, but granulated sugar is cheaper and gives good results. Do check that you don't buy the preserving sugar with pectin added.

3 Crystallizing may be caused if the sugar has not been completely dissolved before boiling the jam, or if too much sugar has been added.

4 If you overcook the preserve it will start to caramelise and darken in colour, impairing the flavour.

5 To test for the setting point: place a little jam or marmalade in a saucer. Allow to cool (take the pan off the heat while testing) then push your finger through to see if the mixture wrinkles. If not, continue boiling until set. On cooling it should also drip off the end of the wooden spoon in flakes.

If using a sugar thermometer, the jam should read 104°C (220°F) or for a firmer set, especially for marmalade, 106°C (222°F).

6 Always pour the preserve into warm sterilised jars and seal immediately.

To label/store
Keep preserves in a cool, dark place – warmth and dampness encourage fermentation and mould, and sunlight bleaches out colour and vitamins. Label jars clearly.

Freezer Tip

When time is not on your side, freeze your fruit or prepare Seville oranges by slicing them, freezing the juice and pips, ready for use later.

Orange Marmalade

Makes 9-12 lb (4-6 kg)

8 Seville oranges

2 large sweet oranges

2 lemons

9 pints (5 litres) water

8 lb (4 kg) preserving sugar, warmed

Halve the fruit, squeeze out the juice and pips. Remove the pith and put into a muslin bag with the pips. Shred the peel to the thickness required. Put the peel, juice, muslin bag and water into a pan and bring to the boil, then simmer gently for 2 hours until peel is tender. Remove bag of pips and, when sufficiently cool, squeeze juice back into pan. Stir in the sugar over a gentle heat until sugar has dissolved. Boil quickly until marmalade is at setting point. Leave to stand 1 hour and then stir. Pour into warm, clean, dry sterilized jars. Seal and label.

To label/store

Label the jar with contents, date and amount. This marmalade keeps well for one year in a cool, dry cupboard.

Grapefruit Marmalade

Makes 5 lb (2½ kg)

1 lb (450 g) grapefruit

2½ pints (1½ litres) water

2½ lb (1.1 kg) sugar

2 tbsp. lemon juice

Halve fruit, squeeze out juice, remove pips and tie in muslin. Cut peel, pulp and pith into strips; mince, or chop in a food processor. Soak overnight in cold water. Simmer for 1½ hours. Remove bag of pips, add sugar and stir until dissolved. Add grapefruit and lemon juices, boil rapidly to reach setting point. Pot as before.

To vary
Lemon or Lime Marmalade
Follow above recipe but use 2 pints (1.2 litres) water and 2 lb (1 kg) sugar to each 1 lb (450 g) lemons or limes.

Scotch Marmalade
Use 2 sweet oranges, 2 bitter oranges, 2 lemons. Weigh the fruit, then allow 3 pints (1.75 litres) water, 3 lb (1½ kg) sugar with 2 tbsp. lemon juice to each 1 lb (450 g) fruit.

Sweet Orange Marmalade
Use 2 pints (1.2 litres) water, 2 lb (1 kg) sugar and 4 tbsp. lemon juice to each 1 lb (450 g) sweet oranges.

Tangerine Marmalade
Use 1 ½ pints (900 ml) water with 3 tbsp. lemon juice to each 1 lb (450 g) tangerines.

Three Fruit Marmalade
Use 1 medium bitter orange, 1 small grapefruit and 1 lemon with 2¼ pints (1.25 litres) water, 2¼ lb (2 kg 50 g) sugar and 2 extra tbsp. lemon juice.

Other fruits can be added for a tasty and different preserve.

Lemon Apricot Marmalade

Makes 5 lb (2½ kg)

1 lb (450 g) lemons

3 pints (1.75 litres) water

1 lb (450 g) dried apricots

3 lb (1½ kg) sugar

2 tbsp. lemon juice

Halve the lemons, squeeze out juice, remove pips and tie in muslin. Cut up peel, pulp and pith and put into the water. Slice the apricots and add to the lemon pulp, with the bag of pips. Simmer for 1¼ hours, remove the pips, add the sugar and lemon juice. Stir and boil rapidly to reach the setting point. Pot.

To vary
Orange and Apricot Marmalade
Use 2 small bitter and 2 small sweet oranges with the apricots and 3 pints (1.75 litres) water, 3 lb (1½ kg) sugar and 3 extra tbsp. lemon juice.

Mint Marmalade
Add 1 tbsp. finely chopped fresh mint to each 1 lb (450 g) marmalade.

Jelly Marmalade
Any fruit can be used to make this.

Use the same proportions as for the grapefruit marmalade. Peel citrus fruit, and remove all pith and pulp. Tie the pith, pulp, pips and half the peel in muslin. Shred remaining peel very finely. Soak peel and muslin bag overnight. Simmer for 1 hour. Remove bag, stir in sugar and lemon juice. Boil rapidly to reach setting point. Pot as before.

Apple Chutney

Makes about 3 lb (1½ kg)

1 lb (450 g) peeled and chopped onion

2 lb (1 kg) peeled and chopped cooking apples

10 fl oz (300 ml) malt vinegar

1 teasp. mixed pickling spice

1–4 oz (25–100 g) sultanas (**or** seedless raisins)

1 teasp. ground ginger

½–1 teasp. salt

12 oz (350 g) granulated (**or** moist brown) sugar

Put the onion and apple into a pan with just enough vinegar to cover; simmer slowly for 10 minutes. Add the spice, fruit, ginger and salt, and a little more vinegar. Simmer steadily until the apple is tender. (Use the minimum of vinegar at this stage, for the best flavour.) Add the remaining vinegar and the sugar; stir over a low heat until the sugar has dissolved, then boil steadily until the chutney is the consistency of jam. Spoon into hot jars and seal.

To vary
Banana Chutney
Substitute banana for apple; flavour with 1–2 tbsp. curry powder.

Carrot and Turnip Chutney
Use 1 lb (450 g) peeled and coarsely-grated raw carrots and 1 lb (450 g) peeled and coarsely-grated raw turnip instead of the apples. Add a few sprigs of parsley and a handful of raisins.

Apple and Mint Chutney
Add 2–3 oz (50–75 g) finely-chopped mint with the 12 oz (350 g) sugar; use a light vinegar and white sugar for a more appetising colour.

Tomato Chutney

Use 1½ lb (675 g) red or green tomatoes, 1 chopped green pepper and 8 oz (225 g) apples instead of all apple. Omit the dried fruit.

Indian Chutney

Increase the amount of ginger to 1½ teasp. and add 1–2 teasp. mild curry powder. Add 2–3 peeled and chopped garlic cloves.

Uncooked Date Chutney

Makes about 2 lb (1 kg)

8 oz (225 g) stoned dates, finely chopped

6 oz (175 g) peeled and chopped cooking apples

3 large onions, peeled and chopped

4 oz (100 g) seedless raisins

8 oz (225 g) light brown sugar

5 fl oz (150 ml) white malt vinegar

1 teasp. ground ginger

1 teasp. ground cinnamon

1 teasp. salt

Mix all the ingredients together, spoon into jars and cover. Leave for 24 hours before serving. Use within 2 weeks.

To vary
Chilli Chutney

Substitute 8 oz (225 g) green peppers for the dates and add 1 tbsp. dried crushed chillies and 1 teasp. chilli powder to the mixture. Continue as for uncooked date chutney. Serve very sparingly with curries; this is extremely hot!

Chestnut and Orange Chutney

Use two 14 oz (400 g) cans drained chestnuts instead of the dates and apple, and 6 small oranges, unpeeled and chopped, instead of the onions. Continue as for uncooked date chutney.

Fresh Coconut Chutney

Grate the flesh from 1 whole coconut and mix with 2 tbsp. chopped parsley, 1–2 finely chopped fresh green chillies, 1 inch (2.5 cm) piece finely chopped fresh root ginger, 1 tbsp. sweet curry paste, 2 tbsp. lemon juice (or vinegar) and 2 tbsp. oil. This dry chutney will keep in the refrigerator for only 2–3 weeks.

Green Tomato Chutney

Makes 3–3½ lb (1.5–1.6 kg)

3 lb (1½ kg) green tomatoes, chopped

1½ lb (675 g) cooking apples, peeled, cored and finely chopped

8 oz (225 g) onions, peeled and chopped

4 oz (100 g) raisins, seedless

4 oz (100 g) dried dates, chopped

8 oz (225 g) Demerara sugar

1 teasp. salt

15 fl oz (450 ml) vinegar

1–2 oz (25–50 g) crystallised ginger, chopped

1 teasp. dry mustard

Put all ingredients into a large enamel or stainless steel saucepan and bring to the boil. Reduce the heat and simmer until just tender and of a thick consistency. Pour into clean sterilised jars. Cover and label.

Store in a cool dark place for up to 1 year.

Fruit Vinegars

Use a fairly acid variety of fruit (blackberries, raspberries, etc.) but not strawberries. The fruit can be over-ripe but must be without marks. For each 1 lb (450 g) of ripe fruit use 1 pint (600 ml) of distilled vinegar. Put fruit and vinegar in a china bowl, cover with a cloth and leave to stand for 3–5 days – but remember to stir it occasionally. Strain off the liquid, add 1 lb (450 g) white sugar for every pint of liquid and dissolve it slowly in pan over a low heat. Boil for 10–15 minutes and then purée through a cloth or sieve. Bottle and store in a cool place.

Mint Jelly

3 lb (1½ kg) cooking apples, washed and chopped

10 fl oz (300 ml) dry cider

*4 tbsp. malt **or** white wine vinegar*

4 sprigs mint

1 pint (600 ml) water

1 lb (450 g) sugar, warmed for each 1 pint (600 ml) juice

few drops of green colouring

6–8 tbsp. freshly chopped mint leaves

Put the apples, cider, vinegar, 4 sprigs of mint and water into a large pan. Bring to the boil then simmer until soft. Spoon into a jelly bag and leave overnight to drip. (Don't squeeze the bag, otherwise the jelly will go cloudy.) Measure the juice, calculate the sugar (see above) and pour the apple juice and sugar into a saucepan. Stir well over a gentle heat to dissolve. Bring to the boil until jelly reaches setting point 220° F, 104° C. Add a few drops of colouring and the mint, and mix well. Pour into clean, warm, sterilised jars. Cover and label.

To vary
Replace the mint with either fresh sage or parsley and thyme.

To label/store
Keeps well for 2–3 months in a dark, cool cupboard.

CURDS

Fruit curds are the most common type as they're made and sold commercially. They are made from citrus fruits: usually lemons, oranges and limes. The rind and juice or puréed fruit is sweetened with sugar or honey, then thickened slowly in a double boiler, or saucepan, with eggs and butter (preferably unsalted). Make fruit curds in small quantities and, once opened, store in the refrigerator. Use within 2 weeks. They can be used for pie and cake fillings, as a sauce with poultry, or spread on hot buttered toast.

Lemon Curd

Makes 3 lb (1½ kg)

6 large lemons, juice and finely grated rind

6 eggs, beaten

6 oz (175 g) butter

1½ lb (675 g) caster sugar

Put all the ingredients into the top of a double saucepan, or in a basin standing over a pan of simmering water. Stir the ingredients until the sugar has dissolved. Stir occasionally until the mixture has thickened and coats the back of the wooden spoon. Remove from the heat and pour into sterilised warmed jars. Seal and label.

To vary
Orange Curd
Replace the lemons with 3 oranges and ½ lemon and use only 1 lb (450 g) sugar.

To label/store
Label with date, quantity. Keep in a cool place for up to 2–3 months. Once opened store in the refrigerator, covered.

Dried Apricot Curd

Makes 1½–2 lb (675 g–1 kg)

8 oz (225 g) dried apricots

5 fl oz (150 ml) wine mixed with 5 fl oz (150 ml) water [**or** 10 fl oz (300 ml) water]

8 oz (225 g) granulated sugar

6 oz (175 g) unsalted butter

3 eggs, beaten and strained

2 tbsp. Kirsch **or** Amaretto (optional)

Soak the fruit in the wine and water for 12 hours, then poach gently. Once soft leave to cool, then blend in a liquidiser or sieve. Follow method for Lemon Curd substituting apricot pulp for the lemon juice and rind. Just before pouring into sterilised jars stir in the Kirsch or Amaretto.

To vary
Add 4–6 oz (100–175 g) seedless raisins, or 6 oz (175 g) shelled walnuts, roughly chopped, to the basic recipe, or replace the apricots with 8 oz (225 g) figs, peaches, prunes or pears.

CHEESES

Fruit cheeses were so called because they were an alternative to the cheese course at mealtimes. Fruit cheeses are made from fruit purées sweetened with brown or white sugar and boiled until thick, then poured into pretty moulds and left to set. Leave for about 24 hours before turning out of the mould.

To label/store
Label with date, content and quantity. Serve with scones, bread or cheese or as an accompaniment to cold meats, roasts and curries. Lemon cheese is made commercially in the form of a spread. Fruit cheeses keep well

for up to 12 months in a cool place, but once opened should be stored, covered, in a refrigerator and used quickly.

Almond and Plum Cheese

Makes 3 lb (1½ kg)

4 lb (2 kg) cooking golden plums

1 lb (450 g) warmed sugar for each 1 lb (450 g) fruit pulp

*4 oz (100 g) ground **or** flaked almonds*

Wash the fruit, put into a heavy based pan and pour in enough water to just cover the plums. Bring to the boil and simmer gently until the fruit is soft and pulpy, stirring occasionally and skimming the stones off as they come to the surface. Push the pulp through a sieve or purée in a blender. Weigh out equal amounts of pulp and sugar. Return fruit and sugar to the pan and dissolve over a low heat. Boil gently until very thick (35–40 minutes) stirring constantly to avoid sticking. Add the nuts. The cheese is done when a spoon drawn through it leaves a clean line. Spoon into warmed sterilised jars and cover when cold.

Blackberry and Apple Cheese

An unusual way to keep the best of summer for a little longer and cheap, too, if you can pick the blackberries from the hedgerow.

Makes 1½ lb (675 g)

2 lb (1 kg) blackberries

1 lb (450 g) cooking apples, peeled and chopped

Juice of 1 lemon

1 lb (450 g) warmed sugar for each 1 lb (450 g) fruit pulp

Put blackberries, apples, lemon juice and ½ pint (300 ml) water in a large saucepan. Simmer until soft. Sieve and weigh pulp. Return to the pan. Add an equal amount of sugar and allow to dissolve. Cool gently, stirring until mixture is very thick and leaves a definite impression when the spoon is removed. For a party-sized dish spoon into a 1½ lb (675 g) loaf tin lined with greaseproof paper. Chill, turn out and serve decorated with fresh fruit. Otherwise pour into warmed sterilised jars or into a sterilised jelly mould. Seal and label.

BUTTERS

Fruit butters are usually softer than fruit cheeses and often spiced. They are made in the same way, but normally contain less sugar so they don't keep quite as well.

To label/store
This type of preserve does not keep a very long time. Make in small quantities and, once opened, use quickly and store in the refrigerator, covered.

Serve the sweet fruit butters sliced with tea loaves, scones or bread.

Banana Butter

A delicious preserve which makes a really different filling for cakes and sandwiches.

Makes 2 lb (1 kg)

8 bananas, peeled and sliced

Juice and finely grated rind of 2 lemons

1 lb (450 g) caster or granulated sugar or 14 oz (400 g) sugar and 2 oz (50 g) thick honey

Simmer the bananas with the sugar and lemon juice in 8 fl oz (260 ml) water and cook slowly in a double saucepan, stirring well, until thick. Spoon into small, clean, sterilised jars. Cover, seal and label.

Apple and Lime Butter

Makes 4 lb (2 kg)

3 lb (1½ kg) apples

3 limes, derinded and chopped

1 pint (600 ml) cider

1 teasp. ground cinnamon

12 oz (350 g) sugar for each 1 lb (450 g) fruit

Wash the fruit and cut into quarters. Simmer the fruit in 1 pint (600 ml) water and the cider until well softened, then rub through a fine sieve. Weigh the pulp and the sugar. Return the pulp with the sugar to the pan and simmer to a thick consistency. Add cinnamon and boil, stirring frequently, until liquid is absorbed. If you want to make it a deeper apple colour add a few drops of food colouring. Pour into small, warmed, sterilised jars, seal and label.

Grape Butter

Makes 1 lb (450 g)

1 lb (450 g) ripe green or black grapes

8 oz (225 g) sugar for each 1 lb (450 g) fruit

Wash the grapes. Place in a heavy-based saucepan with a tightly-fitting lid, and simmer over a gentle heat until tender. Push the pulp through a sieve. Weigh the pulp and sugar. Continue as for Apple and Lime Butter.

Savoury and sweet butters add delicious flavour and piquancy to many dishes – from herb and garlic bread to Bread and Butter Pudding. They are easy to prepare at home and pack into pretty jars and on the label you can put some serving suggestion ideas and how to store. (See page 71.)

All the following recipes should use softened, workable butter, not melted. Carefully mix all the ingredients together and roll, shape, pipe or pile into a dish, and chill thoroughly.

To label/store

Make in small quantities and, once opened, use quickly and store in the refrigerator, covered.

Orange, Curry and Parsley

4 oz (100 g) butter

Finely grated rind of ½ orange

2 teasp. fresh orange juice

3 teasp. parsley, finely chopped

½ teasp. curry powder

Freshly ground black pepper

Garlic and Poppy Seed

4 oz (100 g) salted butter

2 cloves garlic, peeled and crushed

Sprinkle on 2 tbsp. poppy seed

Caper and Anchovy

4 oz (100 g) butter

1 tbsp. anchovy purée

2 teasp. capers

½ teasp. lemon juice

Pimento and Parsley

4 oz (100 g) butter

2–4 tbsp. blanched, chopped pimento

Few drops Tabasco sauce

Roll into a sausage and coat with 4 tbsp. freshly chopped parsley

Tomato and Basil

4 oz (100 g) butter

2 teasp. tomato purée

Pinch sugar

1 tbsp. fresh basil, finely chopped

Watercress and Cheese

4 oz (100 g) butter

¼ bunch washed and drained watercress, puréed

1 oz (25 g) mature cheese, finely grated

Salt and freshly ground black pepper

Ginger and Toffee

4 oz (100 g) unsalted butter

2 tbsp. finely chopped stem ginger

2 tbsp. syrup from the jar

2 tbsp. caster sugar

2 tbsp. toffetti syrup

Mandarin and Cointreau

4 oz (100 g) unsalted butter

2 tbsp. mandarin syrup

1 tbsp. Cointreau

1 oz (25 g) icing sugar

Pipe into rosettes. Sprinkle on caster sugar and orange rind.

Brandy Butter

4 oz (100 g) unsalted butter

4 oz (100 g) icing sugar, sieved

1 tbsp. evaporated milk

1–2 tbsp. brandy (if preferred replace the brandy with other spirit or liqueur)

Peanut Butter

4 oz (100 g) unsalted butter

4 oz (100 g) caster sugar

1 oz (25 g) finely liquidised peanuts (or walnuts, almonds or pistachio nuts)

Choc 'n' Mint

4 oz (100 g) unsalted butter

Few drops of peppermint essence

1–2 oz (25–50 g) melted plain chocolate

2 tbsp. toasted coconut (optional)

SUGGESTED IDEAS FOR USE

Here are some ideas for putting on the labels of your savoury and sweet butters when you come to sell them.

Savoury

Delicious served on top of meats, grilled fish, beefburgers or jacket potatoes.

Use them to fill or stuff chicken, escalopes or chops coated in egg and breadcrumbs and deep fried.

To add extra flavour to scones and biscuits add the melted flavoured butter before cooking.

Toss in or stir the butters through pasta and cooked vegetables.

Sauté mushrooms, onions, sliced cooked potatoes and tomatoes in a flavoured butter of your choice.

For Quick Herb Garlic Bread, slice a small French stick diagonally. Butter both sides of each slice with Herb and Garlic butter. Wrap in foil and heat in oven at Mark 6, 400°F, 200°C for 10 minutes.

Sweet

Use when making sweet sandwiches.

When preparing bread and butter pudding.

On top of Christmas pudding and mince pies.

DRYING

This is one of the oldest methods of food preservation and one of the simplest. Fruits preserved by this method retain only a small amount of moisture so keep well if stored correctly because moulds and bacteria need water to grow. Many fruits and vegetables including herbs can be dried at home. Gather your fruit and vegetables during the autumn and only use the best quality and no inferior produce. Only a few rules have to be followed and no expensive equipment is necessary. You need:

Slatted or perforated wooden trays

Non-ferrous cake-cooling trays

Oven shelves or toasting racks

String or wooden dowelling (and everything *must* be very clean

The ideal drying temperature is between 49°C (120°F) and 66°C (150°F) and there must be an air flow.

Ideal Ways to Dry Foods

An electric conventional and convection oven.

An electric airing cupboard or warming draw.

A very cool gas oven.

An airing cupboard with plenty of ventilation.

Do not over-prepare the ingredients because they can take up quite a lot of room and this process should not be rushed. When the fruit is completely dried make sure it is cold before packing and storing in airtight containers. Label clearly. Store in a dark place.

Use dried fruits in puddings, sauces, savoury casseroles, compotes; soak in cold tea, water, wine etc., for a special treat. Leave to soak overnight, covered.

Ideal Fruits

Cooking and Eating Apples
Pears
Apricots
Plums

Apples
Use ripe, first quality fruit. Peel, core and cut into rings. Dip the even-sized slices or rings into a brine solution of 1 tbsp. salt to 2 pints (1 litre) of water, ensuring they are completely submerged. Leave for 10 minutes to prevent the fruit from going brown. Drain the slices, and dry on kitchen paper. Thread onto wooden dowelling or place on trays. Put into an oven (if not cool enough leave oven door open) for 5–6 hours or longer depending on the thickness. The apples should be soft and give slightly to the touch but they should not brown.

Pears
The fruit should only just be ripe. Peel, core and cut into quarters or eighths. Dip into the brine solution and dry thoroughly as above. Or sprinkle the quartered pears with an ascorbic acid* solution and spread on stacking trays which have been covered with muslin. Dry as for apples.

Apricots
Cut the fruit in half and stone. Place the fruit onto trays and dry as above. To test if

completely dry, the apricot should have shrunk and become leathery and when cut there should be no moisture. Pack as above.

Plums
Dry small plums whole, having first scalded them with boiling water to split the skins. Large plums can be halved and stoned.

*Ascorbic Acid Solution
Buy the ascorbic acid from the chemist and dissolve 1 teasp. in 1 pint (600 ml) water.

Vegetables

It is a little more tricky to dry vegetables than fruit, as they contain less acid and almost no natural sugar. Onions, peppers and mushrooms give the best results.

Cut up vegetables into smaller pieces than fruits as more water has to be lost and the process takes longer.

Mushrooms and peppers
Can be dried by the method described for fruit, using the lowest possible oven temperature. Pack in airtight containers, then store in a cool dark place. Use in stews and soups.

Mushrooms (without stalks)
Can be threaded on strings and hung over the cooker to dry. Use in stews and soups.

Tomato paste
Cut 6–7 lb (3–3½ kg) very ripe, peeled tomatoes in half, scoop out seeds and mash flesh with 1½–2 oz (35–50 g) salt. Leave in jelly or muslin bag over a non-metallic bowl overnight. Dry paste on tray in very cool oven until hard but still pasty. Pack into jars with a top layer of oil. Do not add salt during the cooking process.

Onions and garlic
Onions can either be dried whole and strung up in skins for everyday use, or peeled and sliced. The bulbs themselves will keep for months in a dry place, as will the slices, if kept in an airtight container. Use only sound onions or heads of garlic. Spread out the bulbs (still on their stems) on raised wire mesh which will allow the air to circulate and leave them out of doors in the sun for several days. Cover them if it rains. They are ready when their skins are bronzed (in the case of onions) and papery and the stalks have shrivelled. Knot the onions or garlic inside old stockings and store in a warm dry place, or tie them up in strings (they will sprout if they are kept in a damp atmosphere).

Bruised or damaged onions can be peeled, sliced and dried like fruit. Spread slices on trays covered with muslin and dry for three hours in an oven, or eight hours in the sun. They are ready when brittle. After being conditioned for a day, store them in plastic bags. Use dried slices as a convenience food in stews and soups; they are marvellously tasty if fried for a couple of seconds.

CRYSTALLISING AND CANDYING FRUITS AND NUTS

This process takes a long time but it is worth it, as they make ideal gifts and are much cheaper to produce than to buy in the shops. Pack in pretty baskets or gift boxes and cover well with cling-film.

Glacé fruits
These are fruits which have been dipped and soaked in a very thick sugar syrup, then dried on cooling racks until glossy in appearance.

Candied fruits
The fruit is soaked in hot syrup, to which sugar is added slowly over a period of time. The fruit is then left to dry or is dusted with caster sugar to give a crystallised finish.

Although candied or glacé fruits take a long time to prepare, no special equipment is needed and the process is not difficult to complete. But do allow at least $2\frac{1}{2}$–3 weeks if making these fruits as gifts as, if the process is rushed, the fruit becomes shrivelled and very tough. It is also important not to mix the fruits in the syrup otherwise flavours and colours will also mix.

Choosing and preparing fruit

Canned or fresh fruits are ideal but frozen fruit tends to lose its shape and texture. Choose fresh fruits that are only just ripe and not marked or misshapen; if overripe, the flavour and texture will be spoilt. Here are some of the best fruits to choose:

Fresh: whole stoned apricots, small peaches, pears, plums, figs, strawberries, pineapple, stoned cherries, orange and lemon peel, crab apples.

Canned: peach slices, pears, red stoned cherries, figs, pineapple rings and cubes, mandarin oranges, greengages, damsons.

Whole fresh fruit like peaches, crab apples and apricots should be pricked with a plastic fork. Top and tail or hull the fruit if required. Put 1 lb (450 g) prepared fruit in a pan and add just enough boiling water to cover the fruit. Reduce the heat and poach the fruit until just tender, so that the colour, flavour and texture are not impaired. Reserve 10 fl oz (300 ml) of the cooking liquid.

If using an 8 oz (225 g) can of fruit, drain, then measure the fruit syrup. Set the fruit aside and make up the syrup to 10 fl oz (300 ml) with cold water.

Crystallising the Fruit

Day 1
Fresh fruit
Add 6 oz (175 g) granulated or caster sugar or 3 oz (75 g) granulated sugar and 3 oz (75 g) powdered glucose to 10 fl oz (300 ml) reserved liquid.

Canned fruit
Add 8 oz (225 g) granulated or caster sugar to 10 fl oz (300 ml) water and fruit syrup.

Method: dissolve the sugar (and glucose) slowly in a saucepan and bring to the boil. Put the fruit in a large mixing bowl and gently pour the hot syrup over the fruit. Cover with cling-film. Leave for 24 hours to soak in the syrup. Sometimes a few drops of edible food colouring are needed to brighten fruits like pears or cherries.

Day 2
Fresh and canned fruit
Add a further 2 oz (50 g) granulated or caster sugar.

Method: drain the fruit carefully. Put the syrup into the saucepan, add 2 oz (50 g) sugar and continue as day 1. Leave for 24 hours.

Days 3 & 4
Fresh and canned fruit
As for day 2.

Method: as for day 2. Leave for 24 hours. If using fresh fruit repeat day 2 for another 3 days.

Day 5 or 8
Fresh and canned fruit
Add a further 3 oz (75 g) sugar.

Method: dissolve the sugar as above, reduce the heat, add the fruit and gently poach for 3–4 minutes. Pour the fruit into the bowl and cover with cling-film. Leave for 2 days.

Day 7 or 10
Fresh and canned fruit
As for day 5.

Method: as for day 5. The syrup should now be very thick and clear. Leave for 3–4 days.

Day 11 or 14
Drain the fruit from the syrup and place on wire trays. Place in a very cool oven, Mark ¼, 225°F, 110°C, or in a warming drawer of an oven or in a warm kitchen, loosely covered to keep out dust, until dry.

To glaze: Dissolve 8 oz (225 g) granulated sugar in 2½ fl oz (60 ml) water and bring to the boil. Dip the fruit in boiling water, then in sugar syrup. Leave to dry on a wire rack.

Marrons Glacés

1 lb (450 g) sweet whole chestnuts in the shells or 12 oz (350 g) shelled

dehydrated chestnuts, soaked in cold water overnight

1 lb (450 g) granulated sugar

8 oz (225 g) glucose powder

vanilla essence

Snip the shells of the chestnuts, put a few at a time in boiling water and scald for about 2½ minutes. Peel carefully while hot, removing all the furry brown inner skin. Put the chestnuts into a large pan of cold water and simmer very gently until tender but not broken.

Mix 8 oz (225 g) sugar with the glucose and 5 fl oz (150 ml) water to a syrup. Bring to the boil, add the drained chestnuts, and bring back to boiling point. Remove from the heat but leave in a warm place. Next day boil the syrup with the chestnuts in a pan without a lid and leave covered, overnight. Repeat on the third day and add 6–8 drops vanilla essence before heating the syrup. Lift out the chestnuts carefully and drain on a wire rack. For the glacé finish see instructions above. The chestnuts should be wrapped in aluminium foil or cling-film to prevent them hardening.

Candied Peel

2 oz (50 g) sugar for each orange, grapefruit or lemon

Wash the fruit, remove the peel and cut into quarters. Put the peel into a saucepan with sufficient water to cover. Simmer gently for 1–2 hours until tender, replenishing the water if necessary. Add the sugar, stir until dissolved and bring to the boil. Put on one side to cool, uncovered. Next day boil the syrup and simmer for a few minutes. On the third day, simmer gently until the peel has absorbed nearly all the syrup. Drain and dry as above. Any remaining syrup can be poured into the hollow of the peel before drying.

Toffee Apples

These are ideal to make, especially if you have an abundance of crisp eating apples. Choose ones that are not too big and check that there are no bruises. Wash the apples well and make sure they are thoroughly dried otherwise the toffee will not stick.

12–14 apples

*12–14 clean lollipop sticks **or** wooden sticks*

1 lb (450 g) granulated sugar

1 lb (450 g) golden syrup

*Knob of butter **or** peanut butter*

Prepare a well-greased baking tray on which to stand the apples. Have a pan of boiling water ready to put the toffee saucepan in so that the toffee does not harden whilst coating the apples. Insert the wooden sticks into the apples. Put the sugar and syrup into a large, heavy-based saucepan. Dissolve the sugar over a gentle heat then bring to the boil. Boil the

toffee until it reaches 155°C (310°F) on a sugar thermometer (or if you drop a few drops into cold water the mixture should crack between your finger and thumb). Take the pan off the heat when testing to prevent over-cooking. When ready, stand the saucepan in the boiling water carefully. Add the knob of butter and stir well. Dip the apples into the toffee once for a thin coating and twice for thicker coating. Leave to drip for a few seconds then stand on the tray. Leave to set. (Remember, toffee should be handled very carefully because it can cause a nasty burn.) Wrap the set apples in waxed or greaseproof paper, securing firmly at the base of the stick with a metal tie or small elastic band. Use within 1 week.

For an extra treat when the toffee has set dip the apples into melted chocolate ... packed full of calories ... but delicious!

PIES

Hot Water Crust Pastry

This is so called because the fat and water are heated before being added to the flour to form the dough. It is, in fact, one of the easiest pastries to work with, but do remember that it should be kept warm until required, otherwise it will crack and be difficult to mould. Covering the pastry with a damp tea-towel will prevent cracking – or keep it in a warm place.

1 lb (450 g) plain flour

6–7 fl oz (180–210 ml) water

Pinch salt

1 oz (25 g) butter

3 oz (75 g) lard

Sift the flour into mixing bowl. Bring water to the boil in a saucepan, add salt, butter and lard and stir until fats dissolve. Pour boiling liquid into flour and beat vigorously to make a smooth dough, leaving pan clean. Knead well on a floured surface. The paste should be stiff but pliable enough to mould easily. Add a little hot water if necessary. Work quickly so the pastry stays warm and easy to mould.

Pork Pie

Serves 4–6

8 oz (225 g) hot water pastry

12 oz (350 g) pork, lean and fat mixed (not too lean otherwise it will be dry)

2 teasp. salt

½ teasp. ground pepper

A little sage to taste

3 eggs, hard boiled and shelled (optional)

Filling
3–5 fl oz (75–150 ml) jellied **or** gelatine stock

For the glaze
A little egg wash

Preheat oven to Mark 7, 425°F, 220°C.
Make up the hot water pastry and line a pork pie mould – or a loose-bottomed cake tin will suffice – leaving sufficient crust for lid. Mince the meat, add seasonings and 5 tbsp. water. A little sage may be added at this point if liked. Mix well. Half fill the pastry-lined mould and add the eggs if using, then add the remaining mixture. Moisten the edges, roll out the pastry lid and place on top, pressing edges well together. These can be fluted if you wish. Decorate with leaves made from any remaining pastry. Leave a small hole in the top, through which the jelly can be added when pie is quite cold. Brush the top and pastry decorations with a little egg and water.
Bake at Mark 7, 425°F, 220°C for the first 30 minutes to cook the pastry. Then lower the temperature to Mark 5, 375°F, 190°C for a further 1–1½ hours. If you want a really golden crust remove pie from mould and return to oven, having lightly brushed round the sides with egg, and cook for 10–15 minutes.

To label/store

Sell the pies either in slices or wedges. Keep well wrapped, ideally store in a chilled unit. Label well with contents, quantity and an eat by date. Wrap in clear cellophane or cling-film. Do make sure not to store with uncooked meats etc.

a further 10–15 minutes. Place all the remaining ingredients in a large bowl, mix well and pour the mixture into the flan ring. Return to the oven, reduce temperature to Mark 5, 375° F, 190° C, and bake for 40 minutes or until the filling has set. Leave to cool. Decorate with remaining cream.

Pumpkin Pie

Serves 8–10

5 oz (150 g) lard and margarine

10 oz (275 g) plain flour

1 oz (25 g) ground almonds

1 egg yolk

Milk and sugar to glaze

15 oz (425 g) fresh pumpkin pulp

3 oz (75 g) caster sugar

4 tbsp. golden syrup

8 fl oz. (260 ml) whipping cream, lightly whipped (reserve 2 tbsp.)

1½ teasp. ground cinnamon

1 teasp. ground ginger

pinch ground allspice

Preheat oven to Mark 6, 400° F, 200° C.

Rub the fat into the flour until it resembles fine breadcrumbs. Add the almonds and egg yolk, and enough cold water to bind to make a smooth but not sticky dough. Roll out the pastry to line an 8 inch (23 cm) flan ring. With the remaining pastry make a plait and use it to make a decorative edge. Glaze with a little milk and sugar.

Bake blind for 10 minutes, then remove baking beans and continue cooking for

CHRISTMAS GOODIES

Viennese Christmas Stars

Makes 40–50

6 oz (175 g) margarine **or** butter

2 oz (50 g) icing sugar, sieved

6 oz (175 g) plain flour, sieved

2–3 drops vanilla **or** almond essence

To Decorate
Quartered glacé cherries, small pieces of angelica or halved walnuts.

Preheat oven to Mark 7, 425°F, 220°C.

Cream the margarine and icing sugar with a wooden spoon or an electric mixer until light and fluffy and pale in colour. Fold in the plain flour along with the essence. Pipe the mixture into stars onto a baking tray. Decorate with one of the suggested decorations. Bake for 8–10 minutes or until golden brown. Cool on a wire tray.

Label and store in an airtight tin for 1–2 weeks or in the freezer for up to 6 months.

Christmas Cookies

Makes 30–40

10 oz (275 g) margarine **or** butter

1 lb (450 g) plain flour

9 oz (250 g) caster sugar

pinch nutmeg

¼ teasp. vanilla essence

1 egg, size 3

Preheat oven to Mark 5, 375°F, 190°C.

Rub the fat into the flour until it forms fine breadcrumbs. Add the remaining ingredients. Knead to a soft but manageable dough on a lightly-floured surface and cut into fancy shapes – hearts, bells, Christmas trees, etc. Make a little hole in each so that when the biscuit is cooked a pretty ribbon can be threaded through to hang from the Christmas tree. Bake for 10–15 minutes. Cool on a wire cooling tray. Thread the hanging ribbon through the biscuit. Decorate with glacé icing. Sieve 4 oz (100 g) icing sugar. Add enough cold water to make a smooth piping icing then colour and flavour as you wish.

Florentines

Makes 30

1 oz (25 g) glacé cherries, chopped

1 oz (25 g) mixed peel, chopped

1 oz (25 g) sultanas, chopped

4 oz (100 g) almonds, chopped

3½ oz (85 g) butter **or** margarine

4 oz (100 g) caster sugar

1 tbsp. top of the milk **or** cream

1 oz (25 g) plain flour

4–5 oz (100–150 g) plain chocolate, melted

Preheat oven to Mark 4, 350°F, 180°C.

Place chopped fruit and nuts in a pan with the butter, sugar and milk and heat until bubbling. Add the flour, then put about 6 teasp. on silicone-lined tray, well apart to allow for spreading. Bake for 8–10 minutes until golden. Remove from the baking tray when just warm to prevent sticking. Coat backs with chocolate, and spread evenly with a knife. Then with a fork make a wavy lined pattern before the chocolate has set. Leave in a cool place to set.

To store
Pack in an airtight tin or box for 1 week or freeze for up to 1 month.

Mincemeat

Makes 8-10 lb (4-5 kg)

1 lb (450 g) seedless raisins

12 oz (350 g) sultanas

12 oz (350 g) currants

4 oz (100 g) mixed peel

2 oz (50 g) almonds, blanched and chopped

1 carrot, peeled and grated

8 oz (225 g) suet, shredded

*12 oz (350 g) demerara **or** soft brown sugar*

8 oz (225 g) cooking apples, peeled and chopped

*5 fl oz (150 ml) brandy **or** rum*

Juice and grated rind of 1 orange

Juice and grated rind of 1 lemon

1 level teasp. ground mixed spice

Mince the raisins, sultanas, currants and peel together into a mixing bowl. Add the remaining ingredients. Cover and leave for two days, stirring occasionally and adding more liquor if necessary to keep the mixture moist. Pack into clean sterilized jars. Cover and label.

To store
Keeps very well. It should be made at least a month before using to allow the flavours to mature.

Dundee Cake

Serves 10-12

*8 oz (225 g) butter **or** margarine*

8 oz (225 g) caster sugar

Finely grated rind of 1 small orange

4 eggs

8 oz (225 g) plain flour, sieved

1 level teasp. baking powder

4 oz (100 g) chopped candied peel

1 oz (25 g) almonds, blanched and chopped

2 oz (50 g) glacé cherries, chopped

1 lb (450 g) currants and sultanas, mixed

Topping
1 oz (25 g) split or halved almonds

Preheat oven to Mark 2, 300°F, 150°C.
   Cream butter and sugar; add rind. Beat in eggs gradually; fold in flour, sieved with baking powder. Stir in peel, nuts and fruit. Spoon into an 8 inch (20 cm) tin. Bake for 3 hours. After first 30 minutes top with 1 oz (25 g) split almonds.

To label/store
This cake will keep very well. Label with date made, and store in an airtight tin.

Christmas Pudding

Makes 6 pint (3.6 litres) pudding

8 oz (225 g) plain flour

1 lb (450 g) fresh breadcrumbs

1 level teasp. salt

2 level teasp. mixed spice

Juice and grated rind of 1 orange

Juice and grated rind of 1 lemon

1½ lb (675 g) suet, chopped

1 lb (450 g) brown sugar

1 lb (450 g) currants

1 lb (450 g) sultanas

8 oz (225 g) glacé cherries, quartered

2 oz (50 g) almonds, chopped

1 lb (450 g) raisins, stoned

4 oz (100 g) mixed peel

2 oz (50 g) ground almonds

1½ lb (675 g) cooking apples, peeled and chopped

1 medium carrot, grated

8 standard eggs, beaten

1 wine glass brandy (optional) **or** milk, beer, stout, barley wine to mix

Place the flour, breadcrumbs, salt, mixed spice, grated rinds of the orange and lemon, suet and sugar into a large bowl, and mix thoroughly.

Add all fruit, nuts and grated carrot, stir very well.

Add the eggs to the mixture, followed by the orange and lemon juice and the brandy.

Mix to a soft dropping consistency with the milk, beer, stout or barley wine.

Turn the mixture into greased pudding basins. (Divide as you please, depending on whether you think your market will go for smaller or larger puddings.)

Cover with greaseproof paper and tie down. Cover the greaseproof paper with tinfoil and seal. Steam for 6–8 hours. Do not let the water go off the boil and top up as necessary with more boiling water.

Remove the coverings from the puddings and leave to cool. Cover with fresh greaseproof paper and store in a cool, dry larder.

Note on the label that these puddings need to be steamed again for a further 2–4 hours before eating (or 2–4 minutes in a microwave oven, but re-cover with cling-film, not foil, and prick twice).

Ideally, make these 3 to 4 months in advance to give them time to mature.

ANYTIME

BREADS

Granary Bread

Makes 2 lb (1 kg)

1½ lb (675 g) Granary flour, warmed

8 oz (225 g) wholemeal flour, warmed

1 tbsp. salt

1 oz (25 g) fresh yeast **or** ¼ oz (7 g) dried yeast

1 tbsp. clear honey

1 tbsp. molasses (optional)

Mix the flours together with the salt and rub in the fat. Activate the fresh yeast by creaming it with 5 fl oz (150 ml) warm water and the honey. If using dried yeast, dissolve the honey in 5 fl oz (150 ml) warm water and sprinkle the yeast on. (There is no need to stir dried yeast.) Leave in a warm place for 10–15 minutes until frothy and yeast granules have dissolved. Dissolve the molasses in 15 fl oz (450 ml) warm water. Stir the yeast and molasses mixtures into the dough. Knead, adding more liquid if required. Allow to rise until doubled in size. Knock back and knead the dough well. Shape into loaves. Cover and allow to rise for about 30 minutes. Bake at Mark 6, 400°F, 200°C for 30–40 minutes.

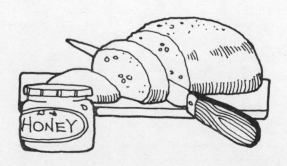

To vary
Muesli Loaf
Replace half the flour with your favourite muesli cereal. Top the loaf with nibbed wheat. It will not rise as much.

Cheese and Onion Loaf

A savoury loaf that can be left whole or served in slices. Very quick to make.

Makes 2 x 1 lb (2 x 450 g) loaves

6 oz (175 g) margarine, softened

1 lb (450 g) self-raising flour

2 teasp. baking powder

2 teasp. dry mustard

1 teasp. salt

½ teasp. freshly ground black pepper

1 onion, peeled, diced and sautéed in 1 tbsp. oil

6 slices of ham, finely diced

2 eggs

6 oz (175 g) cheese, grated

10 fl oz (300 ml) milk

Preheat oven to Mark 5, 375°F, 190°C.
   Place all the ingredients in a mixing bowl and beat together for 2–3 minutes. Spoon into the prepared greased and lined loaf tins. Gently tap the tin on a work surface to remove any air bubbles, and smooth the top. Bake for 40–45 minutes or until well risen and golden brown.

To label/store
Label and date. Keep well wrapped in foil or an airtight tin up to 1 week. Freeze for up to 3 months.

Wholemeal Bread

Makes 4 lb (2 kg)

2 oz (50 g) fresh yeast

3 lb (1½ kg) wholemeal flour

2 level tbsp. caster sugar

4–6 level teasp. salt

*1 oz (25 g) lard **or** vegetable oil*

Blend the fresh yeast with ½ pint (300 ml) warm water, or sprinkle on the dried yeast. Leave to froth. Mix the flour, sugar and salt, then rub in the lard. Stir the yeast liquid into the dry ingredients, adding sufficient warm water [about 1 pint (600 ml)] to make a firm dough that leaves the bowl clean. Turn out on to a lightly-floured surface and knead until it feels firm and elastic and no longer sticky. Shape into a ball, cover with cling-film, or a damp tea towel and leave to rise until doubled in size. Turn the dough out on to a floured surface and knead again until firm. Divide into 2 or 4 pieces and flatten firmly with the knuckles to knock out any air bubbles. Shape to fit 2 x 2 lb (1 kg) or 4 x 1 lb (450 g) tins. Brush tops with salted water and prove until the dough rises to the top of the tins (about 1 hour at room temperature). Bake the loaves in the centre of the oven at Mark 8, 450°F, 230°C for 30–40 minutes. Cool on a wire rack.

Alternative shapes

1 Divide each quarter-portion of dough into 4 smaller pieces, shape into rolls and fit side by side in the tin. Finish as above.

2 Shape each quarter-portion of dough into a round cob, dust with flour and put on to a floured baking sheet. Finish as above.

3 Shape all the dough into a round cob and place on a large floured baking sheet. Partly cut into 4 wedges and scatter cracked wheat or flour over the top. Allow to rise, mark again and bake for 40–45 minutes.

Quick Bread

Make 3 x 1 lb (3 x 450 g) or 26–30 rolls

3 lb (1½ kg) strong plain flour

*1 oz (25 g) butter **or** lard*

3 teasp. salt

1 pkt. easy blend dried yeast

1½ pints (900 ml) warm water

Warm the flour in a large bowl. Rub the fat and salt into the flour. Sprinkle in the yeast and mix in enough water to make a moist sticky dough. Beat well with a wooden spoon or electric mixer for 3–4 minutes – at this stage the dough is too wet to be kneaded. Divide the dough between three greased and floured 1 lb (450 g) loaf tins. Leave covered to rise in a warm place until doubled in size. Bake at Mark 5, 375°F, 190°C for 35 minutes or until golden brown. (Turn out and tap the bottom – if it sounds hollow the loaf is cooked.) Cool on a wire tray.

Toppings

Bread can be topped in various ways either before cooking or 10 minutes from the end of cooking. Brush the top with water for a good crusty loaf; if you want a softer crust use milk.

For a sticky glaze on sweet bread mix together equal quantities of milk and honey and brush on.

For a crunchy topping brush the loaf with a beaten egg then coat lightly with poppy or sunflower seeds, nuts, nibbed wheat, rolled oats, grated cheese, or dried fruit.

Teabreads

These delicious breads can be sold in slices or whole. They are quick to make but only keep well for a short time, but can be frozen for 1 month.

Makes 1 x 2 lb (1 kg) or 2 x 1 lb (450 g) loaves

1 lb (450 g) self-raising flour, sieved

2 level teasp. baking powder

*4 oz (100 g) margarine **or** butter*

4 oz (100 g) caster sugar

2 eggs, size 3

10 fl oz (300 ml), scant, milk

Preheat oven to Mark 4, 350°F, 180°C.

Put the flour into a mixing bowl. Add the baking powder and rub in the margarine. Add the sugar. Add the eggs and just enough milk to make a soft dropping consistency. Spoon the mixture into a greased and lined tin. Bake for about 1½–1¾ hours or until golden brown in colour. Cool on a wire tray. Wrap well in foil.

To vary
Brazil and Apricot
Add 2 oz (50 g) chopped Brazil (or any other nuts) and 4 oz (100 g) chopped dried apricot and ½ teaspoon mixed ground spice.

Banana and Walnut
Add 2–3 peeled mashed bananas and 2 oz (50 g) chopped walnuts just before you add the milk.

Fruit and Nut
Add 4 oz (100 g) mixed dried fruit and 2 oz (50 g) chopped almonds just after the margarine has been rubbed in.

Wholewheat Scones

Makes 15–20

*8 oz (225 g) wholewheat **or** plain flour, sieved*

3 teasp. baking powder

*2 oz (50 g) margarine **or** butter*

Pinch of salt

*5 fl oz (150 ml) milk **or** sour milk*

1 egg, size 3, beaten

Preheat oven to Mark 6, 400°F, 200°C.

Mix the flour and baking powder into a bowl. Rub in the margarine until the mixture forms fine breadcrumbs. Add the salt. Pour in the milk and egg to give a soft dough. Knead until smooth. Roll out to ½ inch (1.5 cm) thick and cut using a round 2 inch (5 cm) pastry cutter, or form into a cake shape and mark into segments. Place on a lightly-greased baking tray and bake for 10–12 minutes or until light golden brown.

To vary
Add one of the following to the above.

Honey
Beat 1½ tbsp. honey with the egg.

Bran
Add 2–3 level tbsp. bran to the flour.

Spicy
Add 1½ teasp. mixed ground spice before rubbing in the fat to the flour.

Fruit
Add 3 oz (75 g) dried fruit after rubbing in the fat.

Cheese
Add 2–3 oz (50–75 g) grated cheese and a little cayenne pepper to the mixture after rubbing in the fat.

Herb
Add 1 teasp. mixed dried herbs and some freshly ground black pepper after rubbing in the fat. Cut into fingers and brush with milk before baking.

CAKES AND BISCUITS

Chocolate Peppermint Slice

Makes 20

2 oz (50 g) soft brown sugar

4 oz (100 g) margarine

4 oz (100 g) self-raising flour

1 teasp. cocoa

pinch salt

4 oz (100 g) icing sugar

few drops peppermint essence

8 oz (225 g) chocolate plain **or** *milk, melted*

Preheat oven to Mark 5, 375°F, 190°C.

Cream sugar and margarine until soft and creamy. Stir in flour, cocoa and salt. Spread mixture on a greased Swiss roll tin and bake for 20 minutes. Whilst still hot, mark into fingers and leave to cool. Mix the sieved icing sugar with ¼ teasp. peppermint essence (or to own desired taste), and a little water. Spread over the biscuit mixture, leave to set, spread with melted chocolate. When cold, cut into fingers.

To store
Store in an airtight tin for 1 week or in the freezer for 2 months.

Flapjacks

Makes about 24 pieces

4 oz (100 g) butter **or** *margarine*

1 oz (25 g) dark brown **or** *caster sugar*

2 tbsp. golden syrup

8 oz (225 g) rolled oats

Pinch of salt

Preheat oven to Mark 5, 375°F, 190°C.

Melt the fat, sugar and syrup together in a saucepan. Add the oats and salt, mixing well. Put into a prepared greased baking tin 9 x 9 inch (23 x 23 cm). Bake for 25–30 minutes or until golden brown. Whilst still warm cut into fingers or squares.

To vary
Cornflake Crush
Replace the rolled oats with 7 oz (200 g) cornflakes or Rice Crispies.

Nutty Chew
Omit 2 oz (50 g) rolled oats and replace with desiccated coconut or coconut chips.

Madeleines

Makes about 36

8 oz (225 g) caster sugar

4 large eggs

¼ teasp. vanilla essence

1 lemon, grated rind

8 oz (225 g) plain flour sieved with 1 teasp. baking powder

6 oz (175 g) unsalted butter, melted

2 tbsp. icing sugar, sieved

1 oz (25 g) glacé cherries

¼ oz (7 g) angelica

Preheat oven to Mark 6, 400°F, 200°C.

Whisk sugar, eggs and vanilla essence together in a bowl over hot water, until thick and creamy and the whisk leaves a thick trail. Fold in the lemon rind and half the flour with a metal spoon using a figure of eight movement.

Then fold in the butter and the remaining flour. Part fill shell-shaped mould trays or madeleine tins. Bake for 10–15 minutes. Decorate with icing sugar, cherries and angelica.

To store
Store in an airtight tin for up to 1 week or 3 months in the freezer.

Meringues

Make into tiny meringues and sandwich together with cream, or leave just by themselves.

Makes about 8–12 medium sized or 16–20 tiny ones

2 egg whites

4 oz (100 g) caster and icing sugar

Pinch salt

Preheat oven to Mark ¼, 225°F, 110°C.

Whisk the egg whites stiffly in a grease-free bowl until stiff. Fold in half the sugar, whisking well so it remains stiff. Fold in the remainder. Pipe or spoon piles of meringue onto a greased baking tray. Bake for 2–3 hours depending on the size or until crisp, but still white. Cool on a wire tray.

To vary
The basic meringue mixture can be varied in many ways.

1 Blend 1 oz (25 g) chocolate powder with the 4 oz (100 g) sugar before folding in to the whites.

2 Add a few drops of vanilla essence to the stiffly-whisked egg whites.

3 Add, with the last lot of sugar, 2–3 teasp. finely grated orange or lemon rind or 2 teasp.

coffee essence, or 1–2 tbsp. slightly warmed honey or syrup, or 2 oz (50 g) finely ground nuts.

Meringue Mushrooms

Make up the basic mixture and colour two thirds red and the remainder brown with edible food colouring. Spoon the red mixture into small mounds on rice paper. Sprinkle with sugar strands. Make the stalks with the rest of the mixture by either piping 1 inch (2.5 cm) long stalks or spooning out little even-sized oblongs. Bake as above. Stick the stalks and tops together with jam.

To store
In an airtight box or tin for up to 2–3 months.

Queen Cakes

Makes 14–16 cakes

4 oz (100 g) butter **or** margarine

4 oz (100 g) caster sugar

2 eggs, beaten

4 oz (100 g) self-raising flour, sieved

1–2 oz (25–50 g) dried fruit

Few drops of vanilla essence **or** fruit juice

14–16 paper cake cases

Preheat oven to Mark 5, 375°F, 190°C.

Cream the fat and sugar together in a mixing bowl until light and fluffy. Gradually beat in the eggs. Fold in the flour and fruit. Divide the mixture evenly between the cake cases on a baking tray or in a patty or bun tin. Bake for 15–20 minutes or until golden brown and well risen. Cool on a wire tray.

To vary
Butterfly Cakes
Make up the above mixture but omit the dried fruit. If you would like *chocolate cakes* omit 2 teasp. self-raising flour and replace with 2 teasp. sieved cocoa powder and 1 teasp. milk.

When the cakes are cooked and cooled cut a small circle from each cake top with a small sharp knife. Cream well together 3 oz (75 g) softened butter and 5 oz (150 g) sieved icing sugar with a few drops of vanilla essence until smooth.

Spoon a little butter cream into each cake or pipe it in. Cut the top circle in half and press into the butter cream to form wings. Decorate the tops with any remaining butter cream and sprinkle on some hundreds and thousands, chocolate vermicelli or sieved icing sugar.

Refrigerator Cookies

Makes about 20

5 oz (150 g) caster sugar

5 oz (150 g) margarine

1 egg, size 3

1 teasp. vanilla essence

10 oz (275 g) plain flour

1 teasp. baking powder

Cream the sugar and fat until light and fluffy. Work in the remaining ingredients. Shape into a roll, wrap in cling-film or greaseproof paper. Chill until firm.

Preheat oven to Mark 5, 375°F, 190°C.

Cut the roll into ¼ inch (6 mm) slices and bake for 10–12 minutes.

The mixture can be kept for up to 2 weeks in a refrigerator before cooking. Store in an airtight tin or freezer once cooked.

To vary

Add one of the following to the basic ingredients:

Ginger

Add 2 tbsp. ground ginger, top with chopped ginger before cooking, then sprinkle with sieved icing sugar.

Coffee

Add 2–3 teasp. coffee essence and omit the vanilla essence.

Shortbread

Makes 30

7 oz (200 g) plain flour

2½ oz (60 g) caster sugar

*5 oz (150 g) margarine **or** butter*

Preheat oven to Mark 3, 325°F, 160°C.

Sift flour into a basin with the sugar. Add butter and 'crumb' the mixture. Then gradually bind it together into a ball. Roll out on a floured surface to about ¼ inch (6 mm) thickness. Cut into rounds with a 2 inch (5 cm) cutter. Put on to a baking sheet, prick a couple of times with a fork and bake for about 15 minutes until just beginning to brown.

Remove from the oven and leave for a couple of minutes – then lift off and put on a cooling tray. Sprinkle tops of shortbread lightly with caster sugar.

Slab Cake

This is the basic recipe.

*12 oz (350 g) butter **or** margarine*

12 oz (350 g) caster sugar

6 eggs, beaten

12 oz (350 g) self-raising flour, sieved

Few drops of vanilla essence

Preheat oven to Mark 4, 350°F, 180°C.

Cream fat and sugar together until pale and fluffy. Gradually beat in eggs, beating well to incorporate plenty of air. Fold in flour with a metal spoon. Spoon mixture into a greased and lined 11 x 8 inch (28 x 20 cm) or 10 inch (25 cm) round baking tin. Bake for 45–60 minutes or until golden and risen.

Petits Fours

Any left-over pieces of Slab Cake can be cut into attractive shapes, such as small triangles, and iced. Pipe a design in a lighter shade.

To vary
Battenberg

Make the basic slab cake mixture. Divide the baking tin lengthways with a wall of greased greaseproof paper or foil. Pour half the mixture into one side of the tin. Colour the remaining mixture pink or brown and pour into the other side of the tin. Bake as for Slab Cake. Cool and trim the sides. Cut each piece in half lengthways. Spread a strip of each colour with warmed sieved apricot jam and place side by side. Top with remaining strips with the colours forming a chequer-board and press well together. Coat the outside of the cake with warmed sieved apricot jam. Roll out 12 oz (350 g) ready-made marzipan thinly in a little caster sugar. Wrap around the cake and seal the join well. Crimp the edges and score a decorative pattern. Make marzipan leaves with the offcuts.

Spicy Treats

6 oz (175 g) plain flour

6 oz (175 g) caster sugar

4½ oz (115 g) margarine or butter

3 tbsp. golden syrup

1½–2 teasp. mixed ground spice or ground ginger

¾ teasp. bicarbonate of soda

Preheat oven to Mark 4, 350°F, 180°C.
Sieve the flour into a mixing bowl and add the sugar. Just *melt* the margarine and syrup in a saucepan and pour in the spice and bicarbonate of soda. Knead until smooth. Roll out to ¼ inch (6 mm) thick on a lightly floured surface. Cut into biscuits using a 2 inch (5 cm) round cutter and prick with a fork. Bake on a very lightly greased baking tray for 10–12 minutes or until golden brown. Cool on a wire rack.

To vary
Cut the raw, rolled out dough into fun animal shapes and decorate the biscuits with currants, chocolate drops etc. for the animal features.

To store
In an airtight container for 2 weeks or in the freezer for up to 3 months.

Traditional Brownies

Makes about 16

4 oz (100 g) chocolate (bitter chocolate gives a stronger flavour), or 3 oz (75 g) cocoa powder and 3 oz (75 g) extra fat

6 oz (175 g) butter or margarine

9 oz (250 g) sugar

3 eggs

few drops vanilla essence

3 oz (75 g) plain flour

½ teasp. baking powder

3 oz (75 g) chopped mixed nuts

little milk

little icing sugar

Preheat oven to Mark 5, 375°F, 190°C.
Melt the chocolate or cocoa and fat in a bowl over a pan of hot water. Cream the butter, sugar and eggs until fluffy. Beat in the melted chocolate, then the vanilla. Fold in flour, baking powder and nuts, adding milk to give a soft dropping consistency. Spoon into a greased, lined 9 inch (23 cm) cake tin. Bake for about 45 minutes. Cut into squares and sprinkle with sieved icing sugar.

To vary
Marbled Brownies
Divide basic mixture in two. Add nuts to one, chocolate to other. Spoon alternately into tin.

Fudge Brownies
Use only 4 oz (100 g) sugar. Cook 5 oz (150 g) brown sugar, little milk and 1–2 oz (25–50 g) butter until syrupy, then add with the chocolate.

Marshmallow Brownies
Add 4 oz (100 g) chopped marshmallows.

Crunchy Wholewheat Brownies

Use wholewheat flour and brown sugar (half basic recipe quantities), honey instead of chocolate, and pecan nuts. Spoon into a 7 inch (18 cm) round cake tin, sprinkle with brown breadcrumbs and sugar, then bake. Drizzle with icing.

Peanut Butter Brownies

Use peanut butter instead of butter, and peanuts instead of mixed nuts.

Fruity Brownies

Use 3–6 oz (75–175 g) chopped dried fruit instead of nuts.

Apple Meringue Brownies

Top with apple slices and meringue. Bake at Mark 3, 325°F, 160°C for 25–30 minutes until meringue is golden brown.

Orange Brownies

Use juice of 2 oranges instead of milk, and brown sugar. Cream in the grated rind. Cook for an extra 15 minutes. Top with segmented fruit.

Coconut Brownies

Use half the chocolate, and use 2–3 oz (50–75 g) desiccated coconut instead of nuts. Toss in toasted coconut when cooked.

Walnut Brownies

Use 4 oz (100 g) walnut halves, or pieces, instead of the mixed nuts. Decorate each square with a piece of walnut.

NIBBLES & BITES

If you have a committee meeting or AGM on a budget these items are good to make, or even serve them at a cheese and wine party.

Pastry Bites

For the basic dough, which makes about 3–4 dozen bites, you will need:

12 oz (350 g) self-raising flour

3 oz (75 g) margarine

½ teasp. salt

As for a scone dough, rub the fat into the flour until the mixture resembles fine breadcrumbs. Flavour as described below. Mix enough water to bind the contents to a soft dough, then roll and twist into small, plain or fancy shapes. Remember to keep shapes small as they puff up when cooked.

Fry the shapes in deep fat or oil (it is hot enough when a cube of bread turns golden in 1 minute) for 2–3 minutes, turning occasionally. Drain on absorbent kitchen paper and sprinkle with salt.

Here are some suggestions for flavourings:

Onion Knots

Mix 1 level teasp. onion salt into about ⅙ of the dry mixture. Bind with a little water to a soft dough; roll out tiny pieces into strips. Tie in knots. Continue as above.

Celery Fingers

Mix 1 level teasp. celery salt into about ⅙ of the mixture, form a dough and shape into about 10 long rolls. Continue as above.

Cheese Twists

Mix about 1 oz (25 g) very finely-grated firm mature Cheddar cheese into ⅙ of the dough. Roll out and cut into about 20 long, thin rolls, twist two together and continue as above.

Marmite Straws

These are also based on the scone dough. Roll dough out to about ¼–½ inch (6–12 mm), spread thinly with Marmite and cut into thin strips. Twist into shapes, then bake in a hot oven, Mark 6, 400°F, 200°C for about 15 minutes until crisp and golden.

Paprika Pretzels

Crumble ½ a chicken Oxo cube into about ⅙ of the crumble mixture and form into a dough with water. Roll out into about 12 strips and shape into rings. Fry as above, then drain and toss in paprika.

Cheese Knots

Makes 20–30

7 oz (200 g) frozen puff pastry, thawed

3 oz (75 g) strong Cheddar cheese, grated

Beaten egg to glaze

Preheat oven to Mark 7, 425°F, 220°C.

Thinly roll out the pastry and top with 2 oz (50 g) of the cheese. Fold pastry in half. Brush with beaten egg and scatter the remaining cheese over the top. Cut into strips ¼ inch x 3 inch (6 mm x 8 cm). Tie in knots. Place on ungreased baking trays and bake for 15 minutes, until golden.

Savoury Straws

Makes 150

8 oz (225 g) margarine **or** butter

1 lb (450 g) plain flour

6 oz (175 g) strong cheese, grated

cold water to mix

¼–½ teasp. dried mustard

To garnish
One of the following: chopped nuts and seeds, grated cheese, rock salt **or** cayenne pepper.

Preheat oven to Mark 6, 400°F, 200°C.

Rub the fat into the flour until it resembles fine breadcrumbs. Add the cheese and mustard. Knead with enough cold water to make a firm pliable dough. Roll out into fingers 3 inch x ¼ inch (8 cm x 6 mm). Brush with a little milk or beaten egg and sprinkle on a garnish of your choice. Bake for 10–15 minutes or until golden brown. Cool on a wire tray. Tie into bundles with pretty coloured ribbon.

Store 1 week in an airtight tin or 6 months in a freezer.

Seedy Sticks

Makes about 70–100

3 oz (75 g) soft margarine

4½ oz (112 g) cream cheese

1½ tbsp. water

3 oz (75 g) plain flour

3 oz (75 g) wholewheat flour

½ level teasp. salt

pinch of cayenne pepper

3 oz (75 g) sunflower **or** sesame seeds (**or** chopped nuts if liked)

Preheat oven to Mark 4, 350°F, 180°C.

Cream margarine, cream cheese, water and plain flour together. Add wholewheat flour, salt, cayenne and half the sesame seeds. Mix well, then chill until firm. Turn out on to a surface and knead lightly. Sprinkle surface with remaining sesame seeds.

Cut dough into 4 pieces and roll each piece with hands in the seeds to 30 inch (66 cm) long. Then cut into 2 inch (5 cm) lengths. Arrange on a greased baking sheet. Alternatively, roll out dough on a surface sprinkled with sesame seeds and cut into ¼ inch (6 mm) strips with a pastry wheel. Cut into 3 inch (8 cm) sticks.

Cook in a moderate oven for 20 minutes. Cool on a wire rack.

APPETISERS

Most larders contain some kind of dried pulse food, so try some of these interesting and nourishing appetisers to hand round at cheese and wine parties or at barbecues. To save fuel costs, soak pulses in cold water overnight with a level teasp. bicarbonate of soda. Drain well. They won't need any cooking and will be soft enough to eat.

Curried Beans with Dates
Toss prepared butter beans in 2 teasp. mild curry powder; add a few chopped dates.

Split Peas and Sultanas
Prepare split peas then toss in hot oil or butter, drain and toss with salt and sultanas.

Haricot Beans with Poppy Seeds
Toss prepared beans in hot oil or butter, drain; toss in celery salt and poppy seeds.

Chick Peas with Sesame
Crush a clove of garlic and fry gently in olive oil. Toss prepared chick peas in the oil. Drain; sprinkle with salt and sesame seeds.

Nuts and Raisins
Monkey nuts (peanuts), although fiddly to shell, are about half the price of peanuts, so are worth using. After shelling them, and removing the brown inner coating, toss in hot butter or oil, drain, then sprinkle with salt. Add raisins and toss well before serving.

CRUNCHY CRACKERS

Here are ways of using up vegetable peelings, which are full of vitamins and minerals:

Carrot Crackers
Save thin peelings from carrots, dry on absorbent paper to prevent splattering and fry in deep fat. Drain on kitchen paper and sprinkle with salt. These peelings cook almost instantly, so take care.

Potato Peelings
First, dry potato peelings on absorbent paper to prevent dangerous splashing. Fry, drain on kitchen paper; sprinkle with salt.

Crispy Onion Rings
Thinly slice 3 medium-sized onions and coat them in seasoned flour [2 oz (50 g) flour, 1 teasp. salt and ¼ teasp. pepper]. Leave to dry for about an hour so that the flour sticks well, then deep fat fry until onions are golden and crisp. Drain; sprinkle with salt.

Bacon Nibbles
Fry 1 oz (25 g) bacon or bacon rind slowly until crisp and crumbly. Drain on kitchen paper and mix into about ⅙ of the basic dough described on page 90. Bind with water and form into tiny balls. Fry as above and drain.

16 Easy Crisps
Very thinly slice 1 or 2 medium-sized potatoes, with a vegetable peeler, wash off the excess starch and blot dry with absorbent paper. Fry the potatoes, a few at a time, for 2–3 minutes in hot fat (when a 1 inch (2.5 cm) cube of bread browns in 1 minute) and lift out on to kitchen paper. Sprinkle with salt.

Curry Powder

This recipe is for a medium tasting curry. Make in large quantities and package into decorative tins and jars. This recipe calls for ground spices but if you can grind your own spices and seeds the flavour will be stronger (and better) than buying them prepared. Accompany the curry powder with your favourite curry recipe.

6 tbsp. ground cinnamon

1½ tbsp. ground coriander

4 tbsp. ground turmeric

4 tbsp. ground cumin

2 tbsp. ground fenugreek

2 tbsp. garlic granules, ground

3 tbsp. mustard powder

3 tbsp. ground cardamom seeds

4 tbsp. ground chillis

*3 tbsp. ground pepper (black **or** white)*

1½ tbsp. ground ginger

Put all the ingredients into a screw top jar and mix together well. Store in well-sealed jars away from daylight.

SWEETS AS GIFTS

Homemade sweets are fun to make as well as being economical and easy to sell. Most of the ingredients are found in the store cupboard, but sometimes the use of a sugar thermometer is needed and it helps stop a certain amount of guesswork. (See page 27 for how to package them prettily.)

Sugar Boiling

Boiled sugar, at different stages, is used for many sweets, caramel toppings, spun sugar; so it is helpful to understand how the sugar changes.

You can start with sugar on its own, or add a small quantity of water, but this slows down the process. Water boils at a much lower temperature than sugar, so it must evaporate before the sugar will boil (100°C/212°F). Heat very gently to dissolve the sugar without burning, then increase the heat until the sugar is at the temperature you need. To measure the temperature accurately, use a sugar thermometer, but there are other easy tests to use. For example, place a sample of sugar syrup onto a cold dish. When cold it will crinkle and hold the mark of a finger run through it if it is ready. Remember that all your equipment must be clean; use a heavy-based pan and have any other equipment ready before you start. A sugar syrup will easily crystallise and be ruined both during and at the end of boiling, so do not stir. Brush the insides of the pan occasionally with water and don't increase the heat until the sugar is totally dissolved.

Soft Ball
(115–120°C/235–245°F) a small drop of syrup put into cold water will form a soft, pliable ball. Use for fondants and fudges.

Hard Ball
(120–130°C/245–265°F) the same test above produces a firm ball of syrup. Use for caramels, marshmallows and nougat.

Soft Crack
(135–145°C/270–290°F) drops of syrup in cold water will separate into threads which are hard but not brittle. Use for toffees.

Hard Crack
(150–155°C/300–310°F) when tested as above it forms threads which are hard and brittle. Use for hard toffees, rock and humbugs.

Caramel
(155°C/310°F) the syrup becomes golden brown. This is used for caramel toppings. Add chopped nuts and 1 teaspoon cream of tartar to the golden syrup. Shake well and pour on to greased foil to make praline (nuts in caramel). Grind this in a liquidiser or break up with a rolling pin. Store for 1–2 weeks in an airtight jar.

Humbug Variations

Makes about 30 twists or canes

2 lb 2 oz (1 kg) granulated sugar

2 tbsp. golden syrup

4 oz (100 g) butter

½ teasp. cream of tartar

Flavouring and edible food colouring

Dissolve sugar in ½ pint (300 ml) water, syrup, butter and cream of tartar. Bring to boil, then to 143°C/290°F. Pour on to a greased marble slab. Use a palette knife to fold edges into centre. As it cools and hardens, cut in half. Add flavouring and colouring to one half. When cool enough to handle pull coloured half into a long rope. Pull and fold other half until it becomes glossier. Quickly, but carefully, twist the two together. Cut with oiled scissors. Mould the two mixtures together to make bull's eyes. Substitute soft brown sugar for white to make humbugs and canes. Traditionally, humbugs are flavoured with peppermint.

Basic Fudge

Makes 12 oz–1 lb (350–450 g)

2 oz (50 g) butter **or** margarine

2 tbsp. golden syrup

1 lb (450 g) granulated sugar

8 tbsp. sweetened condensed milk

¼ teasp. vanilla essence

Place all the ingredients in a large, heavy-based pan with 4 tbsp. water. Slowly dissolve the sugar. Bring slowly to the boil stirring continuously until the mixture reaches 114°C/238°F. Remove from the heat. Whisk by electric or hand whisk until the mixture thickens and is pale in colour. Pour into a buttered 7 inch (18 cm) square tin. Cool. When still just warm cut into squares.

To vary
Almond
Replace the vanilla essence with almond essence. After whisking the mixture when cooked add 3 oz (75 g) warmed flaked almonds.

Ginger
Just before pouring into the tin add 2 oz (50 g) warmed ginger and ½ teasp. ground ginger.

Cherry
As for ginger but use chopped glacé cherries.

To store
Store in a cool dark place in an airtight container. Keeps for 1–2 weeks but will keep slightly longer if individually wrapped.

Quick Chocolate Fudge

Makes about 36 pieces

3 oz (75 g) plain **or** milk chocolate (cooking **or** eating)

1½ oz (40 g) butter

1½ tbsp. single cream **or** top of the milk

¾ teasp. vanilla essence

12 oz (350 g) icing sugar, sieved

Melt the chocolate in a large bowl over a pan of hot water. Add the butter and cream and mix until smooth. Add the essence and slowly add the icing sugar until smooth. Put into a 6 inch (15 cm) square buttered tin. Leave to set then cut into squares.

To vary
For a mocha variation, replace the vanilla essence with 1 teasp. coffee essence.

Chocolate Novelties

Father Christmas, animals and eggs can be made by filling moulds completely with chocolate (it is cheaper to use cooking or coverture chocolate and follow the manufacturers' instructions for melting). For the best results if using eating chocolate (dark, light and white) grate it finely into a mixing bowl. Place the bowl over a pan of hot, not boiling water, so the chocolate melts slowly. Polish the moulds well with cotton wool, before pouring in the melted chocolate. When the mould is filled, gently tap it on a table to remove any air bubbles. Leave to set in a cool place, not a refrigerator. If the novelties are required for hanging on a tree, place some string into the chocolate before it sets. When set tap the mould sharply and the chocolate shape should drop out. Handle carefully, as fingermarks on the chocolate can't be removed. Wrap the set chocolate in foil wrappers or cling film. Store in a cool dark place.

Hollow Novelties

Brush the prepared moulds with 3–4 layers of melted chocolate, allowing each layer to set before applying the next. Leave to set as above. Seal the two chocolate halves together with a little piped or melted chocolate. If liked the moulds can be filled with sweets, softened fondant etc., before sealing together.

To vary

Ready made or home made marzipan and fondant can be made into shapes pressing small quantities of the paste into the moulds. Once they are set they can be dipped into melted chocolate and left overnight to set.

See also page 61 for recipes for chocolate Easter Eggs.

Chocolate Truffles

Makes about 30–40

12 oz (350 g) plain **or** milk chocolate, broken and melted

8 oz (225 g) icing sugar, sieved

2 egg yolks

2 oz (50 g) butter, room temperature

1 tbsp. milk **or** double cream

1 tbsp. brandy or rum **or** 2 teasp. of brandy or rum essence

To Decorate
Chocolate vermicelli

Sieved cocoa powder

Sieved icing sugar

Crushed peanut brittle, then liquidised finely

Paper cases

Mix together the chocolate, sugar, egg yolks and butter. Blend together until smooth then add the cream and brandy. Chill for 30 minutes. Using a teaspoon, spoon out enough paste to form a small ball. Roll in your hand to form a ball, then in one of the coatings. It is a good idea to have the coating in bags. Just shake the truffles then remove carefully and place in paper cases. If you handle too much finger marks will show.

To store
In a cool place in an airtight tin or box in a refrigerator. Freeze for up to 2 months.

Fruity Lollipops

Makes 20

8 oz (225 g) granulated sugar

6 tbsp. water

2 teasp. liquid glucose

10 tbsp. clear raspberry juice **or** any other clear fruit juice or syrup

20 lollipop sticks

Slowly dissolve the sugar in the water and liquid glucose. Bring to the boil without stirring until it reaches the hard-crack stage (143°C/290°F). Mix in flavouring (and additional colouring if required) and boil to 146°C/296°F. Stop cooking immediately and plunge the base of the pan into cold water. Put spoonfuls of syrup on a cold, greased surface, such as marble. While the syrup is still soft, push in the sticks. Secure stick with a few drops of remaining syrup on top. Leave to set. Wrap in cling film or Cellophane. (Work fast on syrup or it cools and becomes too brittle.)

Marzipan Petits Fours

Make about 2 lb (1 kg)

8 oz (225 g) icing sugar, sieved

8 oz (225 g) caster sugar

1 lb (450 g) ground almonds, hazelnuts **or** walnuts

2 eggs, size 3, beaten

1 teasp. rose water **or** vanilla essence

vanilla essence

lemon juice to taste

edible food colouring

caster sugar for dredging

petits fours cases

Mix the sugars and almonds together. Add the eggs, rose water and lemon juice. Knead lightly until stiff. Divide the marzipan in four to six and colour each differently. Roll each piece into a long sausage shape. Cut into 1 inch (2.5 cm) sections and shape into barrels, balls, pyramids, ovals or oblongs. Sandwich with nuts, prunes, dates or glacé fruits if liked and place in petits fours cases.

Marzipan Fruits

Divide 1 lb (450 g) marzipan (use half the above recipe) into 14 pieces. Mix a few drops of various food colourings into the marzipan for the different fruits: grapes, oranges, strawberries, pears, bananas, apples, acorns, lemons, etc. Knead well to blend the colour. Use cloves, angelica, green marzipan or chocolate vermicelli for stalks, leaves etc.

For pitted finish for oranges, roll over a fine grater and for strawberries roll over a coarse grater and roll gently in granulated sugar. Paint with edible food colouring to make the markings of bananas and paint a rosy blush of apples and peaches.

Chequers

Make the recipe as for Marzipan Petits Fours. Divide 8 oz (225 g) marzipan in half. Colour one portion with edible food colouring. Roll out two rectangles to ¼ inch (6 mm) thick. Cut in three lengthways. Stack strips with egg white, alternating the colour. Cut into narrow strips lengthways. Stick layers together with egg white to achieve a chequered look. Slice down. Leave to dry a little before packing so that the egg white hardens.

Marzipan Cherries

Divide 8 oz (225 g) marzipan into 12–14 pieces and form into flat rounds. Wash and dry 12–14 glacé cherries and place on marzipan rounds. Roll into balls, cut in half.

Marzipan Bullseyes

Divide 8 oz (225 g) marzipan into 3; colour 2 green. Roll a green piece into sausage shape. Brush with egg white, wrap in plain marzipan. Roll out other green piece to cover roll. Slice.

No-Cook Coconut Ice

Makes about 45 pieces

10 tbsp. sweetened condensed milk

17 oz (475 g) icing sugar, sieved

9 oz (250 g) desiccated coconut

few drops of red or green colouring

Mix together the milk and sugar. Stir in coconut and knead well. Divide the mixture in half. Knead one half well and place into a buttered tin. Add colour to the remainder and knead well. Top with remaining mixture. Leave to set. Cut into 1 inch (2.5 cm) squares.

To store
Store in an airtight tin or box in tissue-lined layers to prevent it breaking. Keeps well for 2–3 weeks.

As a bonus
Use to fill petits fours like stuffed dates or prunes, or coat the squares in melted chocolate.

Peanut Brittle

Makes 1½ lb (675 g)

1 lb (450 g) soft brown or granulated sugar

8 oz (225 g) golden syrup

5 fl oz (150 ml) water

8 oz (225 g) peanuts, salted or unsalted

½ oz (15 g) butter

½ teasp. bicarbonate of soda

Put the sugar and water into a heavy-based saucepan. Slowly dissolve the sugar over a gentle heat. Bring to the boil and boil to 115°C/238°F, or if you drop some syrup mixture into cold water it should form a soft ball. Add the peanuts and stir well. Remove from the heat, add the butter and bicarbonate of soda. Pour into a 13 x 9 inch (33 x 23 cm) well-greased Swiss roll tin. Leave to cool. When cold break into pieces.

To vary
Sesame and Peanut Brittle
Add 3 oz (75 g) toasted sesame seeds when adding the peanuts.

Coconut chip
Replace the peanuts with coconut chips.

To store
Store in waxed paper in an airtight container for 2–3 weeks.

Popcorn

Really easy to make and a few packets of corn go a very long way. Serve at barbecues, childrens' parties, cocktail parties. The popcorn can be made sweet or savoury. Follow the instructions on the packet and do make sure the saucepan is big and heavy enough to get a good result. Serve in pretty cones.

Chocolate Popcorn
For each 1 pint (600 ml) of popped corn toss in 8 oz (225 g) melted plain or milk chocolate. Mix well. Spoon into small clusters on a lightly greased tin and allow to set. Serve in bright paper cones.

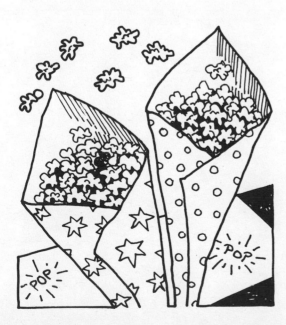

Raisin and Chocolate
Add 3–4 oz (75–100 g) raisins when mixing in the chocolate.

Toffee Popcorn
Dissolve 4 oz (100 g) sugar in a saucepan with 2 tbsp. milk and 2 oz butter. Once dissolved bring to the boil until the mixture just starts to brown. Stir carefully into the warmed popcorn, spoon small clusters onto a lightly-greased tin and allow to set.

Savoury
Sprinkle on 1–2 teasp. salt.

Parmesan
1 2 tbsp. grated Parmesan to 1 pint popcorn.

Curry
1–2 tbsp. curry powder sprinkled onto the corn then shake well.

To store
In airtight tins and containers.

Soft Marshmallows

Makes 1¼ lb (575 g) approx

1 lb (450 g) granulated sugar

*1 tbsp. liquid glucose **or** golden syrup*

2 sachets powdered gelatine

2 egg whites, stiffly whisked

*flavouring (vermouth **or** fruit syrup) and colouring*

1 oz (25 g) cornflour and 2 oz (50 g) icing sugar sieved and mixed

Dissolve sugar and glucose in 5 fl oz (150 ml) water and gelatine in 5 fl oz (150 ml) of hot water. Boil sugar in a large, heavy-based saucepan to 127°C/260°F, and pour into gelatine slowly, whisking well. Pour the mixture slowly down the side of the bowl, whisking all the time (preferably with an electric one). Continue whisking until light and holding its shape. Add flavouring and colouring. Pour into a greased, deep baking tin, dusted with sugar. Leave for 24 hours. Cut into squares then toss in remaining sugar mixture until all the sticky edges have been coated.

To vary
Once the tin has been greased, dust and toss the marshmallow cubes in one of the following:

Hundreds and thousands, toasted coconut, sesame seeds, grated chocolate or strands. Vary the flavour and colour using peppermint, orange and lemon.

To store
Store in layers in boxes or tins, dredging each layer with plenty of icing powder. Keeps for 2–3 weeks in airtight containers.

Treacle Toffee

Makes about 72 pieces

1 lb (450 g) golden demerara sugar

5 fl oz (150 ml) water

3 oz (75 g) butter

¼ teasp. cream of tartar

4 oz (100 g) black treacle

4 oz (100 g) golden syrup

Dissolve the sugar and water in a large saucepan. Add remaining ingredients and bring to the boil. Boil to 132°C/270°F (soft crack stage). Pour into a greased tin. Cool for 5 minutes, then score a pattern of squares or diamonds. Leave to set. When set use a toffee hammer or sharp knife to separate the pieces.

Wrap toffees individually in waxed paper. For a golden-coloured toffee omit the treacle and use 8 oz (225 g) golden syrup.

White Truffles

Makes 10–12

2 oz (50 g) ground almonds

4 oz (100 g) cake crumbs

4 oz (100 g) icing sugar

3 tbsp. honey

1 tbsp. brandy

*2 oz (50 g) crystallised ginger **or** pineapple, chopped*

Mix all the ingredients together and knead lightly. Form into small balls and roll in sieved icing sugar.

To store
The same as chocolate truffles.

RECIPES FOR KIDS

Golden Rules to Remember When Cooking in The Kitchen

1 Do check that a grown up has read through the recipe you have chosen and they have agreed you can make it.

2 Make sure that you have all the ingredients and equipment before you start to prepare or cook the food.

3 Tie your hair back if it is long, and fold back sleeves.

4 Wash your hands and nails well.

5 Wear an apron to help keep you clean, and mop up any spills *immediately*.

6 Check the oven shelves are in the correct position *before* turning it on ... remember it gets very hot when it is on so it is best to ask a grown up for help. *Always* use thick, dry oven gloves when removing dishes from the oven.

7 Never touch electrical equipment with wet hands, or touch the electric or gas hob whilst cooking.

8 Remember sharp knives, electric blenders and mixers are *dangerous*.

9 Hold the saucepan handle firmly when stirring food.

10 If your cooker does not have a timer, write down when you started cooking and when it will be ready – and check the clock! When cooked turn off the heat as soon as you've finished cooking.
P.S.: Don't forget to clean up and do the washing up after you!

Cherry Cake

Serves 10–12

4 oz (100 g) margarine

4 oz (100 g) caster sugar

1 large egg

8 oz (225 g) self-raising flour

pinch of salt

1 oz (25 g) desiccated coconut

6 oz (150 g) glacé cherries

2½ fl oz (60 ml) milk

Preheat oven to Mark 4, 350°F, 160°C.
Line the cake tin, see below. Using a wooden spoon, cream the margarine and sugar together in a mixing bowl until pale and fluffy. Beat the egg in well. Fold in the flour and salt. Add enough milk until mixture drops easily off the spoon. Place the coconut in a bag. Cut the cherries in half with scissors that have been dipped in water to stop them sticking. Toss cherries in coconut and fold them both into the mixture. Spoon into prepared tin and bake for 1–1½ hours. When cooked, allow to cool in the tin slightly before turning out on to a cooling rack.

How to Line a Cake Tin

Place two sheets of greaseproof paper on top of each other on a table. Place the cake tin on the paper and with a pencil draw round it. Cut out the two circles and a strip of greaseproof paper long enough to go round the tin, but a little deeper. Fold one long edge in 1 inch (2.5 cm) then snip at 1 inch (2.5 cm) intervals along it. Put one circle in the tin and the strip with snips in the base. Then fit the second circle on top and grease well with a little oil on a pastry brush.

Chocolate Crispies

Makes 15–20

2 oz (50 g) butter **or** margarine

2 tbsp. golden syrup

2 tbsp. cocoa powder, sieved

1½ tbsp. caster **or** soft brown sugar

Rice Crispies or cornflakes

15–20 paper cake cases

Melt the butter and syrup together in a saucepan. Add the cocoa powder and sugar. Fold in the crispies and mix well together. Place spoonfuls of mixture into the paper cases and leave to set in the refrigerator.

Chocolate Fruit

Dip cleaned, perfect fruit or nuts in melted plain or milk chocolate for a delicious sweet. Break a bar of eating or cooking chocolate into a clean bowl over a pan of hot, *not* boiling, water. Leave to melt and stir occasionally making sure you hold the saucepan handle firmly.

Use fruit that you have picked or that's cheap to buy. If you use cherries or grapes, keep the stalks on as they are easier to dip into the chocolate. Keep the green hull or stalk of strawberries in and half dip the fruit. Place on a lightly-greased baking tray to set.

Eat the same day.

Coconut Pyramids

Makes about 15

2 egg whites (ask someone to help separate the eggs)

6 oz (175 g) caster sugar

6 oz (175 g) desiccated coconut

Rice paper

Preheat oven to Mark 1, 275°F, 140°C.

Line the baking tray with rice paper. Whisk the egg whites stiffly in a clean, grease-free mixing bowl. Fold the sugar and coconut in with a metal spoon. Spoon little piles or mould spoonfuls of mixture into pyramids, and place on the baking tray. Bake for 30–45 minutes or until just started to brown (do ask a grown up to help you remove the tray from the oven with oven gloves). Leave to get cold.

To store

Keep in an airtight tin lined with greaseproof paper for 1 week or in a freezer for 2 months.

Fondant or Marzipan Animals

With a little help from an adult you can make enchanting and delicious cake decorations, tree hangers or just a treat. You can, of course, use your own home-made marzipan to mould little novelties, but bought marzipan or fondant will do just as well. There is no cooking required.

First colour small quantities of marzipan in different shades with food colouring, adding one or two drops and kneading it in.

Once softened with the warmth of your hands, marzipan is easy to mould into any shape.

You will need about 3 oz (75 g) marzipan for each animal. Make up the body, head, legs, tail, ears, eyes, etc. Prepare all the parts you need first, in the required colours, then mould into shape, pressing the pieces lightly together. With practice you can, of course, make any cartoon character you like.

Leave to dry in a cool, airy place if they are for cake decorations or, to harden them up for long-term keeping, brush with egg white. They will keep well in an airtight tin for up to three weeks.

Fondant Peppermint Creams

Makes about 1¼ lb (575 g)

1 small can sweetened condensed milk

1 lb (450 g) icing sugar, sieved

few drops of peppermint essence to taste

green edible food colouring

a little cornflour for dusting

few crystallised violets

2–3 oz (50–75 g) melted chocolate to decorate

Mix together the milk and icing sugar until smooth and firm. Add the essence to taste and a few drops of colouring. Mix evenly through the mixture. Roll out on a surface lightly dusted with cornflour until ¼ inch (6 mm) thick. Cut into shapes with a small cutter. Leave to set for 24 hours in a cool place, loosely covered. Dip half into melted chocolate and leave to set on waxed paper or greased baking tray.

Sugar Mice

Make the Fondant Peppermint Cream recipe, leaving out the green colouring and peppermint essence. Leave the mixture white, or colour half pink and the other half white. Flavour with vanilla essence.

Shape the fondant into mice shapes. Shape some fondant into ears and attach to the head. Press in two small silver dragees for the eyes and attach a small strip of angelica or string for the tail. Leave to harden on a lightly-greased baking tray.

Gingerbread People

Makes about 8–10

*4 oz (100 g) butter **or** margarine*

*4 oz (100 g) caster **or** brown sugar*

10 oz (275 g) plain flour, sieved

2–3 teasp. ground ginger

2½ tbsp. syrup, warmed

Chocolate drops or currants

Preheat oven to Mark 4, 350° F, 180°C.

Cream the fat and sugar together until light and fluffy. Add the dry ingredients and syrup. Knead together and roll out onto a lightly floured surface until ¼ inch (6 mm) thick. Cut out using a gingerbread cutter. Place on to a greased baking tray. Decorate the features of the people – like eyes, mouth, buttons – with the currants. Bake for about 15 minutes or until golden brown. Leave to cool a little before lifting off the baking tray. Tie a little red bow around the neck. Cover in cling film. Keeps up to 1 week.

Home Made Lemonade

Makes 1 pint (600 ml)

1 lemon, washed and cut into pieces

1 pint (600 ml) ice cold water

sugar to taste

6 crushed ice cubes

Place the water and lemon in a liquidiser and blend for 15 seconds on maximum speed. Add the sugar and ice, blending for a further 10 seconds. Strain through a nylon sieve into a jug. Serve chilled.

Jam Tarts

Makes 20

8 oz (225 g) plain flour, sieved

2 oz (50 g) lard

2 oz (50 g) margarine

2½ tbsp. cold water

jar of jam

Preheat oven to Mark 7, 425°F, 220°C.
   Put flour and salt into a bowl. Add the lard and margarine; cut fat into pieces. Rub in with fingertips until it resembles fine breadcrumbs. Add water. Gather together to make a soft dough. Shape into a round. Sprinkle a little flour on to the clean table or board. Roll out pastry using a rolling pin. Roll in one direction and move the pastry round to prevent sticking. Choose a pastry cutter slightly larger than the bun tin holes. Cut out pastry circles and place in the tins. Spoon a little jam into each case. Bake for 10–12 minutes. Remove from the tin when cool. However good the tarts look don't eat them straight from oven! The jam gets very hot.

Melting Oats

Makes about 22

*4 oz (100 g) butter **or** margarine, at room temperature*

*3 oz (75 g) caster sugar **or** soft brown sugar*

1 egg yolk

5 oz (150 g) self-raising flour, sieved

Rolled oats

Nuts and cherries, to decorate

Preheat oven to Mark 5, 375°F, 190°C.
   Cream the butter and the sugar with a wooden spoon for about 2–3 minutes until light and fluffy. Beat in the egg yolk. With a metal tablespoon fold in the flour well. Divide the mixture into 22 small, even balls. Roll each ball into the rolled oats to cover evenly. Place the biscuits on to a very lightly-greased baking tray and flatten the balls slightly with the back of a spoon. Place a quarter of glacé cherry or nuts in the centre. Bake for 20–25 minutes or until golden brown. (Don't forget to ask help from a grown up.) Cool on a wire tray.

To store
In an airtight tin for 1 week or in the freezer for 3 months.

No-Cook Cookies

Makes about 24–26

4 oz (100 g) margarine

4 oz (100 g) golden syrup

4 oz (100 g) caster sugar

8 oz (225 g) cake, biscuit or cereal crumbs

This is the basic recipe and you then choose your flavouring. Melt the margarine, syrup and sugar in a saucepan. Stir in the crumbs.

To vary
Chocolate Crumbles
Use crushed cornflakes instead of crumbs and add 2 tbsp. cocoa. Spoon the mixture in paper cases and chill.

Mint Sandwiches
Use Rice Crispies instead of crumbs. Mix all the ingredients together, plus 4 oz (100 g) plain or milk chocolate. Spread half the mixture into a 2 x 6 inch (2 x 15 cm) cake tin. Melt 6 oz (150 g) marshmallows, add a few drops peppermint essence to taste. Spread over the chocolate. Top with remaining mixture and chill. Cut into squares.

To label/store
These cookies keep for up to a week in an airtight tin or 3 months in a freezer.

No-Fuss Fruit Cake

Makes 1 x 9 inch (1 x 23 cm) round cake

8 oz (225 g) margarine, softened
8 oz (225 g) soft brown **or** caster sugar
5 eggs
4 oz (100 g) mixed peel, chopped
4 oz (100 g) almonds, blanched and roughly chopped
1 tbsp. black treacle
8 oz (225 g) currants
8 oz (225 g) sultanas
8 oz (225 g) seedless raisins
4 oz (100 g) glacé cherries, washed, dried and quartered
9 oz (250 g) plain flour
2 teasp. baking powder

Preheat oven to Mark 4, 350°F, 180°C.

Place all the ingredients into a mixing bowl and beat together well for 3–4 minutes. Spoon the mixture into a greased and lined cake tin. Smooth the top with a round-bladed knife. Bake in the middle of the oven for 2–2¼ hours. Check half way through cooking to make sure the cake is not cooking too quickly, if so cover with foil loosely (ask a grown up to help). When the cake is well risen and golden brown remove from the oven with oven gloves. Leave in the tin for 30 minutes or until cool. Turn out on to a cooling tray. When cold remove the greaseproof lining.

To label/store
This is not a cake for keeping. Store, wrapped in foil, in an airtight tin for 2–3 weeks. If freezing, store whole or in slices, well wrapped, for 4 months.

HALLOWE'EN

Combine a Hallowe'en party for children with a few stalls for selling things and charge a small entrance fee. Here are some ideas.

Creating Pumpkin Faces

First decide whether you are going to create a happy, sad or scary face. All the family can join in the fun, but as pumpkins have such tough skins, it's advisable to let an adult do the actual carving. Don't forget that pumpkin seeds and flesh are edible – so they can be used to make a pumpkin pie.

Cutting a face
Step 1 With a sharp knife cut a thin slice from the stalk end of the pumpkin.

Step 2 With a large metal spoon scoop out the flesh, reserving it in one bowl, and the seeds in another.

Step 3 Once flesh has been scooped out, use a soft crayon or felt-tip pen to sketch a face of your choice on the outside of the pumpkin.

Step 4 Very carefully cut through the pumpkin skin following your sketch lines. Push out the cut sections from the inside.

Step 5 Place a night light, stubby candle or torch in the pumpkin to illuminate it. Do keep naked lights out of the reach of small children.

Trick or Treat

Everyone can have a fun time dressing up in spooky clothes on Hallowe'en. Witches' hats and masks are easy to make and old sheets can be turned into cloaks with a little imagination. Games are the order of the night. Apple bobbing can be hilarious. To play it, fill a bucket or washing-up bowl with water and float apples in it. Players have to pick out the apples using their teeth, with their hands behind their backs.

Another game is The Witch's Eye. Everyone sits in a circle in a darkened room. Items are then passed round that are supposedly part of the dead witch, such as a carrot for her nose.

Trick or treat is an essential part of Hallowe'en in Scotland and the USA. Children call at neighbours' houses and ask if they want a trick or treat. If the children are not given a treat, such as a piece of fruit, sweets or money, they then play a trick on the neighbour. They should *always* be accompanied by an adult.

Sewing seeds

Remove all fleshy pieces from pumpkin seeds. Wash and dry seeds thoroughly. Paint seeds with non-toxic paint and leave to dry. Using a large needle, thread seeds on to shearing elastic to make necklaces or bracelets.

Who's making up?

Children love putting on scary make-up for Hallowe'en. Here's one fun formula that washes off easily with soap and water. For four colours of make-up you need cold cream, red, yellow, blue and green food colouring, four paper cups and a spoon. Put 2 teasp. of cold cream into each cup. Add one or two drops of colouring to each cup. Mix with a spoon.

Seedy Snacks

Scoop out the seeds from a pumpkin, squash or marrow and discard any fleshy, fibrous pieces. Rinse and dry the seeds. Place on a baking tray with 1 oz (25 g) melted butter or margarine, and sprinkle with granular sea salt or onion salt. Bake at Mark 4, 350°F, 180°C for about 20–30 minutes or until golden brown.

GREAT OUTDOORS!

Cooking in the open air, whether on a sophisticated barbecue or a grill over a fire pit, always seems to give food an extra delicious taste. Everyone's keen to help the chef and no-one really minds waiting for their food as, after all, they're (hopefully!) sitting enjoying the sun and fresh air.

The food can be as plain as a hamburger or as fancy as a shoulder of lamb marinated in wine and herbs. Depending on the type of barbecue you are planning – for children or adults, or a mixed party – drinks can range from beer, wine, iced teas and coffee, to ginger ale punch and non-alcoholic fruit cup.

Timing your Cooking

Remember to take into consideration the fierceness of heat on your particular barbecue, as well as the quality of the meat you are cooking, and how well done you like it. It's really a matter of practice, but don't forget that you can always put food like steaks or sausages back for a further few minutes. It takes the charcoal some time to get burning really well, so light your barbecue at least an hour before you want to start cooking.

Flavours to Savour

Add extra flavour and aroma to your barbecued foods: sprinkle the charcoal with a little oak dust; shower the grill racks with sprigs of fresh herbs and place the meat on top; or sprinkle the food with one of the special barbecue spices available. But brush the grill rack with oil first to prevent sticking. The oil could be flavoured too, with garlic, chilli, herbs or nuts if you wish.

You can't do without a barbecue sauce, either, although everyone's favourite is different. Ideally, it should be a mixture of sweet, rich and tangy – even very hot – flavours. Here is a very tasty combination: brown sugar or treacle, tomato ketchup and chutney (preferably apple chutney) in equal quantities, then add a little Worcestershire or chilli sauce to give flavour and fire. This barbecue sauce can be served with most meats, or brushed on before and during cooking. Other good mixtures are chutneys of all sorts – peach or apricot, for instance, can be used as a very quick barbecue baste straight from the jar. French dressings, too, can make a good baster. Or serve soured cream flavoured with chives, horseradish sauce or grated cucumber, as a side sauce.

Quick-To-Cook Favourites

Cheap, chewy bones make lovely munching in the open air. Marinate Chinese spare ribs or breast of lamb bones (tiny riblets, cut up) in a tasty sauce. They need only a quick grilling – about 10 minutes altogether. The secret is to make them crisp and crunchy. But you'll need plenty of paper serviettes for sticky fingers!

Make your own hamburgers from pure beef – just add a little seasoning. You'll find they keep their shape and hold together better if you chill them for a day before cooking. Add chopped onion or fresh herbs if you prefer. Grill for about 8 minutes on each side. Have a tray of garnishes ready to serve with the hamburgers – you'll need chopped onion, grated cheese, mustards, pickles, and even fried eggs for extra large appetities!

Marinated Lamb Shoulder

Ask the butcher to bone out a shoulder of lamb completely (he can leave the knuckle end of the bone for easier handling or carving if you wish). Lay it out flat and marinate it for at least 2 hours, or overnight if you can, in: 5 fl oz (150 ml) white wine mixed with 4–5 teasp. oil, 1 sliced onion, a few black peppercorns, bay leaves, seasoning, a sprig of parsley or rosemary and 1 crushed clove of garlic. Turn and baste once. Then remove, fold back into shoulder shape if you wish, or cook flat for speed. It should take only about 15 minutes each side if cooked flat – 25–30 minutes each side, otherwise. Or it can be grilled. It is best served when the lamb is still pink in the middle. Brush with the marinade juices during cooking.

Barbecued Fish

Certain fish are delicious barbecued; but cook the fish after your meat, otherwise fishy flavours may permeate the other food. Wrap the fish, either whole or fillets, carefully in foil. Keep heads on whole gutted fish if you wish, or remove before cooking. Firm whole fish such as mackerel, herring or fresh sardines can all be cooked resting directly on the barbecue grill rack. Sprinkle with lemon juice, seasonings or herbs and cook 2–3 minutes each side for sardines, or 7–8 minutes each side for large fish. For convenience, bake fish in your oven and transfer to the barbecue for the last few minutes before serving. Wrap in foil, add a little butter, lemon or orange juice and a sprig of fresh herbs and cook for about 30 minutes for whole fish at Mark 5, 375° F, 190° C.

To accompany

Baked potatoes are, of course, firm favourites, but for a change try alternatives like baked corn-on-the-cob or sweet potato. Start them off in the oven, wrapped in foil, to save time. Have a selection of different salads, and let people just help themselves. Garlic or herb-flavoured hot bread or baps also go down well.

Fresh fruit and a selection of cheeses are perfect to serve after your barbecue dishes, but for a hot, really delicious, barbecued pudding, try baked apples, oranges or bananas. Just peel the fruit, place on foil and sprinkle with brown sugar or honey. Wrap up and bake so that the fruit is ready to serve after the main course, with ice-cream or thick soured cream. Fruits can be grilled, too, as the barbecue is cooling down. Or try a flambéed version – bananas with whisky, for instance. Add a spoonful of flaming whisky to each banana before cooking as above.

4
Make it to sell

Hand-knitted or crocheted things are always good sellers at fairs and bazaars but they must be of high quality because you have to charge a fair amount for them, given the time and cost involved in making them. Depending on how many items you have, you can arrange one table for garments and one for knitted toys or else, if you only have enough for one table, place them in groups, displaying one of each item and keeping the others in clear plastic bags. But do keep the uncovered items well back from the reach of small sticky fingers! Or even large ones.

You could approach some of the large spinners or your local wool shop or department store for contributions of balls of wool which you can either make into items to sell or simply offer for sale as they are. Mixed bags of leftover wool also sell well, so ask knitters to give you their leftovers.

CONVERSION CHART

FABRICS

Fabrics and sewing accessories are sold in metric measures in most stores, but in case you still think in imperial measures here is a quick conversion guide.

Seam allowances are generally 1.5 cm (⅝ inch). 2.5 cm is equivalent to 1 inch, and 30 cm is nearly 1 ft. 1 m is considerably more than 3 ft – 3 ft 3⅜ inches to be precise.

For the sewing instructions in this book, the following conversions are as accurate as possible but they are not exact, and you may have to adjust seam allowances accordingly.

cm	inch	cm	ft	inch
1	⅜	30	1	
1.5	⅝	40	1	4
2	¾	50	1	8
2.5	1	60	2	
5	2	90	3	
7.5	3	1 m	3	3½
10	4	2 m	6	7
15	6			
20	8			

Here is an accurate conversion chart

mm	ft	inch
5		³/₁₆
10		⅜
25.4		1
50		1¹⁵/₁₆
100		3¹⁵/₁₆
250		9¹³/₁₆
304.8	1	
500	1	7¹¹/₁₆
609.6	2	
750	2	5½
914.4	3	
1000	3	3⅜
1500	4	11
1829	6	
2000	6	6¾

WOOD

Although professional woodworkers and specifiers usually work in millimetres for accuracy, most local D.I.Y. merchants still work in imperial measures.

Wood is normally sold 'p.a.r.' (planed all round). The actual dimensions are slightly less than the nominal dimensions because the wood has been planed. So a length of wood sold as 2 inch x 1 inch will actually measure 50 mm x 25 mm.

To make a success of a fund-raising craft stall, the items you offer for sale must be attractive and of good quality. Here are a few hints and tips:

If you are using unravelled yarn to make toys, wash it first to remove the kinks, and if you find that you have a pile of yarn in very muted colours, hunt around for bright colours to mix in with it. A grey donkey with a yellow mane and tail and a red saddle will sell more readily than one that is grey all over.

The finish of craft items must be impeccable. See that all loose ends are run in and that seams are sewn neatly and firmly. If you are finishing off something with bias binding, make sure that the stitching isn't so near to the edge that the binding pulls away after one or two washes. Don't be mean with straps and ties. It's easy to shorten apron strings that are too long, but those that are too short are a constant irritation to the wearer.

Where possible, state what fabric is used to make an item, so that the buyer knows if it is washable. This applies, too, to toy stuffings. And while on the subject of stuffed toys, do remember to stuff them adequately. A toy which is supposed to stand or sit upright should do so and not fall over in a dismal heap.

All trimmings on toys should be child-proof. If you are using bought eyes and noses for animal toys, see that they are of the safety type. If using felt for features, sew the pieces on, don't just fix them with adhesive.

Knitted Mitts

Time involved: about 12 hours.

MATERIALS

1 ball (50 g) Pingouin Pingofrance Double Knitting in main colour (M.) and oddments of 2 contrast colours (A. and B.) for coloured mitts; 2 balls for plain mitts; a pair each 3 mm and 3¾ mm (No. 11 and No. 9) Milward knitting needles.

Measurements: to fit average hand.

Tension: 24 sts. and 32 rows to 10 cm square in stocking stitch.

Abbreviations: K., knit; p., purl; sts., stitches; cm, centimetre(s); alt., alternate; beg., beginning; cont., continue; dec., decreas(e)ing; foll., following; inc., increas(e)-ing; inc. 1 k.w., increase by picking up loop between sts. and knitting into back of it; p.s.s.o., pass slip stitch over; patt., pattern; p.w., purlwise; rem., remain(ing); sl., slip; st.-st., stocking stitch; tog., together; t.b.l., through back loop.

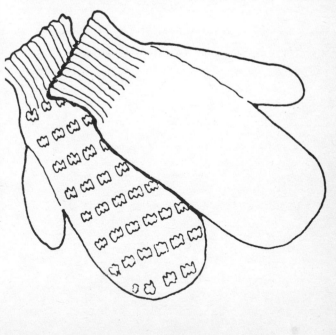

The Coloured Mitts

THE LEFT-HAND MITT
With 3 mm needles and M., cast on 49 sts.
Work 6 cm k.1, p.1 rib, beg. alt. rows p.1.
Change to 3¾ mm needles. Twisting yarns on
wrong side when changing colour to avoid a
hole, cont. in patt. thus: **Next row** With M., k.
Next row With M., p.2, (p.1 winding yarn twice
round needle, p.3) 6 times, p.23.

Shape thumb gusset. 1st row With M.,
k.19, inc. 1 k.w., k.3, inc. 1 k.w., k.2, with A., (k.2,
sl.1 p.w. dropping extra loop, k.1) 6 times, k.1.
2nd row With A., (p.2, sl.1 p.w., p.1) 6 times,
p.1, with M., p.26. **3rd row** With M., k. **4th row**
With M., p.4, (p.1 winding yarn twice round
needle, p.3) 5 times, p.27. **5th row** With M.,
k.19, inc. 1 k.w., k.5, inc. 1 k.w., k.2, with B., k.1,
(k.3, sl.1 p.w. dropping extra loop) 5 times, k.4.
6th row With B., p.1, (p.3, sl.1 p.w.) 5 times,
p.4, with M., p.28. **7th row** With M., k. **8th row**
With M., p.2, (p.1 winding yarn twice round
needle, p.3) 6 times, p.27.

The last 8 rows form the colour patt. Cont.
in this way, working colour patt. over 25 sts.
and inc. 1 st. at both sides of gusset as before
on next row and every foll. 4th row to 59 sts.
Work 3 rows straight. *

Next row With M., k.32, turn and cast on 2
sts. **Next row** P.15, turn and cast on 2 sts.
Cont. on these 17 sts. for thumb. Work 5 cm
st.-st., ending after p. row. **Next row** K.2, (k.2
tog., k.1) to end. **Next row** P. **Next row** (K.2
tog.) to end. Break off yarn, thread through
rem. sts., draw up and fasten off. Join seam.

With right side facing, join M. at base of
thumb and with right-hand needle, pick up
and k. 4 sts. from base, k.2, patt. to end. Cont.
in patt. as set for 9 cm, ending after wrong-
side row.

Shape top. Next row (K.1, sl.1, k.1, p.s.s.o.,
patt. 19, k.2 tog., k.1) twice. Work 3 rows. **Next
row** (K.1, sl.1, k.1, p.s.s.o., patt. 17, k.2 tog.,
k.1) twice. Work 1 row. Cont. dec. in this way
on next row and foll. alt. row. **Next row** (P.1,
p.2 tog., patt. 11, p.2 tog. t.b.l., p.1) twice. **Next
row** (K.1, sl.1, k.1, p.s.s.o., patt. 9, k.2 tog., k.1)
twice. **Next row** (P.1, p.2 tog., patt. 7, p.2 tog.
t.b.l., p.1) twice. Cast off. Join seam.

THE RIGHT-HAND MITT
Divide rem. yarn into 2 small balls. Working
rows from end to beg. and using separate
balls for colour patt. and for plain block, work
as left-hand mitt to *. **Next row** Patt. 25, with
M., k.15, turn and cast on 2 sts. **Next row** With
M., p.15, turn and cast on 2 sts. Complete as
thumb of left-hand mitt. With right side facing,
join M. to base of thumb and pick up and k. 4
sts. from base, k. to end. Complete to match
left-hand mitt.

The Plain Mitts

Using one colour and st.-st., work as
coloured mitts.

Crochet Scarf

Time involved: about 14 hours for a scarf
20 cm wide by 165 cm long.
MATERIALS

4-ply yarn in various colours (one 50 g ball
works about 6 rows 165 cm long); 3 mm
crochet hook.

Measurements: as desired.
Tension: 6 patterns and 14 rows to 10 cm
square.
Abbreviations: Beg., beginning; ch., chain;
d.c., double crochet; tr., treble; lp., loop; rep.,
repeat; sts., stitches.

TO MAKE

Make a ch. the desired length of scarf, with a number of sts. divisible by 4, plus 3.

1st Foundation row 3 tr. in 4th ch. from hook, ** miss 2 ch., d.c. in next ch., * 3 ch., 3 tr. in next ch., miss 2 ch., d.c. in next ch.; rep. from * to end. Break yarn. **

2nd Foundation row Return to beg. of 1st foundation row and join new colour to 1st ch. Working along other side of foundation ch., work 3 ch., 3 tr. in same place; rep. from ** to ** of 1st foundation row. Join same colour to end of 1st foundation row.

Pattern row 3 ch., 3 tr. in d.c., d.c. in 3-ch. lp., * 3 ch., 2 tr. in 3-ch. lp., 1 tr. in d.c., d.c. in 3-ch. lp.; rep. from * to end. Break yarn and join new colour to end of 2nd foundation row. Rep. pattern row.

Continue in this way, working 2 rows in each colour, one on one side of foundation rows and one on the other. Do not run in ends as they will be hidden in fringe. When scarf is big enough, fringe ends with mixed colours.

Blodwen Bunny

Time involved: 3-4 days.
MATERIALS

2 balls (50 g) Emu Supermatch D.K. in white (W.); 1 ball in each of camel (C.), red (R.) and black (B.); small quantity of flesh pink (F.); a pair each 3¼ mm, 3 mm and 2¾ mm (No. 10, No. 11, No. 12) Aero knitting needles; 1½ m narrow lace; 1 m white ribbon; piece of black felt 25 cm x 32 cm; oddments of felt in white and lilac; 1 button; 2 press studs; piece of card for hat brim; kapok.

Measurements: height to top of hat, approx. 46 cm.

Tension: 26 sts. to 10 cm on 3¼ mm needles.

Abbreviations: K., knit; p., purl; sts., stitches; cm, centimetre(s); alt., alternate; beg., beginning; cont., continue; dec., decreas(e)ing; foll., following; inc., increas(e)ing; patt., pattern; p.w., purlwise; rem., remain(ing); rep., repeat; sl., slip; st.-st., stocking stitch; y.b., yarn back; y.f., yarn forward.

THE BODY (2): with 3¼ mm needles and W., cast on 16 sts. Beg. with k. row, work 40 rows st.-st. Break yarn, leave sts. Work another piece in same way; do not break yarn. **Next row** K. across sts. of 2nd piece, turn, cast on 2 sts., then k. across sts. of 1st piece. 34 sts. P.1 row. Dec. 1 st. at both ends of next row and foll. 8th row. **Next row** P. Dec. 1 st. at both ends of next row. Work 9 rows straight. Cast off 3 sts. at beg. of next 2 rows. Work 12 rows straight. Cast off 3 sts. at beg. of next 4 rows. Cast off rem. sts. for neck.

THE ARMS (2): with 3¼ mm needles and C., cast on 18 sts. Beg. with k. row, work 2 rows st.-st. **Next row** Inc. in 1st st., k.7, (inc. in next st.) twice, k.7, inc. in last st. Work 9 rows st.-st. **Next row** K.2 tog., k.7, (k.2 tog.) twice, k.7, k.2 tog. P.1 row. Break C., join in W. Beg. with k. row, work 16 rows st.-st. Cast off 3 sts.

at beg. of next 2 rows. Work 2 rows straight. Dec. 1 st. at both ends of every row to 2 sts. Cast off.

THE FEET (4): with 3¼ mm needles and C., cast on 12 sts. Beg. with k. row, work 2 rows st.-st. **Next row** Inc. in 1st st., k.4, (inc. in next st.) twice, k.4, inc. in last st. Beg. p. row, work 13 rows straight. **Next row** K.2 tog., k.4, (k.2 tog.) twice, k.4, k.2 tog. P.1 row. Cast off.

THE SIDE HEAD PIECE: with 3¼ mm needles and C., cast on 16 sts. Beg. k. row, work 6 rows st.-st.

Shape thus: 1st row Inc. in 1st st., k. to end. **2nd row** Cast on 6 sts., p. to end. **3rd row** As 1st. **4th row** Cast on 2 sts., p. to end. **5th row** K., inc. 1 st. at both ends. **6th row and every foll. alt. row** P. **7th row** As 5th. 30 sts. **9th, 11th and 13th rows** As 1st. **15th row** K. to

last 2 sts., k.2 tog. **17th and 19th rows** As 15th. **21st row** K., dec. 1 st. at both ends. **23rd, 25th and 27th rows** As 21st. 22 sts. **28th and 29th rows** Dec. 1 st. at both ends of each row. **30th row** P. **31st row** (K.2 tog.) to end. 9 sts. **32nd row** P. **33rd row** (K.2 tog.) 4 times, k.1. P. 1 row. Cast off. Work another piece to match, reversing shapings.

THE HEAD GUSSET: with 3¼ mm needles and C., cast on 6 sts. and work 14 rows st.-st. Inc. 1 st. at both ends of next row. Work 49 rows st.-st. Dec. 1 st. at both ends of next row and foll. alt. rows to 2 sts. K.2 tog. Fasten off.

THE EARS (2 pieces F. and 2 pieces C.)**:** with 3¼ mm needles, cast on 8 sts. Work 2 rows st.-st. Inc. 1 st. at both ends of next row and every foll. 4th row to 16 sts. Work 9 rows straight. Dec. 1 st. at both ends of next row and every foll. 4th row to 4 sts. Cast off.

THE SKIRT: with 3¼ mm needles and B., cast on 175 sts. and k. 2 rows. Join in W. and patt. thus: **1st and 2nd rows** With W., k. to end. **3rd row** With B., k.1, * keeping y.b. sl.1 p.w., k.3; rep. from * to last 2 sts., sl.1, k.1. **4th row** With B., p.1, * keeping y.f. sl.1 p.w., p.3; rep. from * to last 2 sts., sl.1, p.1. **5th and 6th rows** With W., k. **7th row** With B., k.3, * keeping y.b. sl.1 p.w., k.3; rep. from * to end. **8th row** With B., p.3, * keeping y.f. sl.1 p.w., p.3; rep. from * to end. These 8 rows form the patt. Rep. them 6 times more. **Next row** With W., k.1, (k.4, k.2 tog.) to end. **Next row** With W., k.1, (k.3, k.2 tog.) to end. **Next row** With B., k.1, (k.2, k.2 tog.) to end. **Next row** With B., k.1, (k.1, k.2 tog.) to end. **Next row** With B., k.1, (k.2 tog.) to end. Cast off.

THE APRON: with 2¾ mm needles and W., cast on 18 sts. Work 36 rows st.-st. Cast off.

THE SHAWL: with 3 mm needles and R., cast on 3 sts. Work 3 rows st.-st. Cont. in st.-st., inc. 1 st. at both ends of next row and foll. alt. rows to 11 sts. Work 25 rows straight. Break yarn and leave sts., then work another piece in same way. **Next row** K. across sts. of last piece, turn, cast on 12 sts., k. across sts.

of 1st piece. 34 sts. Work 3 rows straight. Dec. 1 st. at both ends of every row to 2 sts. K.2 tog. Fasten off.

TO MAKE UP

Press all pieces. Join shoulder, side and inside leg seams of body. Join arm seams. Sew arms in place. Stuff body and limbs firmly. Join feet in pairs. Stuff and sew to legs. Sew head gusset to side pieces, placing the cast-on edge to edge of 6 cast-on sts. at front, and ending at centre back. Join rem. front seam from nose to neck. Stuff head firmly and sew to body. Join ears together (1 F. and 1 C.). Stuff lightly and sew to each side of head. Make white bobble and sew to back for tail.

Embroider claws on feet and front paws with B. Cut half circles of felt in white, 2 smaller in lilac and 2 still smaller ones in black. Using one of each colour together, sew in place for eyes, placing small fringe pieces in black at back for eyelashes. Embroider nose and mouth as in illustration. Cut 8 cm lengths of red yarn and make fringe along outer edge of shawl. Cross shawl over at front and secure with press studs at front and back. Join back seam of skirt, leaving 8 cm open at top. Sew button at waist, then make loop on other side to correspond; tail will protrude through skirt opening. Sew lace round 3 sides of apron; sew apron to centre of skirt at waist. Sew lace round wrists and ankles. For hat, cut 2 circles of black felt 17 cm in diameter, then cut 8 cm diameter circle from centre of these. Cut strip 24 cm x 9 cm. Join short ends of strip. Sew 8 cm diameter circle to one end of tube for crown. Cut card to same shape as 17 cm diameter pieces. Sew the 2 felt pieces together at outer edge. Insert card inside to stiffen, then sew brim to other end of tube. Cut hole 2 cm in diameter at each side of brim, for ears to be put through. Neaten holes with buttonhole stitch. Trim underside of brim with lace. Sew ribbon to inner edge of crown to tie under chin.

The Mutt

Time involved: About 36 hours.
MATERIALS

1 ball (50 g) Emu Supermatch D.K. in dark colour (D.) and 1 ball in light (L.); oddment orange yarn for ball; a pair 3 mm (No. 11) Aero knitting needles; oddments of felt in black, white and orange; 4 pipe cleaners; piece thin foam rubber to line ears; kapok.

Measurements: approx. 32 cm high.
Tension: 28 sts. to 10 cm.
Abbreviations: K., knit; p., purl; sts.,

stitches; cm, centimetre(s); alt., alternate; beg., beginning; cont., continue; dec., decreas(e)ing; foll., following; g.-st., garter stitch; inc., increas(e)ing; p.s.s.o., pass slip stitch over; p.w., purlwise; rem., remain(ing); rep., repeat; st.-st., stocking stitch; t.b.l., through back loop; y.f., yarn forward.

THE BODY (make 1 in L. and 1 in D.)**:** cast on 50 sts. Cont. in st.-st., dec. 1 st. at both ends of 7th and every foll. 6th row to 38 sts.; then at both ends of every foll. 4th row to 30 sts. Dec. 1 st. at both ends of next row and foll. alt. rows to 20 sts. Cast off.

THE HEAD (make 1 in L. and 1 in D.)**:** cast on 20 sts. and cont. in st.-st. K.1 row. Cast on 2 sts. at beg. of next 4 rows. 28 sts. Inc. 1 st. at both ends of every row to 34 sts.; then at both ends of alt. rows to 38 sts. Inc. 1 st. at both ends of foll. 4th row. Work 3 rows. Dec. 1 st. at both ends of next row and foll. alt. rows to 28 sts. Cast off 2 sts. at beg. of next 2 rows. Cast off rem. sts. (this is top of head).

THE FEET (2): with D., cast on 8 sts. for top of foot. Work in st.-st., inc. 1 st. at both ends of every row to 14 sts. Cont. in stripes of 2 rows L., 4 rows D., inc. 1 st. at both ends of every row to 28 sts. Work 1 row straight, then inc. 1 st. at both ends of next row. **Next row** K.13, cast off 4, k. to end. Working on last set of sts., cont. in stripes, dec. 1 st. at inner edge on every p. row to 10 sts. Cont. straight until 5 L. stripes from beg. have been worked. Work 3 rows D. Cast off. Join yarn to inner edge of rem. sts. and complete to match.

With D., cast on 6 sts. for sole of foot. Inc. 1 st. at both ends of every row to 12 sts. Inc. 1 st. at both ends of next 2 p. rows; then at both ends of foll. 4th row. 18 sts. Cont. straight until work measures 8½ cm from cast-on. Dec. 1 st. at both ends of next 2 k. rows; then at both ends of every row to 6 sts. Cast off. Work another sole to match.

THE EARS: with D., cast on 6 sts. Work in stripes as top of foot and shape thus: **1st row** Inc. at both ends of row. **2nd and alt. rows** P. **3rd row** Inc. in 1st st., k. to end. **5th row** Inc. in 1st st., k. to end. **7th row** Inc. in 1st st., k. to last st., inc. in last st. **9th row** Inc. in 1st st., k. to end. **11th row** Inc. in 1st st., k. to end. **13th row** Inc. in 1st st., k. to end.

Cont. straight until 5 L. stripes from beg. have been worked. Work 4 rows D. Dec. 1 st. at both ends of next row and foll. alt. rows to 11 sts.; then at both ends of every row to 5 sts. Cast off. Work another piece to match, then work 2 more pieces, reading k. for p. and p. for k.

THE ARMS (2): with D., cast on 10 sts. Work in stripes as ears, inc. 1 st. at both ends of every row to 26 sts. Cont. straight until 5 L stripes have been completed. **Next row** With D., k.1; (k.2 tog.) to last st., k.1. **Next row** P. Rep. last 2 rows once more. Cast off.

TO MAKE UP

Press. Join side seams of body. Join head seams, leaving opening at neck edge. Join back seam of feet; sew on soles. Sew feet to body, the 4 cast-off sts. at top to side seam; leave opening between feet for stuffing. Cut 2 half-circles of orange felt and 2 quarter-circles in each of black and white, for eyes, small circle of black felt for nose. Sew in place on face, stuffing each piece lightly to round out. Embroider mouth. Join arm seams. Stuff head, body, feet and arms. Sew up opening at lower edge. Sew head to body. Sew on arms. Cut foam to shape of ears. Sew ears together, inserting foam and leaving base open. Slip a pipe cleaner up each side of ears and stitch lightly to hold in place. Close opening at base and sew on ears. Make pom-pom of orange yarn and tack to arms.

Pat Panda and Pip

Time involved: About 12 hours each.
MATERIALS

For Pat Panda: 1 ball Patons Beehive Shetland Chunky in each of white (W.) and black (B.); a pair 4 mm (No. 8) Milward Disc knitting needles. For Pip Panda: 1 ball (50 g) Patons Beehive 4-ply in each of white (W.) and black (B.); a pair 3 mm (No. 11) Milward Disc knitting needles. For each panda: 2 safety eyes; oddment of black felt; ribbon for neck; stuffing.

Measurements: height from top of ears: Pat Panda, 27 cm; Pip Panda, 16 cm.

Tension: 8 sts. to 5 cm using 4 mm needles and chunky yarn. 14 sts to 5 cm using 3 mm needles and 4-ply.

Abbreviations: K., knit; p., purl; sts., stitches; cm, centimetre(s); alt., alternate; beg., beginning; cont., continue; dec., decreas(e)ing; foll., following; inc., increas(e)-ing; st.-st., stocking stitch; tog., together.

Pat Panda

THE BODY: with B., cast on 16 sts. Beg. p. row, work in reverse st.-st. (p. side right side), inc. 1 st. at both ends of 2nd row and every foll. row to 22 sts. Inc. 1 st. at both ends of foll. alt. rows to 28 sts. Work 20 rows straight. Dec. 1 st. at both ends of next row and foll. 2 alt. rows, then every row to 12 sts. Work 2 rows straight. Cast off. Work another piece the same, using W.

THE BACK HEAD: with W., cast on 12 sts. Beg. p. row, cont. in reverse st.-st., inc. 1 st. at both ends of 3rd row and every foll. row to 24 sts. Work 10 rows straight. Dec. 1 st. at both ends of next row and foll. 2 alt. rows. Dec. 1 st. at both ends of every row to 12 sts. Cast off.

THE FRONT HEAD GUSSET: with W., cast on 14 sts. P.1 row. Cont. in reverse st.-st.,

inc. 1 st. at both ends of next 2 rows. Dec. 1 st. at both ends of every foll. alt. row to 4 sts. Work 1 row. Cast off.

THE SIDE HEAD: beg. at neck edge. With W., cast on 6 sts. Beg. p. row, work 2 rows reverse st.-st. Inc. 1 st. at both ends of next 4 rows. Keeping front edge straight, inc. 1 st. at end of next row and beg. of foll. row. 16 sts. Work 2 rows straight, thus ending front edge.

Cast off 4 sts. at beg. of next row. Dec. 1 st. at beg. of every foll. alt. row to 9 sts. Dec. 1 st. at both ends of every foll. alt. row to 3 sts., then at side edge on foll. alt. row. K.2 tog. Fasten off. Work another piece to match, reversing shapings.

THE ARMS (2): with B., cast on 16 sts. Work 18 rows reverse st.-st. Cast off.

THE LEGS (2): with B., cast on 18 sts. Work 20 rows reverse st.-st. Cast off.

THE FRONT PAWS (2): with W., cast on 4 sts. P.1 row. Cont. in reverse st.-st., inc. 1 st. at both ends of next 2 rows. Work 3 rows straight. Dec. 1 st. at both ends of next 2 rows. Work 1 row. Cast off.

THE FEET (2): with W., cast on 5 sts. P.1 row. Cont. in reverse st.-st., inc. 1 st. at both ends of next 2 rows. Work 4 rows straight. Dec. 1 st. at both ends of next 2 rows. Work 1 row. Cast off.

THE EARS (4): with B., cast on 6 sts. Beg. p. row, work 2 rows reverse st.-st. Inc. 1 st. at both ends of next 2 rows. Work 4 rows straight. Dec. 1 st. at both ends of next 2 rows. Cast off.

TO MAKE UP

Do not press. With right sides tog., join body pieces, leaving neck (cast-off edge) open. Turn to right side and stuff. Join side head pieces tog. from neck to cast-off sts. at nose. Sew in head gusset. Sew back and front head tog., leaving neck open. Turn to right side and stuff, ensuring nose is stuffed firmly. Sew head to body.

Join arm and leg seams. Sew feet and paws in position. Turn to right side, stuff and sew to body, legs in sitting position. Join ears tog. in pairs and sew in position. Cut 2 ovals of black felt. Sew eyes to centre of felt, then sew in position on face. Embroider nose and mouth with black yarn as shown. Tie ribbon in bow round neck.

Pip Panda

Work as for Pat Panda, using 3 mm needles and 4-ply yarn.

Doll Parade

Time involved: About 8 hours each.
MATERIALS

For soldier: scraps of 4-ply yarn in black (B.), red (R.) and pink (Pk.); piece of black tape and length of gold thread. For sailor: scraps of 4-ply yarn in navy (N.), pink (Pk.), white (W.) and black (B.); piece of white felt 7 cm x 10 cm; 5 cm diameter circle of card; length of red yarn. For Frenchman: scraps of 4-ply yarn in sand (S.), navy (N.), tan (T.) and white (W.); small piece of red felt; lengths of blue and black yarn. For Frenchwoman: scraps of 4-ply yarn in sand (S.), red (R.), tan (T.), navy (N.), white (W.) and black (B.); small piece of red felt; piece of leather or felt 12 cm x 6 cm for skirt; length of gold thread; a pair 2¾ mm (No. 12) Aero knitting needles; stuffing.

Measurements: height approx. 21 cm.

Tension: 29 sts. and 57 rows to 10 cm square in g.-st.

Abbreviations: K., knit; p., purl; sts., stitches; cm, centimetre(s); alt., alternate; cont., continue; dec., decreas(e)ing; foll., following; g.-st., garter stitch; inc., increas(e)ing; p.s.s.o., pass slip stitch over; rem., remain(ing); rep., repeat; sl., slip; tog., together.

The Soldier

THE LEGS (2): with B., cast on 25 sts. and k. 5 rows. **6th row** (right side) K.11, sl.1, k.2 tog., p.s.s.o., k.11. K. 1 row. **8th row** K.10, sl.1, k.2 tog., p.s.s.o., k.10. K.1 row. **10th row** K.7, cast off 7, k. to end. * 14 sts. Work 39 rows g.-st. (every row k.). Leave sts. on spare needle.

THE HANDS (2): with Pk., cast on 3 sts. K.1 row. Cont. in g.-st., inc. 1 st. at both ends of next row and foll. alt. rows to 13 sts. Leave sts. on safety-pin.

THE BODY: with right side facing, work

joining row thus: using R., k.7 sts. from 1st leg, k. across sts. from 1st hand, k. rem. sts. from 1st leg., then k. 7 sts. from 2nd leg, k. across sts. from 2nd hand, k. rem. sts. from 2nd leg. 54 sts. Work 29 rows g.-st. **Next row** K.6, cast off 15, k.12 including st. on right-hand needle, cast off 15, k.6. 24 sts. ** K.3 rows.

Change to Pk. and k. 5 rows, inc. 4 sts. evenly on last row. 28 sts. K.5 rows. Change to B. and k.5 rows, inc. 4 sts. evenly on last row. 32 sts. K. 13 rows. **Next row** (K.2 tog.) to end. K.1 row. **Next row** (K.2 tog.) to end. Draw thread through rem. sts.

TO MAKE UP

Sew inside leg, hat and head seams, leaving back open. Join top foot, shoulder and hand openings. Stuff and close back opening. With matching yarn, sew front to back from inside of hand to within 2 cm of shoulder to form arms. With Pk. work a bullion knot for nose. *** Sew tape to front and back for belt. With gold thread embroider buckle and buttons down front of jacket. Make 5 cm chain for hat strap and attach at sides.

The Sailor

THE LEGS: with N., as soldier to *. **Next row** K.7, cast on 9, k. to end. 23 sts. Cont. in g.-st., dec. 2 sts. at centre of foll. 8th rows to 15 sts. K. 6 rows, dec. 1 st. at centre of last row. 14 sts. Leave sts. on spare needle.

THE HANDS: as soldier.

THE BODY: with N., as soldier to **. K.1 row. Change to Pk. and k. 7 rows, inc. 4 sts. evenly on last row. 28 sts. K.9 rows. With W., k. 2 rows. With B., k. 2 rows. With W., k.1 row. **Next row** (Inc. in next st., k.1) to end. K. 4 rows. **Next row** (K.2 tog., k.1) to end. K.1 row. **Next row** (K.1, k.2 tog., k.1) to end. K.1 row. **Next row** (K.2 tog., k.1) to end. K. 1 row. **Next row** (K.2 tog.) to end. **Next row** K.1, (k.2 tog.) to end. Draw thread through rem. sts.

TO MAKE UP

Placing card circle in top of hat and joining lower trouser opening, make up as soldier to ***. Embroider eyes and mouth. With long edges tog., fold felt in half and make a mark 1 cm from fold and 3 cm up from short edge. Beginning at top outside corner, cut diagonally to mark, then cut to fold, curving slightly. Attach felt collar to body. With W., make crochet chain for lanyard.

The Frenchman

THE LEGS: as soldier, but using colours thus: with S., cast on and k. 1 row, then work 6 rows N., 4 rows T., 38 rows N.

THE HANDS: with T., as soldier.

THE BODY: as soldier to **, using colours thus: (4 rows N., 4 rows W.) 3 times, 4 rows N., 3 rows W. K. 1 row. Change to T. and k. 7 rows, inc. 4 sts. evenly on last row. 28 sts. K. 9 rows. Change to N. and k.2 rows. **Next row** (Inc. in next st., k.1) to end. K.1 row. **Next row** (K.1, inc. in next st., k.1) to end. 56 sts. K.3 rows. **Next row** (K. 2 tog.) to end. K.1 row. Rep. last 2 rows once more. **Next row** (K.2 tog.) to end. Draw thread through rem. 7 sts.

TO MAKE UP

Using T. for nose, make up as soldier to *** Embroider eyes, moustache and knot on top of beret. Cut triangle of felt 14 cm across and 6 cm deep. Fold in half and, beginning from centre of folded edge, cut in a curve to outside corner. Tie felt scarf round neck and stitch in place.

The Frenchwoman

THE LEGS: as soldier, but using colours thus: with S., cast on and k.1 row, then work 6 rows R., 42 rows T.

THE HANDS: as Frenchman.

THE BODY: as soldier until 25 rows g.-st.

have been worked after joining row, but working 2 rows N., 2 rows W. throughout, ending 2 rows N. **Next row** With W., k.12, sl.1, k.2 tog., p.s.s.o., k.24, sl.1, k.2 tog, p.s.s.o., k.12. K. 1 row. **Next row** With N., k.11, sl.1, k.2 tog., p.s.s.o., k.22, sl.1, k.2 tog., k.11. K.1 row. **Next row** With W., k.6, cast off 11, k.12 including st. on right-hand needle, cast off 11, k.6. 24 sts. K.1 row. Change to T. and complete as Frenchman, using R. instead of N.

TO MAKE UP

Using T. for nose, make up as soldier to ***. Embroider eyes, mouth and knot on top of beret. Make felt scarf as Frenchman. Thread lengths of black yarn through sts. along edge of beret to form hair, pull back and tie with red yarn.

With short sides tog., fold skirt fabric in half and, beginning 2 cm down fold, cut up to top edge, curving in slightly. Cut the corresponding outside edge in a similar way. Attach skirt round waist and insides of arms, leaving side open. Trim lower corners into curves. Sew 2 pieces of red felt, 5 cm x 1 cm, to front and back to make belt. Embroider buckle with gold thread.

Crochet Lace Edgings

Time involved: Between 3–5 hours per metre.

MATERIALS FOR 1st EDGING

2 balls (20 g) Anchor Mercer-Crochet Cotton No. 40 (sufficient for top edge of 1 double sheet and all round open edges of 2 pillowcases); 0.75 mm Aero steel crochet hook.

Measurements: edging is 2 cm wide.

Tension: 7 rows of block pattern to 3 cm.

Abbreviations: Ch., chain; cont., continue; d.c., double crochet; cl., cluster; lp(s)., loop(s); p(s)., picot(s); rep., repeat; sp(s)., space(s); s.s., slip stitch; tr., treble; t.c., turning chain.

TO MAKE

Make 14 ch. **Foundation row** 1 tr. in 8th ch. from hook, 1 tr. in each of next 3 ch., 2 ch., miss 2 ch., 1 tr. in last ch., turn. Cont. in block pattern thus: **1st row** 3 ch. (to stand as 1st tr.), 2 tr. in sp., 1 tr. in next tr., 2 ch., miss 2 tr., 1 tr. in next tr., 2 tr. in sp., 1 tr. in centre ch. of t.c., turn. **2nd row** 3 ch. (to stand as 1st tr.), 2 ch., miss 2 tr., 1 tr. in next tr., 2 tr. in sp., 1 tr. in next tr., 2 ch., miss 2 tr., 1 tr. in top of t.c. Rep. these 2 rows until work is long enough, when slightly stretched, to edge top of sheet or opening edge of pillowcase, ending after 2nd row; do not turn.

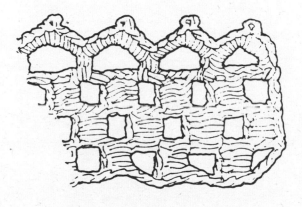

1st edging row Working along one long edge, work d.c. in sp., (7 ch., d.c. in next sp.) to end, turn. **2nd edging row** Into each 7-ch. lp. work 4 d.c., 3 ch. and 4 d.c. Fasten off.

Damp and pin out to measurement. When dry, attach to extreme edge of sheet or pillowcase opening.

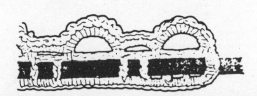

MATERIALS FOR 2nd EDGING

Anchor Mercer-Crochet Cotton No. 40 (one 10 g ball makes approx. 198 cm of edging); 1.00 mm Milward steel crochet hook; Offray ribbon 3 mm wide.

Tension: depth of edging, 1.5 cm.
Abbreviations: see 1st edging.

TO MAKE

Make 8 ch. **1st row** 1 tr. in 8th ch. from hook, 5 ch., turn, 1 tr. in 6th of 8 ch. (a sp. made), * 5 ch., turn, miss 2 ch. of previous 5 ch., 1 tr. in next ch. (another sp. made); rep. from * for length required, having a multiple of 4 sps. plus 3. **2nd row** 2 d.c. in 1st sp., * 7 ch., miss 1 sp., 1 d.c. in next sp., 5 ch., miss 1 sp., 1 d.c. in next sp.; rep. from * to within last 2 sps., 7 ch., miss 1 sp., 8 d.c. in next sp. and continuing to work along other side of 1st row work 3 d.c. in each sp. to within last sp., 6 d.c. in last sp., s.s. in 1st d.c. **3rd row** S.s. in next d.c., * into next lp. work (1 d.c., 2 ch.) 7 times and 1 d.c., 5 d.c. in next lp.; rep. from *; omitting 5 d.c. at end of last rep., s.s. in next d.c. Fasten off.

Damp and pin out to measurement. When dry, thread ribbon through sps. of 1st row.

MATERIALS FOR 3rd EDGING

As 2nd edging. One 10 g ball makes approx. 122 cm.

Tension: depth of edging, 2.6 cm.
Abbreviations: see 1st edging.

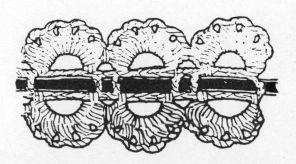

TO MAKE

Make 8 ch. **1st row** 1 tr. in 8th ch. from hook, 5 ch., turn, 1 tr. in 6th of 8 ch. (a sp. made), * 5 ch., turn, miss 2 ch. of previous 5 ch., 1 tr. in next ch. (another sp. made); rep. from * for length required, having a multiple of 4 sps. plus 3.

2nd row 2 d.c. in 1st sp., * 7 ch., miss 1 sp., 1 d.c. in next sp., 5 ch., miss 1 sp., 1 d.c. in next sp.; rep. from * to within last 2 sps., 7 ch., miss 1 sp., 6 d.c. in next sp., continuing to work along other side of 1st row, work ** 7 ch., miss 1 sp., 1 d.c. in next sp., 5 ch., miss 1 sp., 1 d.c. in next sp.; rep. from ** to within last 2 sps., 7 ch., miss 1 sp., 4 d.c. in next sp., s.s. in 1st d.c.

3rd row 3 ch., leaving last lp. of each on hook work 3 tr. in next lp., thread over and draw through all lps. on hook (a cl. made), 3 ch., into same lp. work (a cl., 3 ch.) 3 times and a cl., * 1 d.c. in next lp., into next lp. work (a cl., 3 ch.) 4 times and a cl.; rep. from * along side until 5 cls. have been worked in last 7-ch. lp., 3 ch., miss 1 d.c., 1 s.s. in each of next 4 d.c., 3 ch., ** into next lp. work (a cl., 3 ch.) 4 times and a cl., 1 d.c. in next lp.; rep. from **, omitting 1 d.c. at end of last rep., 3 ch., miss 1 d.c., 1 s.s. in each of next 3 d.c. Fasten off.

Damp and pin out to measurements. When dry, thread ribbon through sps. of 1st row.

MATERIALS FOR 4th EDGING

As 2nd edging. One 10 g ball makes approx. 74 cm.

Tension: depth of edging, 3.2 cm.

Abbreviations: see 1st edging.

TO MAKE

Make 8 ch. **1st row** 1 tr. in 8th ch. from hook, 5 ch., turn, 1 tr. in 6th of 8 ch. (a sp. made), * 5 ch., turn, miss 2 ch. of previous 5 ch., 1 tr. in next ch. (another sp. made); rep. from * for length required, having a multiple of 2 sps. plus 1.

2nd row 1 d.c. in 1st sp., * 3 ch., 1 d.c. in next sp., 3 ch., into next sp. work 1 d.c., 3 ch.

and 1 d.c.; rep. from *, ending with (3 ch., 1 d.c. in next sp.) twice, 5 ch., turn. **3rd row** 1 d.c. in 1st lp., 3 ch., 1 d.c. in next lp., * 3 ch., into next lp. work 1 d.c., 3 ch. and 1 d.c., (3 ch., 1 d.c. in next lp.) twice; rep. from *, ending with 2 ch., 1 tr. in next d.c., 1 ch., turn.

4th row 1 d.c. in 1st tr., (3 ch., 1 d.c. in next lp.) twice, * 3 ch., into next lp. work 1 d.c., 3 ch. and 1 d.c., (3 ch., 1 d.c. in next lp.) 3 times; rep. from *, working last d.c. into 3rd of 5 ch., 5 ch., turn. **5th row** 1 d.c. in 1st lp., * 3 ch., 1 d.c. in next lp.; rep. from *, ending with 2 ch., 1 tr. in last d.c., 1 ch., turn.

6th row 1 d.c. in 1st tr., * 3 ch., 1 d.c. in next lp.; rep. from *, ending with 3 ch., 1 d.c. in 3rd of 5 ch., 5 ch., turn. **7th row** As 5th row, omitting turning ch. Fasten off.

The Heading With right side facing, attach thread to 1st sp. on other side of 1st row, 7 ch., 1 d.c. in 4th ch. from hook (a p. made), 1 ch., 1 tr. in next sp., * 4 ch., d.c. in 1st of these ch. (a p. made), 1 ch., 1 tr. in next sp.; rep. from * to end. Fasten off.

Damp and pin out to measurement. When dry, thread ribbon through sps. of 1st row.

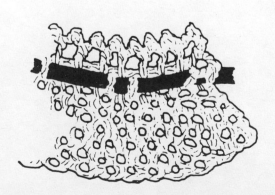

IDEAS TO CHOOSE FROM

One of the best ways to raise money is to make things to sell: Craft items, toys – soft and wooden, cuttings from plants and so on. These can be sold at charity shops, summer fêtes, Christmas bazaars, coffee mornings and so on.

The items you choose to make will depend on your particular skills – and on the type of sale outlet. Seedlings and cuttings, for example, are quick and easy to produce for a garden stall at a summer fête. A patchwork quilt, however, involves a lot of work and can cost quite a bit to produce if you have to buy fabrics for it. Display it on the wall of the local charity shop or craft shop (you may even be able to ask a local antique dealer to display it and give the proceeds of the sale to your named charity). Then the quilt can be realistically priced and you will find a buyer who can pay the price – casual buyers at craft fairs are not likely to be prepared to pay the full value. Alternatively, painstakingly stitched craft items can be sold at auction during a fête – but publicise the auction beforehand so that prospective bidders come prepared to pay a high price! Or you can raffle such items.

The section on Presentation on page 27, tells you how to display your goods in the best way.

FASHION STALL

BOW TIES
Time involved: 7 minutes.
Materials: 36 cm of 4 cm wide ribbon; 46 cm of 2.5 cm wide ribbon; Velcro.
To make: cut 30 cm of 4 cm wide ribbon and fold ends to centre. Bind remaining 6 cm round centre. Stitch bow tie to centre of 46 cm length. Fasten ends with Velcro.

BERET
Time involved: 1–1½ hours.
Materials: 70 cm of 90 cm wide, firm fabric such as felt or cotton drill; 1 m ribbon.
To make: in fabric, cut out four circles each 30 cm in diameter; cut 17 cm diameter centres out of two of these circles to leave rings. Also in the fabric, cut a headband 56 cm x 7 cm.

With right sides together, place each inner ring on each circle. Then with wrong sides together, pin circles together. With 1 cm seam, stitch through all thicknesses round outer edges of circles. Turn right side out; press.

Neaten ends of headband. With right sides together and 1 cm seam, stitch one long edge of headband to the double raw edge of inner rings. Fold headband in half to inside, turn in remaining raw edge and stitch to stitching line. Thread ribbon through end of headband and tie in a bow. Topstitch seams and edges.

SKATING SKIRT
Time involved: 1½ hours.
Materials: (for sizes 10–12): 1.20 m of 90 cm wide firm fabric, such as felt; 2 cm wide elastic (to fit waist); paper for pattern; scraps of fabric for appliqué.
To make: in paper, cut a pattern to required length plus hem by your hip measurement plus 1 cm. Fold pattern into six equal panels. Open out and slit along folds leaving 1 cm uncut along one edge.

Place pattern on fabric and spread out panels until the uncut, or hips, edge forms a semi-circle. Mark round outer edges of pattern, adding 1.5 cm seam allowance, and cut out. Cut out a waistband 7 cm deep by hip measurement plus 3 cm.

With right sides together, stitch panels together. Turn right side out. Stitch one long edge of waistband to top edge of skirt. Fold in half, turn in remaining raw edge and stitch to wrong side of skirt. Thread elastic through waistband, adjust

for fit and secure ends. Slipstitch opening.

Cut contrasting coloured fabric scraps into abstract shapes and appliqué to skirt.

PVC APRONS
Time involved: 1–2 hours.

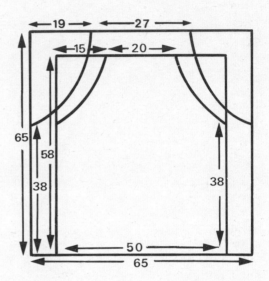

Materials: for a larger apron (9–10 years): a piece of PVC 65 cm square; for a smaller apron, a piece of PVC 58 cm x 50 cm wide; 2 m of 2.5 cm wide tape or petersham ribbon; thread; scraps of PVC for motif (optional).
To make: cut out PVC following the diagram. Turn under 1 cm all round, clipping into the hem allowance round curves and trimming excess fabric from corners. Make tape ties 75 cm long for larger apron, with a 50 cm loop for neck (for smaller apron, 60 cm ties and 50 cm neck loop).
Variations: use blocks and circles of PVC in contrasting colours to make, for example, a train motif. Hold shapes in place with double-sided adhesive tape and zig-zag stitch in place. Or appliqué a

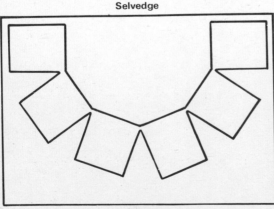

Selvedge

Selvedge

rocket motif on the apron, or popular children's names. Alternatively, use the remnants from cutting out the apron shape to make patch pockets. (If you make up several aprons in bright colours you can mix and match the pocket colours.)

JEWELLERY

Jewellery is always popular at craft fairs and fêtes and it is often cheap and easy to make. The first thing to do is to find a good supplier of fittings (earring hooks, necklace clasps, brooch mounts and so on). Then spend some tIme developing your own designs to suit your skills. Here are some basic techniques and variations.

PAPIER MÂCHÉ BEADS

Time involved: a few hours, plus drying time.

Materials: old newspaper, wallpaper paste, Vaseline, knitting needles, paint and/or varnish.

To make: tear newspapers into long tapering strips, varying the width and length according to the shape required. Long narrow strips will make rounder beads, short wide strips will make long beads. Dip the paper into wallpaper paste, mixed according to the instructions on the packet. Draw out strips one at a time, removing excess glue. Wrap round a lightly-greased knitting needle (start with the wide end of the strip of paper to make a gently graded shape). Allow to dry right through (about 24 hours). Remove from needle, then paint with brightly-coloured gloss enamel paint or poster paint. Allow to dry, then paint on a protective coating of varnish.

PAPIER MÂCHÉ SHAPES

Papier mâché can be used to make a wide range of shapes, crescents, stars etc. to make earrings, pendants, beads. Use small squares of paper to give a smooth finish. Build up layers.

Time involved: a few hours, plus drying time.

Materials: old newspapers, wallpaper paste, wire.

To make: bend wire to make a frame for the shape you want to make. Cover wire with layers of glue-soaked paper. For large shapes, leave to dry after about three layers of paper have been built up. Build up more layers when dry. For earrings and pendants, leave a wire loop exposed to thread on to earring hooks or thongs. Finish with paint and varnish as for beads.

WOODEN JEWELLERY

Time involved: 30–60 minutes for a necklace, plus drying time for paint and varnish.

Materials: lengths of 25 mm x 25 mm batten for square beads; lengths of 25 mm dowel for cylindrical beads; glasspaper; paint or varnish; thongs or string, and clasps as required.

Special equipment: saw, drill and drill bit, vice.

To make: cut wood into short lengths, about 30–25 mm long according to size of the bead you want. Select a drill bit to suit the string the beads will be threaded on to. Drill a hole down the centre of each bead. Smooth with glasspaper. Paint or varnish the bead, ensuring you do not clog up the hole.

Hints: if you thread beads on to leather thongs you will be able to make very simple jewellery which can be tied at the back (to avoid the need for clasps and fiddly knots). By knotting the thong at each end of the bead you will not need as many beads, and they will be anchored firmly in place.

WIRE JEWELLERY

Most jewellery accessory suppliers will also supply silver wire. This can be bent gently to make interesting arrangements, without the need for welding. Note: if you buy wire by weight, you will get about 56 metres per kg of 14–16 gauge wire.

The only special tools you need are a pair of fine, round-nosed pliers and a pair of wire cutters.

SPRING EARRINGS

Take a length of 14–16 gauge wire (about 1.5 mm thick). Make a small loop at one end. Use pliers to bend the wire round a 12.5 mm diameter length of dowel. Slip off dowel and thread on to earring hook.

WIRE AND BEAD NECKLACE

Thread 8 large, brightly-coloured beads on to a 45 cm length of 14–16 gauge silver wire. Use fine-nosed pliers to bend one end of the wire into a loop and the other end into a hook, ensuring that there are no sharp ends to scratch the neck.

BAGS FOR FUN

Bags come in all shapes and sizes, for lots of different uses. Here are a few ideas. If you plan to make several bags, try to buy fabric and sewing yarns in bulk to keep the costs down. Or try the fabric stalls in local markets.

CORDUROY DUFFLE BAG

Time involved: a couple of hours.
Materials: 1 m of 90 cm wide corduroy; 50 cm x 80 cm of lining; 80 cm of 82 cm wide pelmet Vilene; Vilene Funtex in a variety of colours; assorted ribbons and sequins for trimming, if desired; Vilene Bondaweb for bonding; approx. 1.50 m dressing-gown cord; matching thread.
To make: in corduroy, cut 1 piece 80 cm x 57 cm (for sides); 2 circles, each 25 cm in diameter (for base); 1 piece 68 cm x 8 cm (for strap). In lining, cut one piece 80 cm x 49 cm. In pelmet Vilene, cut 1 piece 78 cm x 46 cm (for sides); 1 circle 25 cm in diameter (for base); 1 piece 68 cm x 3.5 cm (for strap). For motif, make a pattern of your choice (a clown, a flower, a cat) and cut out in different colours of Funtex.

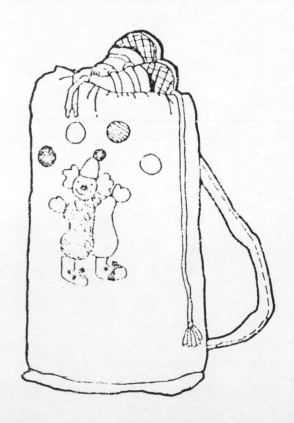

Sew corduroy with right sides together, with 1 cm seams. Using Bondaweb, bond the motif to centre of corduroy on right side.

Stitch pelmet Vilene base to wrong side of one corduroy base. Stitch rectangle of pelmet Vilene to wrong side of lining all round, allowing 1 cm lining overlap at bottom and sides, and 2 cm at the top.

Stitch short edges of corduroy bag sides. Stitch remaining corduroy base in place for lining. Unpick about 2 cm of seam, 7 cm from top edge. Topstitch all round opening.

With wrong sides together, slip lining into bag positioning it 2 cm from top edge. Turn raw edge of lining under 2 cm. Turn in raw edge of corduroy 6 cm, slipping it under lining; press. Stitch close to folded edge of lining through all the thicknesses to form a channel for cord. Thread cord through channel. Neaten raw edges of corduroy strap. Wrap round pelmet Vilene with edges overlapping on underside; bond or slipstitch in place. Stitch ends of the strap to the bag.

SPORTS BAG
Time involved: 1–2 hours.
Materials: 60 cm of green PVC fabric; a circle of yellow, 23 cm in diameter; 1.4 m striped petersham ribbon; red sewing thread; double-sided adhesive tape.

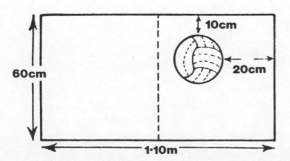

To make: cut a rectangle of green fabric 1.1 cm x 60 cm. Position the yellow circle of fabric on the green rectangle, hold in place with double-sided adhesive tape and stitch the football markings (follow diagram) using a zig-zag or satin stitch (work out the proportions first on paper and mark the stitching lines on the ball in pencil).

Fold in half, right sides together, and stitch down the two shorter sides, 1 cm from raw edges. Leave a 10 cm opening on one side. Turn under edges down slit opening. Turn over 4 cm around top edge to inside and stitch with two rows of stitches, 2.5 cm apart. Thread ribbon through channel and join ends.

We chose green for a field and yellow for a football to give general appeal, but you could use local or school team colours.

DRAW-STRING BAGS
These bags can be made up in PVC, quilted, or heavy cotton fabric, to hold sewing or hair accessories, lotions and creams. Adjust the proportions of the bag to suit the remnants of fabric you have and the intended use.
Time involved: 15–20 minutes.
Materials: a rectangle of fabric 25 cm x 43 cm, 10.5 cm square of fabric for base; ½ m of bias binding; ½ m of piping cord.
To make: join short edges of rectangle with a French seam (i.e., join with ½ cm seam, wrong sides facing, then turn inside out and make another seam, enclosing raw edges). Set base into one end of tube, neatening raw edges. Turn under double hem round top of bag.

Stitch strip of binding round bag, 7 cm from bound edge, to form casing for draw-string. Thread piping cord through and tie ends.

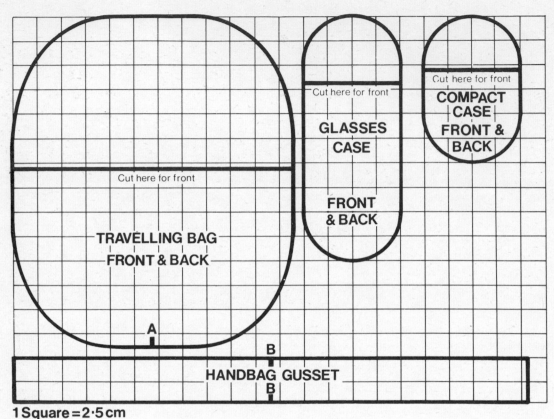

Cut here for front

GLASSES
CASE

FRONT
& BACK

Cut here for front

COMPACT
CASE
FRONT &
BACK

Cut here for front

TRAVELLING BAG
FRONT & BACK

A

B

HANDBAG GUSSET

B

1 Square = 2·5 cm

BEAUTY TRAVEL SET

Little quilted make-up cases and bags are always popular and can be used to protect glasses, hold compacts, comb, make-up, contact lens equipment, etc.

Time involved: 1–2 hours.

Materials: 35 cm of 90 cm wide quilted fabric, 4 m of contrast bias binding; 3 buttons.

To make: cut out pieces following diagram above. Bind top edges of front panels and short edges of gusset. Join gusset to front of bag, wrong sides facing; trim and bind seam allowances together. Join gusset to back in same way, and join front panel of glasses case to back panel and front panel of compact case to back panel. Bind seam allowances and flaps at the same time.

KNITTING NEEDLE CASE

Time involved: about 1½ hours.

Materials: piece of firm fabric 58 cm x 78 cm for case; piece 36 cm x 10 cm for band; 80 cm toning furnishing braid; seam binding (optional); 2 press studs.

To make: turn in edge of case fabric all round and stitch, or trim with binding. Turn up 21 cm of the 78 cm for lower pocket and stitch down at sides. Turn over top section to meet pocket and run a line of stitching 1 cm from fold, to form flap.

Stitch pocket section vertically into various-sized channels to hold needles. Leave large channel at one end to hold sets of double-pointed needles.

Turn in hem all round band and stitch, or trim with binding. Stitch a length of braid along each long edge on right side. Roll up case with needles inside, to judge circumference, wrap band round and mark positions for press studs. Sew on press studs.

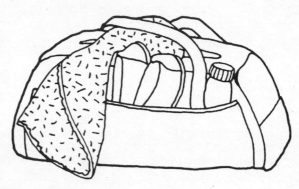

HANDY HOLDALL

This lightweight bag can be used to keep knitting tidy – or be sold as a beach bag.

Time involved: 30 minutes–1 hour.

Materials: 1 m of 90 cm wide heavy cotton fabric; 2 cm of 5 cm wide petersham ribbon or webbing for handles; piece of card 50 cm x 20 cm to stiffen base; thread.

To make: for top of base, cut 2 pieces of fabric, each 80 cm long x 20 cm wide. For sides, cut two pieces, each 50 cm wide x 30 cm deep. For pocket, cut a piece 45 cm wide x 14 cm deep. Mark the centre of each piece.

Cut a 35 cm long slit for opening in top bag piece. Bind edges with 2.5 cm wide bias strip cut from remaining fabric, easing corners to fit. With right sides together, matching centres and taking 1 cm seams, stitch bag base to lower edge only of each side piece. Press seams and open out bag.

Cut ribbon in half for handles. Lay bag out flat, right side up, and pin handles in place, 18 cm apart. Stitch close to edge, starting 10 cm down from top edge of one side, continuing right round bag, and ending 10 cm below top edge of other side.

Turn in raw edges of pocket piece and neaten. Topstitch in place on one side of bag. With right sides together, matching

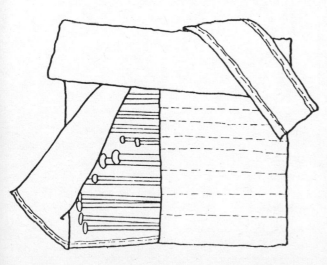

centres and taking 1 cm seams, stitch top and remainder of base to side (top and base meet halfway down sides). Turn right side out.

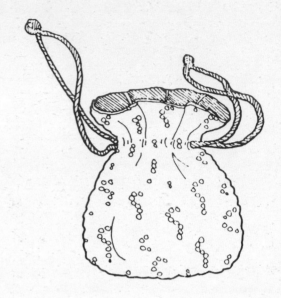

SEQUINNED DRAW-STRING PURSE

Time involved: 20 minutes.

Materials: scraps of sequinned fabric 60 cm x 35 cm; satin, cotton or other lining fabric 60 cm x 35 cm.

To make: cut front and back in both sequinned and lining fabric, following diagram. With right sides of sequinned fabric together, stitch around curved edges, stopping at top straight edge, and leaving gaps between notches unsewn. Stitch around curved edges and sides of lining, leaving a 7–8 cm lining gap at bottom.

DRAWSTRING PURSE

FRONT & BACK

1 Square = 2·5 cm

Place lining over bag, right sides together, and stitch lining to top straight edges. Turn bag inside out through gap in lining. Slipstitch gap closed and push lining inside bag. Work two rows of machine stitching round bag in line with gaps, the first 9 cm, the second 11.5 cm, from the top edge. Cut braid in half. Thread through channel. Knot both pairs of ends. Draw up with both cords, pulling one through each opening in channel.

PAPER CARRIER BAGS

These are a great idea for a Christmas bazaar and can be sold for use as gift wraps.

Time involved: 30 minutes.

Materials: a piece of stiff paper (e.g. pretty wallpaper or brown paper) 55 cm x 96.5

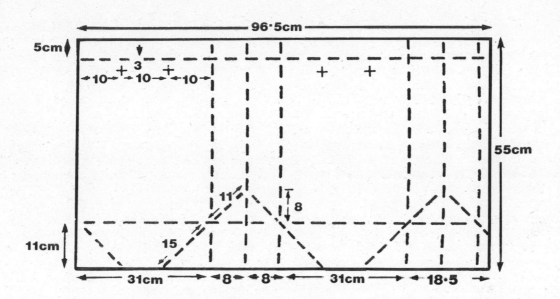

cm; paper glue, pencil and ruler; paper scissors; cord for handles; trimmings.

To make: draw the design of the bag (see diagram) on to your chosen paper. Cut out paper for the bag along the solid lines. Dotted lines are fold lines.

Fold the paper and crease along all fold lines using a ruler as a guide. Fold inwards except along the centre line of each group of three folds.

Spread glue along the side flap and press in place on the other side of the carrier bag. Fold under the top edge and glue. Fold under the bottom flap and glue. Cut holes in the top of the bag where indicated with a + on the pattern. Push one length of cord through each set of holes and knot the ends.

Once you have the basic pattern, it's easy to adapt the pattern to make bags of different sizes and you can use papers in a variety of colours and textures.

Cheap but attractive decorations include doilies, ribbon bows, stencils (you can use doilies as stencils), or, just spray plain brown paper with gold or silver paint. To use doilies as stencils, lay doily on side of bag and spray with chosen paint colour. Leave for a few seconds and lift doily off carefully. Repeat for front.

COVER IT UP!

Many standard household items can have covers made to fit them – to keep them clean, or looking tidy, to make them more efficient (tea-cosies, hot-water bottle covers), or just for decorative effect. Here are some ideas to get you started.

HOT WATER BOTTLE COVER
Time involved: about 1 hour.
Materials: about 50 cm each of 90 cm wide fabric, wadding and lining; scraps of patterned fabric; about 3 m of 2.5 cm wide bias binding; popper fastening; matching threads.
To make: draw round hot-water bottle on paper (or directly on to chosen material

and lining), adding 2.5 cm for seams all round and a flap for neck. Cut out one back and one front in fabric, wadding and lining. With right sides out, place wadding between lining and fabric on front piece; tack round edges. Repeat for back. Choose a simple motif to decorate the cover: a cat, a rabbit or a flower, for example. Draw on paper, then pin on to fabric and cut out two motifs.

Using close-space machine satin stitch, appliqué one motif to front and one to back. Stitch extra trimmings in place if necessary (buttons for eyes, etc.).

Bind edges of front and back with bias binding. With wrong sides facing, stitch the two pieces together, leaving top edge open. Sew popper to flap.

MIRROR COVER

Time involved: 30 minutes.
Materials: small mirror with polished edges; narrow elastic; remnant of cotton

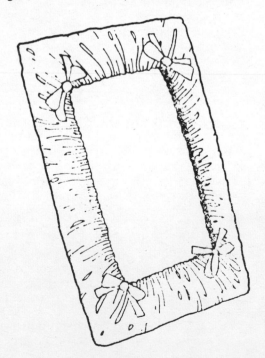

fabric; satin ribbon; matching thread.
To make: cut one piece of fabric to fit mirror back, plus 1 cm for turnings. Measure outer perimeter of mirror. Cut a piece of fabric twice as long as perimeter by about 3 cm (to make a 3 cm wide cover) plus 4 cm for turnings.

With right sides together, join short edges of strip. Gather one long edge of strip and stitch to mirror back piece, pulling up gathers to fit. Along remaining raw edge, turn under and stitch a 1.5 cm double hem. Stitch again to form casing for elastic. Fit cover on mirror and pull up elastic to fit; knot ends to secure. Make satin ribbon bows and sew to corners.

TISSUE BOX COVER

Time involved: 15–30 minutes.
Material: cotton fabric; narrow lace for trimming; tissue box.
To make: measure top and sides of tissue box; cut two pieces of fabric, one to fit top and one to fit all round sides, plus 1 cm seams.

Cut a slit into top section to allow for access to tissue. Trim raw edge of slit with lace. With right sides together, join ends of long piece, then stitch to top section. Neaten raw edges. Display one or two samples on tissue boxes but sell covers without a tissue box for economy.

TEA COSY

Time involved: 15–30 minutes.
Materials: 2 pieces reversible quilted fabric, each 30 cm wide by 22 cm deep; contrasting plain fabric for binding.
To make: cut the quilted pieces into curved tea-cosy shapes. Cut 6 cm wide strips from plain fabric and bind lower edges. Join the two sections with a French seam, catching a hanging tab into the crown.

HEN TEA COSY

Time involved: a couple of hours.

Materials: 40 cm of 136 cm wide brown fur fabric; 23 cm square of red felt; 15 cm square of yellow felt; small pieces of black and white felt; lightweight wadding, 34 cm x 37 cm; lining fabric, 34 cm x 37 cm; cotton wool; thread; craft glue.

To make: cut 2 bodies, 2 wings, (1 body and 1 wing in reverse) 1 front gusset and back gusset from fur fabric; 2 combs and 2 wattles in red felt; 2 beaks, 2 wings, 2 wing feathers and 2 oval eye shapes in yellow felt; 2 eye centres in black felt; 2 large eye backings in white felt.

NOTE: as you cut out the pieces, mark the dots shown in diagram on the wrong side of the fabric to match when stitching. Topstitch the two combs together, leaving

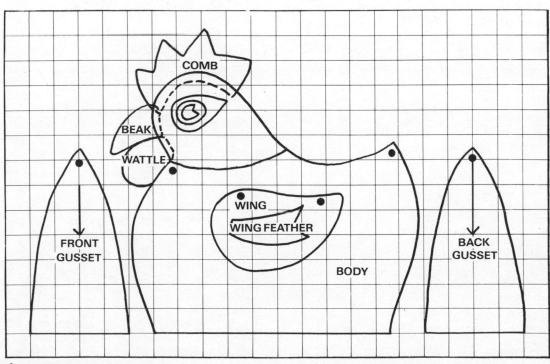

1 square = 3cm

curved edge open. Stitch front and back gussets to both body pieces, matching dots. Pin comb in place on right side of one body. Position other body piece over it and pin, tack and stitch remaining seam. Turn right side out. Lightly stuff head.

Fold wadding lengthways. Stitch short edges together. Repeat for lining fabric. Slip lining inside wadding, slip both inside hen. Turn up a seam at lower edges and slipstitch lining to fur fabric.

Stitch felt wings to right sides of fur wings, leaving open between dots. Turn right side out and slipstitch opening. Stitch wing feathers to fur wings. Stitch wing to body as marked. Oversew beak pieces together, leaving short edge open. Stuff and stitch head. Repeat for wattles. Stitch and glue eye pieces as indicated.

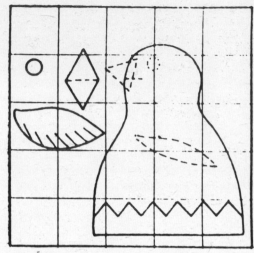

Scale: 1 square = 1 cm

CHICK EGG COSIES
Time involved: 15 minutes.
Material: yellow felt, 21 cm x 15 cm; pieces of orange and black felt; cotton wool, thread and glue.

To make: for each chick, cut out: 2 bodies in yellow felt; 2 wings and 1 beak in orange felt; 2 eyes in black felt. Oversew body pieces together round edge, wrong sides together, leaving open at base. Stuff head with cotton wool. For open beak, fold along dotted line, press and stitch to head along fold. For closed beak, cut along dotted line, glue two points together, then glue opposite edges to head as marked. Glue eyes and wings in position.

● Use the same diagram and dimensions as a guide for making your own variations: Humpty Dumpty, Easter Bunnies, kittens with whiskers, etc.

CUSHIONS
Cushions are popular and easy to make and with a little extra work they can look really special. Here are some general notes to get you started, plus ideas for decorative finishes.

Stuffing: if you want to make cushion pads as well as covers, the best stuffing is down, or feather-and-down, but these are also the most expensive. You can buy bags of foam chips or acrylic stuffing in department stores or local markets, but it's cheaper to re-use old cushion stuffing (tout around friends for throw-outs!). Or you can use old stockings and tights: wash them well, cut off any elastic and cut the nylon into small pieces. For bolster-shaped cushions, roll up a length of foam to form a tube. But, as long as you have a few cushion pads to display your covers, you can sell the rest of the covers without pads.

Cushion pads: if you are stuffing your cushions, it is certainly worth making a separate undercover to hold foam or stuffing so that you can remove the top cover for washing. As far as possible use scraps for the under-cover – old sheets, faded curtain linings or even old summer dresses. If you don't have any suitable fabric, buy the cheapest you can find – calico and dress lining, for example. If you are lucky enough to have feather for stuffing you will need feather-proof fabric.

Cover: when you are choosing a fabric for the top cover, there's no need to limit the choice to furnishing material – some of the prettiest fabric remnants are in the dress department. If you are using a fabric with a bold motif, position the motif centrally on each cover. Sheeting is an economical alternative.

The outer cover should be exactly the same size as the pad cover. Make up the cover (for flat cushions) from two pieces of fabric, allowing 1.5 cm all round for turnings. Stitch them together with right sides facing and raw edges matching, leaving an opening through which the pad can be inserted.

To give a neat finish, clip across the corners, or cut notches in seam allowance if the cushion is round. Press well, first on the wrong side, then right side out. In the opening you can fix a zipper or Velcro or, to cut costs, simply stitch it closed by hand. This can be unpicked when you want to wash the cover. Alternatively, make an 'envelope' opening, like that on a pillowcase.

Piping: piping gives a professional finish to any cushion. Make it with fabric cut on the bias – or use 25 mm wide bias binding. Stitch piping around the edge of one piece of fabric, on right side of panel, with edge of binding just inside raw edge of fabric panel. Sandwich the covered piping cord between the two layers of fabric as you stitch them together.

Appliqué: use squares of lace trimmed with broderie anglaise, strips of plain or embroidered ribbon (easily stitched with straight machine stitch), handkerchiefs, lace doilies and lengths of cord and colourful tassels.

For a more individual effect try making appliqué initials or motifs from furnishing fabrics – flowers, birds and so on. For these more intricate shapes, cut out the motif about 2 cm larger all round. Pin and tack the motif to the right side of the cushion then zig-zag stitch in place with the stitch length set to 0. Cut away the excess fabric close to the edge of the zig-zag stitches.

Always limit decoration to one side of the cushion cover, and stitch in place before you make up the cover.

COVERED COATHANGERS
Time involved: 30 minutes–1 hour.
Materials: 30 cm of 120 cm wide fabric; 30 cm of medium weight 4 oz wadding; one wooden coathanger; pot pourri (optional); small artificial flowers (optional) and matching ribbons.

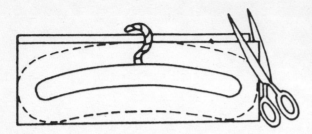

To make: make a paper pattern by tracing around the hanger, allowing an extra 4 cm for seams and bulk of wadding. Cut out from folded fabric (see diagram). Cover wood with wadding. Wind narrow ribbon around the metal hook and secure at base with a stitch. Sew along bottom edge and sides, right sides together, leaving top open. Put cover on to the hanger. Add one tablespoon of pot pourri if using and stitch the opening up by hand, making sure the cover is a good fit.

TABLE LINEN

If you have to buy fabric to make table linen, invest in co-ordinating colours so that you can make up attractive sets of table linen – or allow your customers to choose their own mix and match sets. Sheeting fabric is fairly economical and available in a wide range of colours. Mix pastel plains with stripes, or choose bright primary colours. Avoid using printed fabric for napkins because it is not usually reversible. Real linen is not worth using unless you are providing really attractive 'heirloom' napkins – the best idea is to keep prices down to attract casual shoppers.

TABLE NAPKINS
Time involved: about 5 minutes per napkin.
Materials: 40 cm of 228 cm wide sheeting fabric or 120 cm of 90 cm wide poplin; matching or contrasting sewing thread.
To make: cut fabric into squares (38 cm for sheeting, 40–45 cm for 90 cm wide fabric). Press under a 0.5 cm double hem. Trim excess fabric from corners. Stitch, using a decorative embroidery stitch if you have a suitable attachment for your sewing machine. Alternatively, neaten edges with a close zig-zag or overlock stitch.

NAPKIN RINGS
Time involved: 5–10 minutes.
Materials: remnants of fabric cut into strips 13 cm x 7 cm; thread.
To make: join short edges of fabric to make a ring. Fold under 1 cm down one long edge and press. Fold fabric two or three times to make a ring about 3 cm wide. Slipstitch round inside to neaten.
Variations: embroider initials or motifs on to outside of napkin ring. Trim with ribbon bows.

QUILTED MATS AND RINGS
Time involved: 1–1½ hours.
Materials: 50 cm of 120 cm wide reversible quilted fabric; about 8 m of 2.5 cm wide bias binding; 3 m of 3 mm wide polyester satin ribbon.
To make: from the quilted fabric cut strips 20 cm x 6 cm for napkin rings (see diagram opposite). Cut mats 30 cm x 40 cm. To edge the mats, open out bias binding, and, right sides together, raw edges matching, stitch in place all round mats. Fold binding over raw edge and stitch in place by hand, or by machine using a zig-zag stitch. Cut corners off one short end of each napkin ring strip to make a point and edge in the same way as the mats. Cut the ribbon into

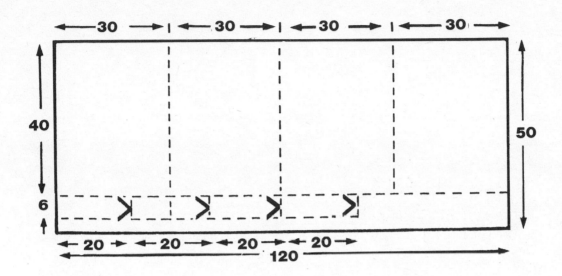

four 75 cm lengths to tie round the rings. (Alternatively, secure with Velcro.)

FRUITY PAN-HOLDERS
Time involved: 20 minutes each.
Materials: for each holder, scraps of red and green fabric; 25 cm x 20 cm each of wadding and heat-resistant fabric e.g. Milium; checked fabric cut into 2.5 cm wide bias strips; yellow and green or red thread. If you have to buy fabric it's worth making several of these to make the best of the fabric.
To make: make paper patterns from diagram, following solid line for strawberry and dotted line for apple. For each pan-holder, cut two pieces in fabric scraps and one each in wadding and the heat resistant fabric.

Using machine satin stitch, appliqué stalks and patches. Work the 'seeds' on the strawberry with two or three machine satin stitches. With right side out, place wadding and heat resistant fabric between outer sections; pin. Bind edges with bias strips and add a hanging loop.

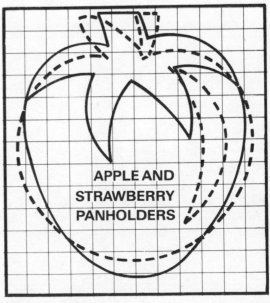

APPLE AND STRAWBERRY PANHOLDERS

Scale: 1 square = 1cm

Apple – – – –   Strawberry ———

BABY MAKES

TOWELLING ROBE

A simple square of towelling with a hood in one corner makes a cosy robe to dry off a baby at bathtime.

Time involved: 30 minutes–1 hour.

Materials: 1.20 cm of 90 cm wide cotton towelling; 3.70 m of 25 mm wide bias binding; one sew-on motif (make yourself or buy).

To make: from the towelling cut two squares, one 90 cm x 90 cm and one 25 cm x 25 cm. Fold the smaller square in half diagonally and tack it to one corner of the larger square to form hood (see diagram). Bind all edges with bias binding and sew motif to hood.

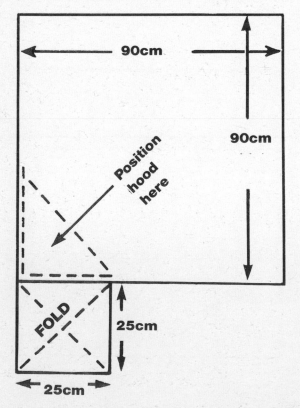

WOVEN SATIN RIBBON PRAM QUILT

Choose delicate pastel satin ribbons to make a really beautiful quilt for a newborn baby.

Time to make: 2–3 hours.

Materials: two pieces of plain white cotton fabric, 49 cm x 59 cm; 46 cm x 56 cm of heavy-weight polyester wadding, a piece of Vilene light supershape iron-on interfacing, 38 cm x 49 cm; satin polyester ribbon by Offray (available from leading department stores): 12 m of 12 mm wide white, 11.10 m of 12 mm wide blue or pink, 3.50 m of 3 mm blue or pink; a piece of polyester satin, 90 cm x 58 cm; 30 cm of 15 mm wide Velcro.

To make: place one piece of cotton fabric on top of the other, right sides together, and place the wadding on top. Stitch the three layers together round three and a half sides. Trim wadding at seams, then turn to right side and slip-stitch opening.

Lay a thick blanket and a cloth on a table to use as an ironing board. Place the Vilene on it, adhesive side uppermost. Cut the 12 mm white ribbon into 24 x 49 cm lengths and, with right sides uppermost, pin these side by side to the Vilene.

Cut the 12 mm blue or pink ribbon into 29 x 38 cm lengths and, again with right sides uppermost, weave these through the white ribbons. Pin to secure. When all ribbons are woven into position, cover with an old cloth and press lightly with a cool iron. When ribbons have bonded to Vilene, remove all pins and turn weaving to wrong side. Press thoroughly. Use a steam iron or damp cloth if necessary.

Cut the satin into a rectangle 58 cm x 50 cm, two strips 10 cm x 58 cm and two strips 10 cm x 50 cm. Lay longer strips down each side of woven panel, right sides together and raw edges matching, and press open, with all raw edges outwards. Lay the shorter strips across the top and

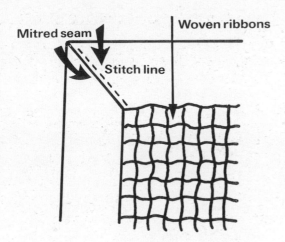

Mitred seam

Woven ribbons

Stitch line

bottom of the panel, turning ends under to make a mitred corner. Stitch and press seam allowance as before. Topstitch at corners (see diagram above).

Cut the 3 mm blue or pink ribbon into two 90 cm lengths and two 85 cm lengths. Stitch in place along the join of the weaving and the border satin, leaving equal lengths free at each corner for a bow. Tie bows.

With right sides together, pin ribbon front to plain satin back. Machine stitch all round, leaving a 30 cm opening in one short side. Turn to right side and press. Stitch Velcro to either side of opening. Put quilt into cover and close up.

To vary:

Make up the quilt in plain polyester satin and appliqué popular names on the quilt; or offer quilts for sale to order, with a choice of embroidered or appliquéd names and birthdays.

RAINBOW PLAY MAT

A quilted play mat in bright, primary coloured stripes with a PVC backing for 3–6 month old babies.

Time involved: 1–2 hours.

Materials: 1.20 m of yellow PVC (at least 112 cm wide); 1.40 m of 8 oz wadding, 94 cm wide; five 30 cm strips of 112 cm wide cotton/polyester poplin in green, white, yellow, blue and red; sewing thread.

To make: (seam allowance, 1.50 cm). From the PVC, cut a square 112 cm x 112 cm. Cut and join together pieces of wadding to make a square 112 cm x 112 cm. Hold in place with large tacking stitches. Cut each piece of coloured poplin into two strips, each 14 cm wide. Right sides together, machine stitch together to make top of mat. Press seam allowance to one side.

Tack wadding to wrong side of joined strips. On right side of striped fabric, top-stitch down one side of each seam (see diagram), using matching thread. With right sides together, pin PVC to striped fabric. Machine stitch round three and a half sides. Turn to right side and slip-stitch opening.

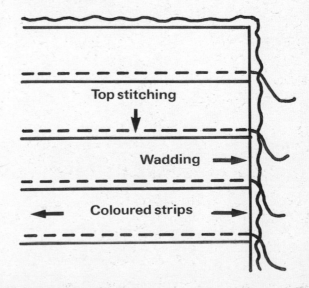

Top stitching

Wadding ⟶

Coloured strips ⟵   ⟶

CHANGING MAT/HOLDALL

Time involved: 2–3 hours.

Materials: 1.20 m of 120 cm wide cotton; 80 cm of 90 cm wide cotton towelling; 1 m of 94 cm wide medium weight polyester wadding; about 95 cm of 5 mm wide elastic; 10 cm of 15 mm wide Velcro.

To make: following the pattern opposite cut, from cotton fabric, one main piece (A), one lining for flap (B), two handles (C), and pockets (D, E, F). From towelling, cut one piece 81 cm x 40 cm for the changing mat and two pieces 31 cm x 40 cm for the side flap linings.

On all the pockets, turn over a 1 cm wide double hem and stitch with two lines of stitching 7 mm apart to form a casing. Gather the other long edge of each pocket to 31 cm (using a long machine stitch). Cut three 31 cm lengths of elastic and thread through casing at top of pockets.

Arrange pockets on top of towelling side flaps with wrong side of pockets facing right side of towelling, raw edges matching. Machine stitch close to edge, along two sides and bottom. Machine stitch two divisions in long pocket (F), to make smaller pockets suitable for holding talc, feeding bottles, etc.

With right sides together, stitch top flap lining (B) and towelling side flaps to main towelling piece to make lining to match main fabric piece (A) (see diagram). Press seams open.

To make each handle (C), fold in half lengthways, line with wadding and stitch sides and ends, turning in raw edges. Stitch handles to right side of main part of

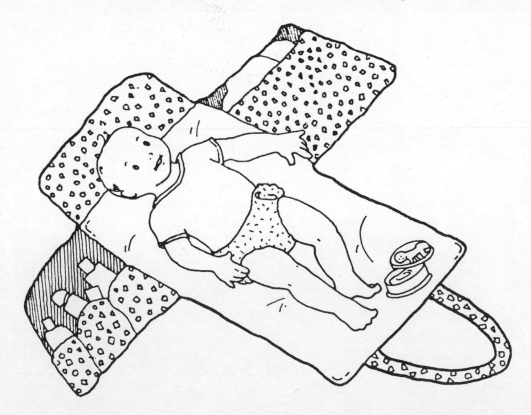

bag, at points marked with an X.

Cut a piece of wadding the same size as main piece of bag (A), and tack it to the wrong side of this piece. With right sides together, stitch main piece (A) to towelling and flaps, leaving an opening large enough to turn the bag through. Turn out to right side and slip-stitch opening. Stitch Velcro to each side of bag and flap to fasten.

– – – – CUTTING LINE   5 Small squares=10cm

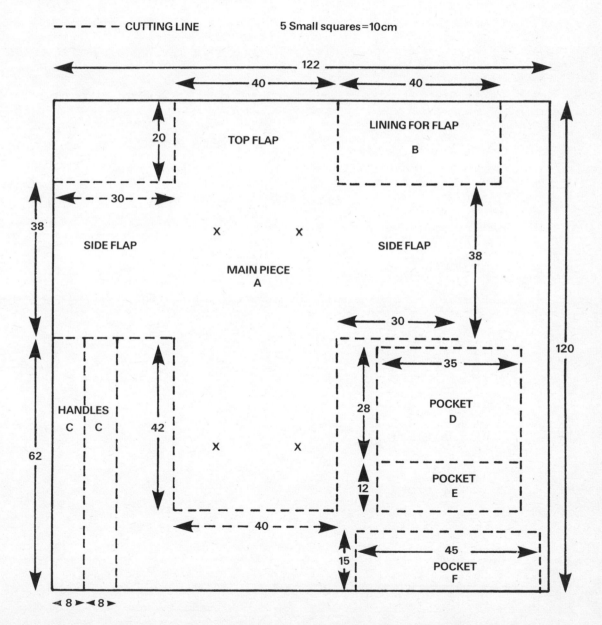

QUILTED COTTON SMOCK

This smock is for a baby of about 6–9 months old but the simple shape can be easily adapted for a larger or smaller baby.

Time involved: 1–2 hours.

Materials: 50 cm of 120 cm wide reversible quilted cotton fabric; about 8 m of 25 mm wide bias binding.

To make: following the diagram opposite, cut one front piece and two back pieces, and two pockets, as shown.

Bind each piece all the way round with bias binding. Pin and tack side seams and top shoulder seams together, overlapping by about 1 cm. Stitch (by hand or machine if you're using one). Stitch underarm seams by hand. Pin and tack pockets in position on front of smock. Sew in place, by hand.

Cut four 20 cm lengths of bias binding for the ties. Fold each one lengthways, with wrong sides together, and stitch, tucking in raw ends. Sew them to each side at the back of the smock.

QUILTED LINING AND COVERLET FOR MOSES BASKET

For newborn babies, a Moses basket is a cheap alternative to a carry cot – and it makes a very attractive gift. But the cost of making it (and buying the basket) only makes it suitable for sale at craft events where customers will be expecting to spend a fair amount of money.

Time involved: 2–3 hours.

Materials: for basket about 80 cm long x 40 cm wide; 1.70 cm of 90 cm wide quilted fabric; 1.70 m of 90 cm wide plain cotton fabric; 7.70 m of 2.5 cm wide bias binding; matching thread.

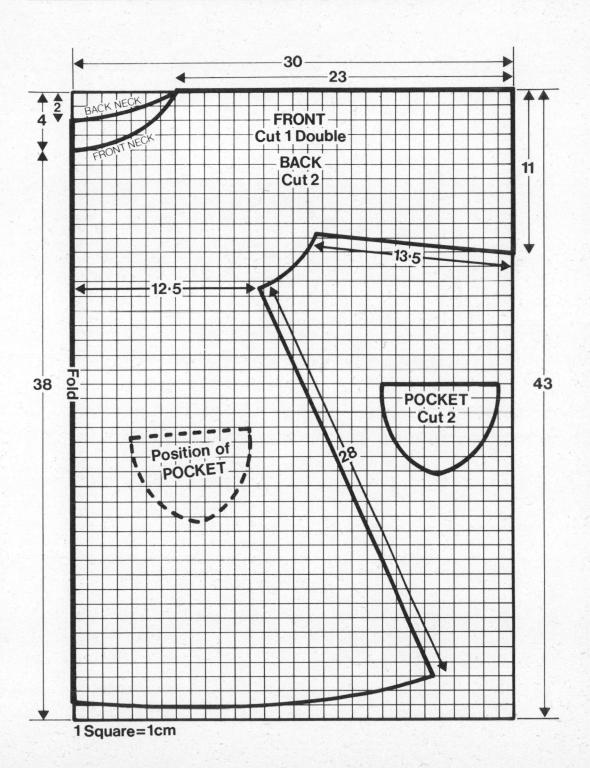

30

23

2

4

BACK NECK

FRONT
Cut 1 Double

BACK
Cut 2

FRONT NECK

11

12·5

13·5

Fold

38

28

POCKET
Cut 2

43

Position of
POCKET

1 Square = 1cm

To make: measure the base inside basket at the widest points, lengthways and widthways. From quilted fabric, cut out one rectangle lengthways to these measurements, adding 4 cm for seams all round.

With wrong side up, place base piece inside basket and mark round the corners. Cut corners to shape, retaining seam allowance.

Using quilted base piece as a pattern, cut out one piece the same size from plain fabric. Measure all round inside of the basket and the internal height at the highest point. From quilted fabric, cut out one piece lengthways to these measurements, adding 4 cm for seams all round. Using this quilted side piece as a pattern, cut out one piece the same size from plain fabric.

With wrong side out, place quilted side piece inside the basket and pin the two short edges together at the foot of the basket. Check fit; if necessary, make two small darts on either side of centre point at the head of the basket to take up any excess fabric. Remove side piece; tack and stitch darts and seam. Trim wadding from seam.

Make up matching plain fabric side piece in the same way.

Place quilted base and side piece in the basket. Mark the seam line all round the base piece. With right sides together, pin, tack and stitch side piece to base. Trim seam. Repeat with plain fabric pieces.

With wrong sides together and matching raw edges and seams, pin quilted lining to plain lining. Tack round edges.

Place complete lining inside the basket. Mark round the top edge, following the top edge of the basket. Remove lining and stitch edges together on marked lines. Trim top edge close to stitching. With the right sides together and raw edges matching, pin, tack and stitch one long edge of bias binding to inside lining. Fold bias binding over raw edges and slipstitch folded edge to outside of lining.

For carry-cot ties, cut four pieces of bias binding, each 54 cm long. Fold each length in half lengthways and turn in raw edges at each end. Pin, tack and stitch all round tie. Mark positions of ties on either side of handle and stitch centre of each tie to top edge of the lining.

For coverlet, cut a rectangle of quilted fabric and a rectangle of plain fabric, each 40 cm x 75 cm. With wrong sides together, pin, tack and stitch rectangles close to raw edges. Bind edges as before.

TOY TIME

POP-UP PUPPET DOLLS

Here's an idea for making toys from scraps – pop-up dolls on sticks in the shape of a clown or Father Christmas. But you can develop your own characters and finishes according to the scraps you have.

Time involved: 1–2 hours.

Materials: for each puppet – one table tennis ball; a few grains of rice; 300 mm of 9 mm dowel; pink felt, 13 cm sq; clear handicraft glue; felt for body, 31 cm x 13 cm; scraps of white, red and black felt; 2 paper cups; about 25 cm x 12 cm felt to cover cup; narrow braid or ric-rac. For clown – scraps of yellow felt and wool; 8 cm gathered lace. For Father Christmas – 13 cm x 5 cm red felt for hood; scrap of blue felt; scraps of white fur fabric.

To make: make a hole in the ball just large enough for the dowel. Put a few grains of rice into the ball, then push it on to the rod. Cut a circle (13 cm diameter) from the pink felt. Gather it round the edge and glue it to the head. Pull up the gathers, leaving a smooth surface on one side for the face. Glue and stitch it at neck.

Mark out two tapering shapes for the body, ensuring that they will fit round the rim of the cup. Cut out. Cut out two pink hands; pin them between the body shapes as shown, and stitch sides together. Turn to right side, gather neck edge, pull the body on to the rod and stitch to head at neck.

To decorate clown: stitch lengths of wool to centre of head for hair. Glue it at back and sides. Stitch gathered lace to cover neck join. From felt, cut three yellow buttons, two white eyes with black dots, one red mouth and two red triangles for cheeks. Glue them in position. **To decorate Santa:** cut a white beard from fur, glue it round neck. Slipstitch back edges together. Glue on scraps of fur for hair and moustache. Fold and glue hood to head, gathering and stitching it round neck. Slipstitch back edges together. Cut two white eyes with blue dots and one red nose, glue in place.

Cut the rim off one cup, then glue it inside the other. Make a hole in the centre base of both cups and push the rod through the hole. Glue round the outer rim, pull the body over it, press down and leave to dry. Cut a felt cover, 1 cm longer than the cup, and glue it to cup, with join at the back. Snip the lower edge, fold under and glue to base. Glue a circle of felt to the base to neaten it. Glue braid round the rim of the cup.

PRICKLES THE HEDGEHOG
Time involved: about ¾ hour.
Materials: brown fur fabric 13 cm x 11 cm; brown felt 13 cm x 8 cm; kapok; 2 small black beads; oddments of black felt.
Measurements: approx. 12 cm x 5 cm.
To make: make paper patterns from diagram on page 146 (2 mm turnings allowed). Lay patterns on fabric (arrow shows direction of pile). Cut out from fur fabric, 2 bodies (1 reversed); from brown felt, 1 base and 2 nose pieces. Sew nose pieces to bodies from A to B. With right sides together, join body and nose pieces from C to A to D to E. Sew on base, leaving

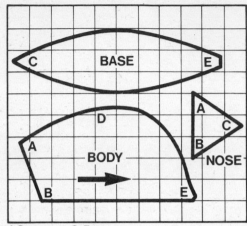

1 Square = 2·5cm

To make: make paper patterns from diagrams (3 mm turnings allowed). Lay patterns on fabric, following arrows for direction of pile, and cut out as follows: in fur fabric, 1 front gusset, 2 side bodies (1 reversed), 2 side heads (1 reversed), 2 head gussets (1 reversed), 4 ears (2 reversed); in black felt, 8 shoes, 1 nose, 2 small circles for eye pupils; in white felt, 2 circles for eyes, slightly bigger than pupils.

With right sides together, join side bodies together from A to B. Make darts on front gusset at dotted lines. With right sides together, join front gusset to body from C to D to E to B to E to D to C. Turn to right side and stuff. With right sides together, join head gussets together from A to F. Join side heads to gusset from G to H. Turn to right side and stuff.

Sew head to body, placing A on head to A on body and F at centre of front gusset. With right sides together, join ears together in pairs, leaving bottom edge open. Turn to right side and close opening. Sew ears into position. Make darts on nose to form it into dome shape. Turn to right side, stuff and sew into position on face.

Sew pupils to eyes and sew eyes in position. Join shoes together in 4 pairs. Turn to right side, slip on to end of each leg and secure. Clean pile from seams.

an opening at E. Turn to right side and stuff. Close opening. Sew on beads for eyes (if for small child, embroider eyes instead). Cut out small circle from black felt and sew to front of nose.

THE LAMBKIN

Time involved: about 1 hour.
Materials: 40 cm square of white sheepskin-type fur fabric; piece of black felt 9 cm x 15 cm; scrap of white felt; kapok.
Measurements: height from top of head, 16 cm.

PERCY PENGUIN

Time involved: about 1 hour.
Materials: 30 cm square black felt; 25 cm square white felt; oddments yellow felt; piece cardboard 10 cm x 7 cm; kapok.
Measurements: height, 23 cm.
To make: make paper pattern from

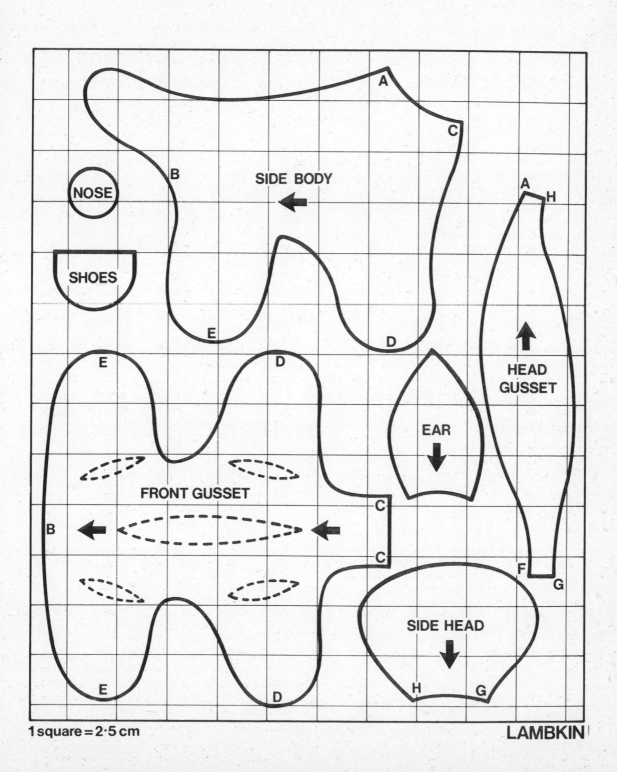

NOSE

SIDE BODY

SHOES

A

C

A H

HEAD GUSSET

B

E

D

E

D

EAR

FRONT GUSSET

B

C

C

F

G

E

D

SIDE HEAD

H

G

1 square = 2·5 cm

LAMBKIN

diagram. Lay pattern on felt and cut 2 side pieces, 1 head gusset, 2 flippers and 1 base in black; 2 flippers and 1 front in white; 2 beaks, 4 feet and 2 small eye squares in yellow.

For sewing, we used white embroidery thread and stab-stitch. Join flat nose pieces of side pieces together, then sew in head gusset, matching X to X. Join back seam. Sew in white front. Sew flippers together, 1 side white, 1 black, leaving opening at one end. Sew feet together in pairs. Sew beak together, leaving opening at one end. Stuff beak and sew to nose. Stuff head and body firmly, insert cardboard base shape, then sew on base. Stuff flippers lightly, sew up opening, then sew in position. Sew feet to front edge.

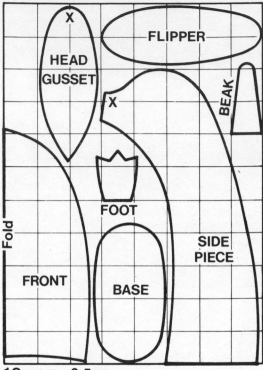

1 Square = 2·5 cm

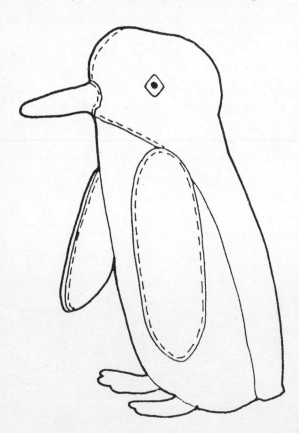

DONALD DOLPHIN
Time involved: about 1 hour.
Materials: 30 cm square of felt in main colour; strip of felt 12 cm x 40 cm in contrast; oddments of red, black and white felt; 10 cm square medium-weight Vilene; ¼ kg (¾ lb) bird seed, lentils or similar easy-moving material for filling.
Measurements: length from nose to tail, 35 cm.
To make: make paper pattern from diagram. Lay pattern on felt and cut out in main colour 2 body pieces, 2 fins and 1 tail. From contrast cut 1 underbody, 2 fins and 1 tail. Cut 1 tail in Vilene. Cut 1 mouth in red, then cut 2 quarter circles in white and 2 smaller ones in black for eyes. Stitch top

edges of body together, then sew in underbody, leaving 2.5 cm open at each side at nose (marked X) and an opening at back for filling. Sew mouth inside end marked X. Sew fins together in pairs and stitch either side of body at dotted line. Backstitch across top fin (marked with dotted line) to prevent filling entering fin. Sew tail pieces together with Vilene between. Place black eye pieces over white and sew in place. Half fill body with seeds, sew on tail.

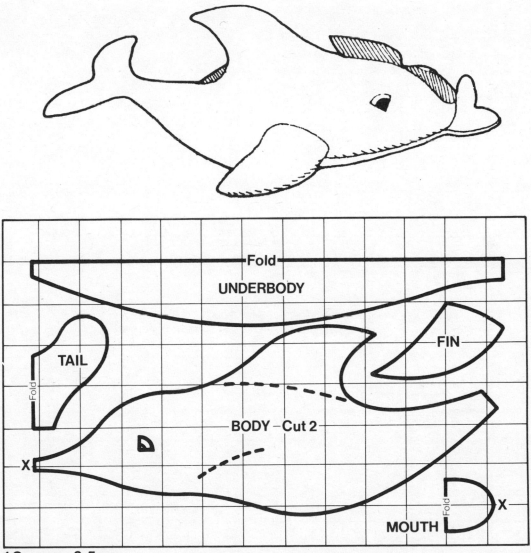

Fold
UNDERBODY

FIN

TAIL
Fold

BODY — Cut 2

X

MOUTH
Fold
X

1 Square = 2·5 cm

THE SCOTTIE AND SPANIEL

Time involved: about 1 hour each.

Materials: 25 cm square black felt; 25 cm square white felt; scraps of tan, red, green and yellow felt; black embroidery thread; kapok for stuffing.

To make: make paper patterns from diagram and use to cut out felt pieces. For each dog, oversew 2 underbody pieces together along top edge. Remainder of animal is stab stitched together, working along dotted lines shown in diagram. Sew in head gusset, then continue along body and legs, leaving one side of body open for stuffing. Stuff firmly and sew up opening.

Sew on foot pads and ears. For Scottie, sew or glue on scraps of black and white felt for eyes, red felt tongue. Sew strip of

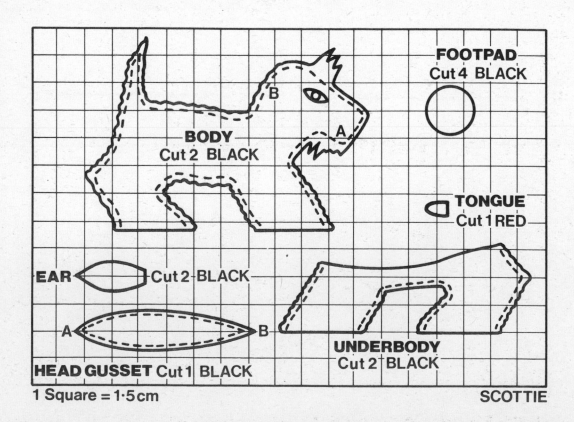

FOOTPAD
Cut 4 BLACK

BODY
Cut 2 BLACK

B

A

TONGUE
Cut 1 RED

EAR ◄►|► Cut 2 BLACK

A ◄ ► B

HEAD GUSSET Cut 1 BLACK

UNDERBODY
Cut 2 BLACK

1 Square = 1·5 cm

SCOTTIE

yellow felt round neck for collar and embroider this with black cross stitches. For spaniel, sew on tan patches. Sew on green felt collar and embroider this with black running stitches. Embroider eyes, nose and mouth.

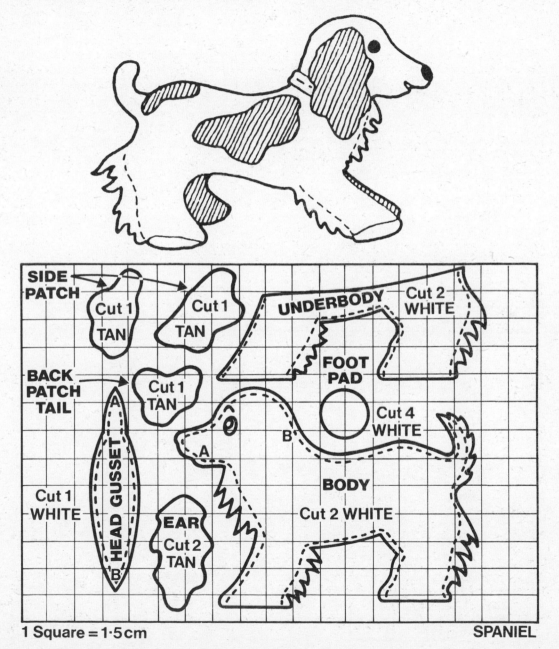

SIDE PATCH

Cut 1 TAN

Cut 1 TAN

UNDERBODY

Cut 2 WHITE

BACK PATCH TAIL

Cut 1 TAN

FOOT PAD

Cut 4 WHITE

A

A

B

Cut 1 WHITE

HEAD GUSSET

B

BODY

Cut 2 WHITE

EAR Cut 2 TAN

1 Square = 1·5cm

SPANIEL

SCRAP-BAG FAMILY

Time involved: about 2–3 hours each.
Materials: for the main body and head of each toy you need a piece of fabric or felt 53 cm x 18 cm. For clothes, oddments of felt, fabric, Vilene, shirring elastic, narrow lace, braid, embroidery thread, yarn for hair, 2 hooks and eyes, matching thread, kapok.
Measurements: each toy is 18 cm tall.
To make: make paper patterns from diagrams on pages 156 and 157. The main body is the same for all toys and ½ cm for turnings has been allowed on all pattern pieces. If using soft fabrics, cut Vilene interlinings for ears.

THE MINSTREL

Cut in black fabric 2 main bodies, 1 front face and 2 back heads (1 reversed). Cut 2 jacket fronts and 1 jacket back in red felt. Cut 4 trouser pieces (2 reversed) in striped fabric. * Sew body pieces together, leaving neck open. Turn to right side and stuff.* Join back seam on head. Gather face to fit head. Sew head and face together, leaving neck open. Turn to right side and stuff. Join head to body. Join back and front seams of trousers from crotch to waist. Join inside and outside leg seams. Make hems at waist and leg edges. Turn trousers to right side and thread shirring elastic through waist hem. Join shoulder, side and sleeve seams of jacket. Turn to right side.

Cut 2 small circles white felt, 2 larger circles black felt, then 2 larger circles in white felt, for eyes. Place together, smallest on top, and sew in place. Cut circle in white for nose, oval in red for mouth. Sew in place. Cut 8 cm lengths black yarn. Fold in half and sew 2 rounds all round face. Tie ribbon bow at neck.

BABY BEAR

Make body as Minstrel. Cut 2 front heads (1 reversed) and 4 ears. Cut 2 back heads (1 reversed). Join ears together in pairs. Join back seam on head. Join front seam from A to B and B to C. Join front and back

together, inserting ears 3 cm each side of centre seam. Turn to right side, stuff firmly and sew to body. Cut 2 pieces of fabric 23 cm wide by 14 cm long for dress. With wrong sides facing, join seam at each side for 5 cm down from top. Turn to other side and join side seams for 5 cm from lower edge. Make small hem round armholes. Turn to right side. Thread shirring elastic 4 cm down from top, draw up to fit neck and secure. Trim lower edge and neck frill with ric-rac braid. Cut fabric panties 23 cm wide and 6 cm long. Join short edges. Trim one long edge with lace. Make hem at other (waist) edge, thread elastic through and secure. With seam at centre back, catch through at lower edge to form legs.

Cut circles of blue felt for eyes and sew in place. With black thread, embroider nose and mouth.

BOBTAIL RABBIT
Cut 2 main bodies, 2 side heads (1 reversed), 4 ears and 1 head gusset in fabric. Cut 1 bolero back and 2 fronts in felt. Make body in the same way as Minstrel.

Sew ears together in pairs, turn to right side. Sew head gusset to side pieces from A to B, inserting ears at C. Sew front head seam from A to D. Turn head to right side and stuff firmly. Sew to body.

Join shoulder and side seams on bolero. Turn to right side. Make small bow tie and sew to neck. Make small fluffy tassel and sew to rear for tail. Cut 2 small circles of blue felt and sew on for eyes. Embroider nose with black thread.

BOY FRED
Cut 2 main body pieces, 1 face and 2 back heads (1 reversed) from fabric. Cut 4 trouser pieces (2 reversed). Cut 2 sweater pieces and, from same fabric, a strip 16 cm x 5 cm for collar.

Make body, head and trousers as Minstrel. Join sweater shoulders to V. Join side and sleeve seams. Make hem at lower and sleeve edges. Join short edges of collar. Sew collar round neck, fold in half

to right side and slip-stitch. Fold in half again.

Cut in felt 2 pieces for cap peak, 1 piece for cap crown and a strip 16 cm x 3 cm for cap band. Join short edges of band together, then sew crown to one edge of band. Sew peaks together, then sew inner curve to cap band from side to side. Stuff cap lightly.

Cut 10 cm lengths of brown yarn. Place on head from ear level to ear level, allowing 4 cm to fall over face and remainder down back. Stitch strands to head, then trim at back and front. Sew cap in position. Cut 2 small circles of black felt and sew on for eyes. Embroider eyebrows with black thread, nose and mouth with red thread.

GIRL SALLY

Make body and head as Boy Fred. Cut out bolero in felt, but cut both front lower edges straight. Join shoulder and side seams. Trim fronts with braid. Sew on 2

hooks and eyes to fasten. Cut 2 sleeves 10 cm wide and 5 cm long from fabric. Join short edges of sleeves, then sew sleeves into armholes of bolero. Make hems at lower edges, thread shirring elastic through, draw up and secure. Cut skirt 36 cm wide and 9 cm long in fabric. Join back seam. Make hem at both edges. Thread shirring elastic through at waist; draw up and secure. Make panties as Baby Bear.

Cut 28 cm lengths of yellow yarn. Spread evenly across top and back of head. Beginning 2 cm in front of top seam, sew yarn across top of head and down back seam. Plait ends. Using blue felt for eyes, work face as Boy Fred.

MILLICENT MOUSE

Cut 2 main bodies, 2 heads (1 reversed) and 2 ears in fabric. Cut 2 ears in pink felt. Work from * to * on Minstrel. Join head pieces together, leaving A to B open. Turn to right side and stuff firmly. Sew ears together in pairs (1 fabric, 1 felt), turn to right side and sew to head. Sew head to

body. Make narrow tube of fabric and sew to back for tail.

Cut 2 pieces of fabric 18 cm wide and 10 cm long for dress. Join shoulder seams for 2 cm, leaving 14 cm for neck opening. Join side seams for 6 cm from lower edge. Make hem at sleeve edges and neck. Turn to right side. Trim lower edge and neck with lace. Thread shirring elastic through neck and waist and pull up to size. Cut 2 circles of blue felt and sew on for eyes. Embroider nose with pink thread. Thread thick cotton whiskers through nose, knotting each side.

JOHANN PIG

Make body as Minstrel. Cut 1 head gussel, 2 side heads (1 reversed), 4 ears and 1 nose. Sew head gusset to side pieces from A to B, then sew front seam from C to D. Sew on nose. Turn head to right side and stuff firmly. Sew to body. Sew ears together in pairs and sew to head. Cut 2 ovals white felt and 2 circles black felt. Place black on white and sew on for eyes.

Make 2 French knots for nostrils.

Make shorts in felt as Minstrel's trousers, cutting at dotted line. Cut small square for bib and sew to front. Cut 2 small strips for braces, sew one to each side of bib, cross over at back and sew to back of shorts. Make jacket as Minstrel. Cut strip 27 cm x 2 cm for scarf and fringe ends.

Cut 1 hat brim in felt. Cut strip 10 cm x 4 cm for crown. Join short ends of crown, then join top. Turn crown to right side and fold in top to form pleat. Stuff lightly. Sew crown to brim, leaving 2 cm round outer edge. Cut strip of felt for hat band and fringe small piece for feather. Sew in place. Sew hat to head. Make narrow tube for tail, draw up one long edge to make it curl, sew to back.

HAMISH MACDOG

Make body as Minstrel. Cut in body fabric 2 side heads (1 reversed), 1 head gusset and 2 ears. Cut 2 ears in paler fabric for linings.

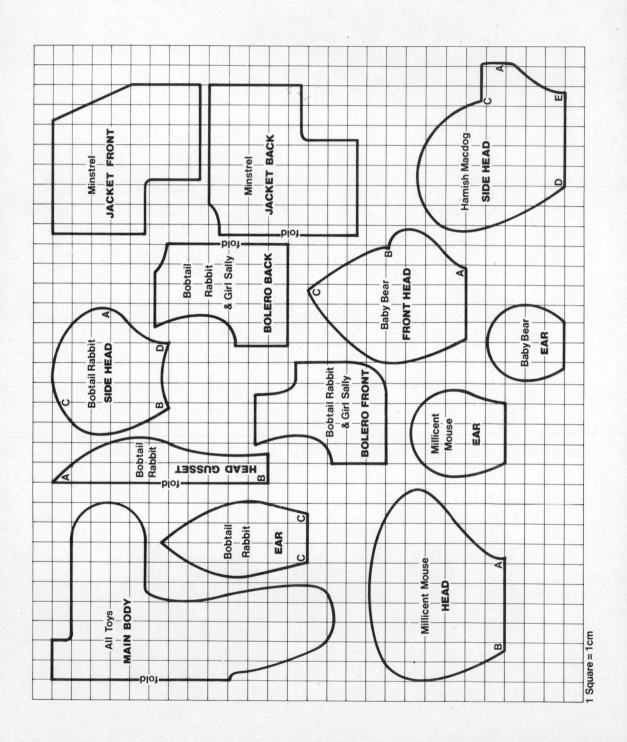

1 Square = 1cm

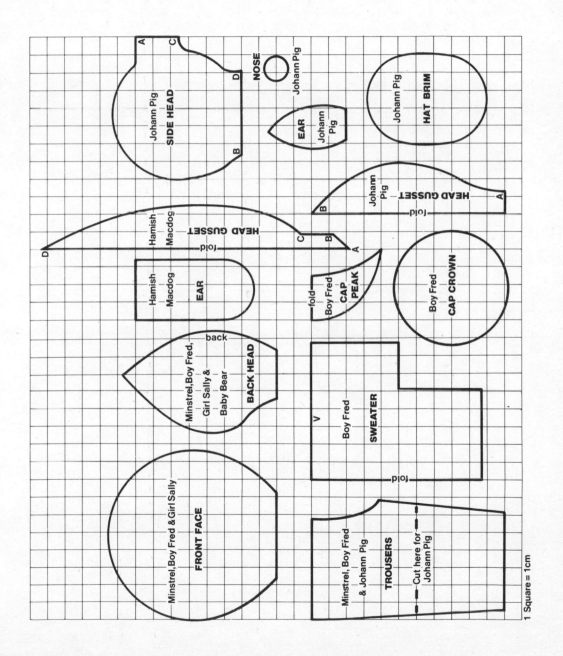

Sew head gusset to side heads, matching A, B, C and D. Sew front head seams from A to E. Turn to right side, stuff firmly and sew to body. Sew ears and ear linings together in pairs and sew to head.

Make trousers and jacket as Minstrel. Cut piece of lace and sew to neck as jabot. Cut circle 10 cm in diameter in fabric for beret, gather all round edge and draw up to 11 cm circumference. Bind edge, then stuff lightly. Make tassel and sew to crown. Sew to head. Cut 2 circles in white felt and 2 in black felt and sew on for eyes. Embroider nose in black thread.

1 square = 1 cm

TOY BUNNIES

Time involved: 15–30 minutes.
Materials: remnant of fabric, 20 cm x 18 cm; filling, e.g. wadding, polystyrene beads or dried lavender; thread; wool and ribbon or other trimmings.
To make: following diagram, cut out two bunny shapes in fabric. Embroider eyes and nose or sew on beads. With right sides together, stitch the two pieces, leaving a gap at bottom. Clip curves; turn right side out. Fill with wadding, polystyrene beads or dried lavender; slipstitch opening to close. Make wool pom-pom and sew to back. Tie ribbon round neck.

CHICKEN BEAN BAG

Time involved: 1–2 hours.
Material: paper for pattern; remnant of heavy cotton or corduroy fabric; 15 cm square of yellow felt; small pieces of black and white felt; polystyrene beads or dried peas or beans; thread; fabric glue.
To make: following the diagram for the hen tea-cosy on page 133, draw a pattern for the bean bag, adjusting the scale to 1 square = 1.5 cm. This will give a chicken about 15 cm high and 18 cm long. Draw the gussets to the same scale, and a base panel 15 cm x 5 cm.

Cut out paper patterns. Fold fabric in half and cut two bodies and two wings. Cut felt pieces as for tea-cosy. Join front and back gusset pattern pieces to each end of base pattern piece and cut out one long gusset, tapering at each end. Stitch felt wings to right side of fabric wings, leaving open between dots. Turn right side out and slip-stitch opening.

Position wing feathers on wing and wing on body as marked. Stitch through all layers along dotted lines on wing feather.

Stitch eyes in place on head, anchoring felt in the centre with a French knot or a couple of back stitches. Topstitch combs together on all sides and trim seams.

Stitch front and back body to gusset, right sides facing, matching dots. Pin comb in place. Stitch head and back seam, leaving a 5 cm opening in back. Fill with beans. Make up beak and wattle as for hen tea-cosy.

MIGUEL THE MEXICAN

This irresistible little chap sits in a round margarine pot – and his head doubles as a lid.

Time involved: 30 minutes.

Materials: two pieces of fabric for arms, 6 cm square; matching fabric for body, 26 cm x 22 cm (preferably striped fabric); 10 cm square of pink felt; handicraft glue; 225 g size round plastic tub and lid; circle of card to fit base of tub; 23 cm square of yellow felt; cotton wool, brown wool, scraps of red felt; thread.

To make: fold one small square of striped fabric in half, right sides together, and stitch to form a tube. Turn right way out and turn under a 1 cm hem at the cuff. Cut a pink felt hand and stitch in to cuff. Repeat for other arm. With right sides together, stitch longer edges of larger piece of fabric together, turn out and insert the card disc at one end. Turn under 1 cm of fabric and glue to card. Glue the card inside the base of the tub.

For the head, cut two circles of yellow felt to fit inside the rim on the top and bottom of the lid. Glue in place. Cut two face shapes from pink felt (see diagram). Oversew curved edges together, stuff with cotton wool, glue and then stitch the

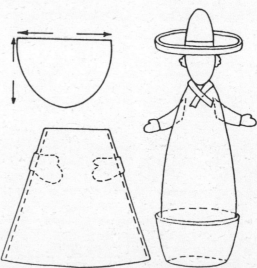

straight edges to the bottom of the lid in the centre. Stitch through both layers of felt and plastic. Cover the stitches with some tiny loops of wool stitched round the head as hair. Complete the crown of the hat by cutting two face shapes, making them slightly longer, in yellow felt. Stitch, stuff and fix to the top centre of the hat in the same way as the face. Glue on a narrow red felt hat band. Gather the open end of the body and stitch to the head at the neck.

Cut a small triangle of red felt, tie it round the neck as a scarf and stitch in place. Stitch the arms to the body. Embroider black eyes, eyebrows and moustache and a tiny red mouth. Fold the Mexican's body into the pot and replace lid.

SWAN MOBILE

Time involved: 1–1½ hours.
Materials: 12 pipecleaners; scraps of pink wool; black felt-tip pen; 80 cm white marabou trim and 10 cm pink ostrich trim (both available from leading department stores); thread; two 25 cm lengths of craft wire.

To make: for each swan, take two pipecleaners and curve them to form the neck. Bend a third pipecleaner into an oval shape to form the body, and then connect it to the neck by bending the ends of the neck pipecleaners round it, as shown. For the head, bind a little wool round the top of the neck leaving about 0.5 cm for the beak. Knot to secure. Colour the beak with black felt-tip pen. Cut a 20 cm length of white marabou, fold it in three and stitch it to the body. Cut a 2.5 cm length of ostrich trim and stitch to the swan's back. Make three more swans in the same way.

Hang each swan on a length of nylon thread, used double. Thread it through the body and up through the neck so that the swan will hang straight. Tie one swan to each end of the two wires, then suspend one wire from the centre of the other using nylon thread. Bind the ends of the wires with some cotton thread to stop the swans slipping off. Hang the mobile on a length of nylon thread.

Other ideas for mobiles
The hanging motifs must be fairly light to catch the slightest breeze.
● Cut out nursery motifs (teddy bears, clowns etc.) in felt, glueing features in place, using contrasting colours
● Fold paper into concertina stars
● Drill holes in the top of short lengths of copper pipe: hang from a ring (e.g. a plastic bangle) so the pipes can jangle together. Add other metal oddments, such as washers
● Draw fairy tale characters (or trace from children's books). Cut out of thin card and paint with poster paints for a 'story book' mobile

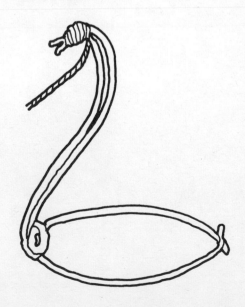

ABACUS

(Not suitable for children under three years old).

Time involved: 1-2 hours.

Materials: 1440 mm of 12 mm x 38 mm hardwood; 1224 mm of 9 mm dowel; three 1 m lengths of heavy gauge piano wire or fine dowel (available from craft and model shops); two butterfly nuts and bolts; woodworking adhesive; heavy-duty glue for sticking metal to wood; 50 coloured beads; matt polyurethane varnish; fine glass paper.

Measurements: the frame measures 415 mm x 420 mm.

To make: cut the hardwood into two 420 mm lengths for side pieces and two 300 mm lengths for the supports. Cut the 9 mm dowel into two 400 mm lengths for the top and bottom bars and one 424 mm length for the support bar. Cut the wire (or dowel) into five 410 mm lengths for struts, and file ends smooth.

Drill two 2.5 mm deep holes for the 9 mm dowel centrally on one side of each of the longer pieces of hardwood, 30 mm in from each end (see diagram). Drill five holes (large enough for the wire or dowel) centrally, 60 mm apart and 7.5 mm deep. Drill one hole through each side piece, centrally 250 mm up from the base, for the supports.

Drill 2.5 mm deep holes in the two support pieces centrally, 30 mm from one end for the dowel support. Drill another hole in each support piece for the butterfly nuts, 20 mm from the other end. Rub all the pieces of hardwood down thoroughly, rounding the corners off evenly.

Lay one side piece on a flat surface, holes upwards. Apply wood glue to the top and bottom holes, then insert the two lengths of dowel. Dip the end of each wire in heavy-duty glue and insert into the five smaller holes. Thread the beads onto the wires. Repeat to fix second side piece to other ends of dowel and wire. Lay frame flat and hold firmly with strong elastic bands until dry.

Fix the support bar between the hardwood supports in the same way. When completely dry, check that the rods holding the beads cannot be removed, then fix the butterfly nuts through the holes and stand the frame up. Cut off the ends of the supports at an angle so that the frame stands steadily. Give the wooden section of the frame three or four coats of polyurethane varnish, rubbing down lightly between each coat with glasspaper.

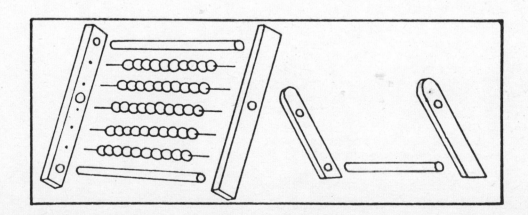

FINGER PUPPETS

Time involved: a few minutes.
Materials: scraps of felt; strong adhesive.
To make: invent your own designs according to the felt scraps you have. Cut two pieces of felt in a thimble shape to fit finger snugly. Stitch round edges leaving base open. Cut pieces of felt to desired shapes. Glue round base. Cut face and features in coloured felt; glue in place.

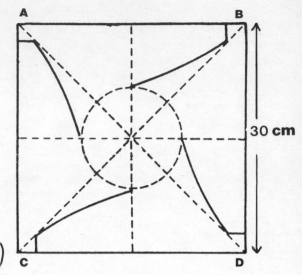

WINDMILL

Time involved: 5–10 minutes.
Materials: 30 cm of 6 mm dowel; 8 cm length of flower wire (from craft shops); 1 oblong and 1 round bead; two 14 cm squares of wrapping paper stuck back to back; 2 cm diameter 'washer' cut from a plastic tub or pot; strong adhesive.
To make: cut and make holes in the wrapping paper, as shown in the diagram. Wind one end of the flower wire round the end of the dowel. Thread wire through bead, then through windmill, turning points A,B,C and D into the centre. Then thread on plastic washer, turn the end of the wire back on itself and push on the round bead to cover it. Add a blob of glue to secure it. On your selling label you should state that this toy is unsuitable for children under three years of age.

CHILDREN'S CORNER

Here are some ideas of things the under tens can make to help out at the school fête, or take to sell at a charity fair.

MUSTARD AND CRESS

Time involved: 10 minutes to sow the seeds, then a few days gentle care.
Materials: one packet of mustard seeds; one packet of cress seeds; about 10 empty, washed margarine containers; remnants of soft white fabric, or paper handkerchiefs.
To prepare: 12 days before the fête, line the bottom of the containers with fabric or tissue. Soak well, then sprinkle mustard seeds on one half of the surface. Line the pots up on a tray and cover with newspaper.

Check the seeds every day and keep them damp (but not sitting in a pool of water). You may find it easiest to keep them damp by spraying every day with a plant spray.

Once the shoots are about 1 cm high, lift the newspaper off. Four days after planting the mustard, plant the cress.

PAPIER MÂCHÉ MASKS

Time involved: 30 minutes each day over several days.
Materials: a balloon for each mask; Vaseline or baby cream; piles of old newspapers; a small packet of wallpaper paste; paints.
To make: ask a grown up to help you to mix some wallpaper paste in a bucket, following the instructions on the packet. Blow up the balloons and smear half of each balloon with Vaseline or baby cream. Tear the newspaper into tiny squares, about 2 cm square (it doesn't matter if the shapes come out a bit uneven!). Dip the squares into the paste. Stick all over the greased balloon and build up about 7 or 8 layers of paper. Leave to dry for a couple of days.

Burst the balloon. Trim the edges of the mask and cut holes for eyes and nose. Make two small holes near the ear positions and tie a piece of elastic round the back of the mask. (Test it on your head before you tie it to see how tight it needs to be.) Paint the mask – make it a clown or a cat, or a goblin or a skeleton!

ALLSORTS JEWELLERY

Time involved: 5 minutes each day over several days.
Materials: large packet of liquorice allsorts; clear varnish; shirring elastic.
To make: lay out the allsorts on newspaper. Paint with a coat of varnish. Allow to dry for several hours. Turn over and repeat. Do this three times, until the allsorts are well coated. Take a length of shirring elastic and thread on to a large-eyed needle. Thread varnished allsorts on to elastic and tie ends to make bracelets.

FROM THE GARDEN

Pot plants, dried flower arrangements and cuttings are always top sellers at fêtes. They cost next-to-nothing to produce and even the most amateur gardener can tackle them.

STEM CUTTINGS

Many indoor and outdoor plants can easily be propagated by cuttings.
Time involved: a couple of minutes per cutting, plus a few weeks of gentle care before the sale.
Materials: good potting compost; clean yoghurt pots; parent plants (see list below); hormone rooting powder (for

more reluctant specimens); plastic bag or plastic bottle.

To prepare: cut healthy, 10—15 cm long shoots from the growing tips of plants, slicing diagonally across the stem with a sharp knife or secateurs (see diagram). Remove lowest leaf (or more if leaves are close together). For woody stem cuttings, dip in water, then hormone rooting powder. Tap off excess powder then push firmly into a yoghurt pot full of compost. Cover with a plastic bag or cover with a clear plastic bottle with top cut off (to make a mini-greenhouse). Place soft cuttings in a jar of water for a couple of weeks to root before planting (keep any leaves above the water level). Remember to keep soil moist and to stand cuttings on a sunny windowsill when rooted.

Suggested plants: tradescantia, Swedish ivy, coleus, geranium, busy lizzie, fuchsia, rhoicissus.

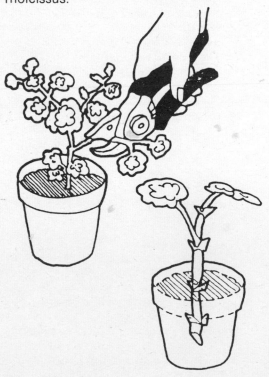

LEAF CUTTINGS
Time involved: as stem cuttings.
Materials: as stem cuttings.
To prepare: either stand a leaf in water, or tuck into a pot of sandy compost. A plant will develop at the base of the leaf, usually in a couple of weeks.

Alternatively, slit the veins on the underside of the leaf and lay it on a bed of compost, pinning it down with wooden or wire pegs if necessary. The baby plants will spring up from the slits and can be divided and planted individually.
Suggested plants: African violet, begonia.

OFFSETS
Offsets are produced by some plants – perfect little plants on the end of the runners, or growing out of the leaf of a plant, and so on.
Time involved: as stem cuttings.
Materials: as stem cuttings.
To prepare: cut off offsets with runners, or break off gently and pot into individual little pots, like empty yoghurt cartons.
Suggested plants: spider plants, strawberries, piggy-back plant, kalanchoë, cacti, dracaena (divided suckers at the base of the plant).

GROWING FROM SEED
If you grow your own bedding plants, it is no effort to grow a few extra for a summer fête.
Time involved: an hour or so for planting, plus general care over about 6 weeks. Sow in April or May for June fairs.
Materials: seed trays (or improvise with cleaned plastic supermarket packaging, such as mushroom punnets); seeds; seed compost; old newspaper.
To prepare: sow trays according to the instructions on the seed packet. Pick out seedlings, thinning them according to the instructions, when a couple of leaves have developed. Remember always to hold

seedlings by the leaves as stalks are easily damaged. The day before the fête, ease the seedlings, complete with compost, out of the seed tray. Divide into appropriately-sized clumps and wrap in damp newspaper. Pack in cardboard cartons overnight.

Suggested plants: alyssum, lobelia, tagetes, pansies, petunias, busy lizzie.

NOTE: Some seeds can be sown straight into individual little pots (empty yoghurt pots). (2 or 3 per pot ensures reasonable results.)

Suggested plants: morning glory, nasturtium, sweet pea.

PRESERVING FLOWERS

As well as propagating plants, you can use flowers and foliage from your garden in many ways: make pictures or cards out of pressed flowers; dry flowers and make arrangements in cheap baskets or sell them in bundles; make pot pourri to sell by weight or to use when making up sachets. Make sure that the flowers or grasses you wish to preserve are fresh to start with. There are several methods of preserving flowers:

AIR-DRYING

Time involved: a few weeks' drying time.

Materials: some suitable flowers include statice, helichrysum, gypsophila, liatris, larkspur.

To prepare: tie a few sprigs together with plant twists and hang upside down in a dry, dark place. Remove the leaves as they shrivel up and leave hanging until the flowers are crisp to the touch. This can sometimes take several weeks.

SILICA GEL

Time involved: a few minutes to prepare, a few days to dry.

Materials: arrangement of flowers; an airtight tin to hold it; silica gel crystals to cover.

To prepare: line an airtight tin with 4 cm of crystals. Support flower heads on florist's wire if necessary and place on a bed of crystals. Cover with more crystals and leave for two to three days. Remove gently when flowers are crisp to the touch. To speed up the process, you can dry the flowers in a microwave oven using a cardboard box. For a 650 watt microwave oven follow these approximate times:

1 minute: carnations; $2-2\frac{1}{2}$ minutes: asters, daffodils, roses; 4–6 minutes: delphiniums, irises. Cover flowers in silica gel crystals in a cardboard box and put in oven for the appropriate time. Remove and leave for 12–24 hours until crisp to the touch.

GLYCERINE

Time involved: a few minutes to prepare; a couple of weeks to preserve.

Materials: branches of suitable foliage (beech, ivy, eucalyptus); glycerine.

To prepare: crush or split the ends of the stem. Stand in one part glycerine to two parts near-boiling water. Some leaves, such as ivy, can be totally immersed. Leave for two to three weeks. Check if the mixture needs topping up. The leaves will eventually go brown and will have a shiny, slightly oily look.

PRESSED FLOWERS

Time involved: a few minutes to pick and press, a few weeks' waiting time while they are being pressed.

Materials: blotting paper; heavy books or flower press.

To prepare: place between sheets of blotting paper and leave under heavy books for 2–3 weeks, or use a flower press. Ideal for leaves, petals and delicate flowers. Use to make a flower picture in a frame, an interesting design on a paperweight, or to decorate cards.

POT POURRI

Time involved: 15 minutes to mix.
Materials: 5 handfuls of dried rose petals; 3 handfuls of dried lavender heads; 1 tbsp. each of ground cinnamon, nutmeg and allspice; 1 tbsp. gum benzoine; orris root (fixative); 10 drops rose geranium oil.
To prepare: blend spices with petals and lavender. Add fixative and oil. Mix well and place in bowls.

CRYSTALLISING PETALS

Time involved: a few minutes per petal, plus drying time.
Materials: suitable flowers, leaves or petals (e.g. roses, violets, borage, mint); egg white; caster sugar.
To prepare: make sure the petals are dust and moisture free. Lightly whisk a small egg white. Dip flowers in or paint on with a small brush. Sprinkle the entire surface with caster sugar. Dry on a tray overnight or in a very slow oven on the lowest setting for several hours. Store in an airtight jar. Use to decorate cakes and sweets, or sell in bags as decorations or as sweets to eat.

PLANT POT HANGERS

Time involved: 1–2 hours.
Materials: 52 m of Dryad 7 ply jute; a 7.5 cm diameter macramé ring for the base of the hanger.
To make: cut 12 lengths of yarn, each 4 m long. Knot the centre of each length on to the ring (diagram 1). Put the strands into six groups of four. The hanger is made from strings of knots (sinnets), each made up from flat knots as follows. The centre two strands form the core of each sinnet. Make a left/right half knot (diagram 2) with the two outer strands, then make a right/left half knot with the same two strands (diagram 3) to complete the flat knot. Repeat these two steps several times for each sinnet.

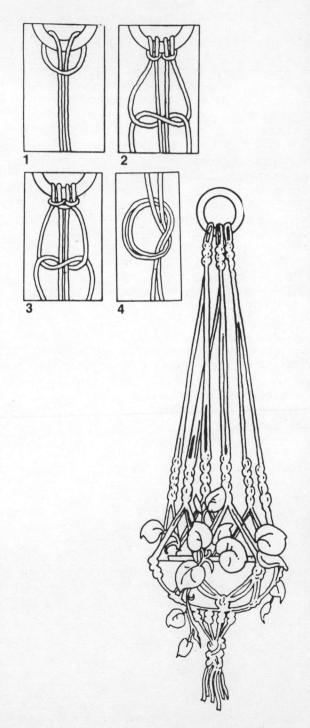

Take one centre strand and one outer strand from each of two adjacent sinnets. Knot the two outer strands together with an overhand knot (diagram 4) about 10 cm away from the end of the sinnet to form the core of the next sinnet. Make another six sinnets, using the strands which had been core strands as outer knotting strands. Re-group the strands again with overhand knots as before, but this time make twisted sinnets by making left/right half knots only.

Make 16 of these, then draw all the strands together and tie close to the ends. For the tassel, cut six x 60 cm lengths of yarn. Knot centres to the ring between the sinnets and tie adjacent strands to tassels with overhand knots.

ANYTHING GOES!

WRITING FOLDER
A simple desk set which you can make up in pretty floral, striped or check fabric. Display one or two sets complete with notepaper, pen and envelopes.
Time involved: 30 minutes–1 hour.
Materials: piece of thin card, 26 cm x 54 cm; two pieces of thick card, each 26 cm x 19 cm; two pieces of fabric, one 30 cm x 68 cm and one 30 cm x 44 cm; adhesive, such as Pritt; scraps of thin card and plain fabric; writing pad, 18 cm x 14 cm; and matching envelopes (optional).

To make: fold thin card along dotted lines as shown in diagram and reinforce it by sticking on the two thicker pieces. Cover outside of folder with larger piece of fabric, folding in a 2 cm hem all round and covering both outside and inside of flap portion. Stick fabric in place.

On smaller piece of fabric, fold in a 2 cm hem all round; press. Stick to inside of folder to neaten. Fold in flap and stick 2 cm flap hem to folder to make 'pouch' for envelopes. Cut a 20 cm x 2.5 cm strip of card; cover with plain fabric. Fold in 1.5 cm at each end and stick strip to right-hand side of folder to hold writing pad. Cut and cover a 7 cm x 2 cm strip in the same way. Wrap it into a circle and stick to folder to hold pen. Cut and cover a 4 cm square of card and stick two sides only to folder to make a stamp holder. Slot in writing pad and envelopes.

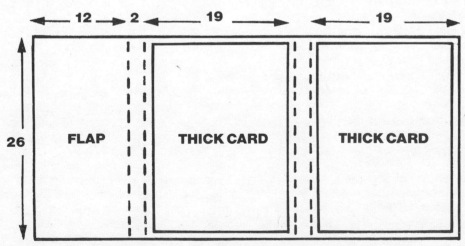

Fold line. All measurements are in centimetres.

PIN BOARD
Time involved: 30 minutes.
Materials: an off-cut of insulation board, 50 cm x 60 cm; 60 cm of 90 cm wide felt; drawing pins; adhesive; 2 m each of red, yellow, blue and green seam binding.
To make: cover board with felt, sticking edges to back. Mark 15 cm intervals along top and bottom edges of board, and 12.5 cm intervals down each side. Criss-cross binding over board, following marks. Secure binding with drawing pins at each edge; stick ends to back. Push in a drawing pin at each binding crossover. Display one with attractive postcards/ pictures behind binding strips and, to give added visual appeal, you can use coloured drawing pins.

MEMO BOARD
Time involved: 30 minutes.
Materials: an off-cut of insulation board, 35 cm x 65 cm; PVC fabric, 45 cm x 80 cm; adhesive; drawing pins; cork tile.
To make: cut a strip from PVC, 5 cm x 45 cm. Use rest to cover board; stick in place. Fold PVC strip in half lengthways. Stick and pin one end to back of board on one side. Make loops in strip for pens and secure to board with drawing pins. Stick cork tile to left-hand side of board, to cover up end of pen and paper strip.

PHOTOGRAPH ALBUM/SCRAP BOOK
Turn a cheap scrap book into something special by decorating the cover.
Time involved: 1–2 hours.
Trimming ideas: use self-adhesive vinyl, in plain, check or floral patterns. Decorate with shapes cut from contrasting plain colours.
● Cover the album with pictures cut from magazines and bulb catalogues. You can either use a large single picture, or make an interesting montage using several pictures. Protect with transparent self-adhesive vinyl. For recipe books, cover with pictures from cookery articles in magazines, or kitchen catalogues.
● Cover with wallpaper. Cut slits in the wallpaper to make holders for a plain postcard, labelled 'Recipes' or 'Wedding' or 'Family album'
● Cover with fabric, trimmed with ric-rac braid, ribbon or lace.

SCRAP BAGS
Ask around for leftover material from home dressmakers and cut into squares with pinking shears. Pack into clear plastic bags to sell as patchwork pieces. The squares in each bag should be the same size but you can do bags of big squares and bags of small squares. Choose colours and patterns and materials that complement one another – greens, yellows, flowers for springlike patchwork; oranges, browns, leaves for an autumnal patchwork, for example. Approach your local department or haberdashery store for contributions.

LINING A BASKET
Baskets lined with fabric can be sold for a variety of uses: for the dressing table, to hold baby changing equipment (cream, baby wipes, talcum powder and pins), for rolls or bread, to hold pot pourri, for sewing accessories and so on. But it's not worth tackling a project like this unless you can buy the baskets cheaply from market stalls or specialist cane and wicker stores.
Time involved: 15–30 minutes.
Materials: basket; remnants of cotton fabric; broderie anglaise trimming; matching thread.
To make: cut fabric to size of inner base plus 1 cm for turnings. Cut another strip to

depth of basket, plus 2 cm for turnings, and twice its circumference. With right sides together, join strip to form a circle. Gather each long edge. Tack and stitch base to one long edge of strip, pulling up gathers to fit. Cut broderie anglaise to fit round top of basket. Stitch to remaining long edge of strip, pulling up gathers to fit. Neaten the seam.

HANGING HAIR TIDY

Time involved: 1–1½ hours.
Materials: small wooden hanger; piece of cotton fabric, about 60 cm x 90 cm; narrow lace and ribbon for trimming.
To make: cut two pieces of fabric for the back, each to width of hanger and about 40 cm deep plus 1 cm for seams. Also in fabric, cut a strap for combs, 5 cm deep by width of hanger plus 1 cm for seams, and a pocket piece, about 18 cm deep by width of hanger plus 1 cm for seams.

In bag front, cut an oval slit 20 cm long. Turn in raw edges and trim with lace. Turn in top raw edge of pocket and stitch. Attach lace trim. With wrong side of pocket to right side of bag, topstitch pocket to front of bag. With right sides together and 1 cm seam, stitch along raw edges of strap. Turn right side out and topstitch to front of bag, about 5 cm down from slit. Topstitch divisions for combs.

With right sides together and 1 cm seam, stitch front to back, leaving opening in top seam. Turn right side out and slipstitch opening to close. Place coat hanger inside bag. Wind ribbon round hook and secure with a few stitches.

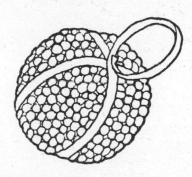

POMANDERS

Time involved: 1 hour.
Materials: for each pomander you need 1 orange, lime, lemon or tangerine; about 2 m of ribbon; a 20g tub of cloves; a selection of trimmings – silk flowers, tassels, bells and so on.
To make: cut two lengths of ribbon, one slightly longer than the circumference of the orange, the other about 1m longer so there is plenty to hang it. Wrap each length of ribbon around the orange, pinning or gluing it in place (pins stuck straight into the orange will be quite secure). Attach the short ribbon first, then the long length, pinning the ends together at the top of the orange as shown in diagram.

Fill the gaps between the ribbons with cloves, sticking the pointed ends into the orange and being careful not to crush the heads. If you have difficulty doing this, make holes with a skewer first.

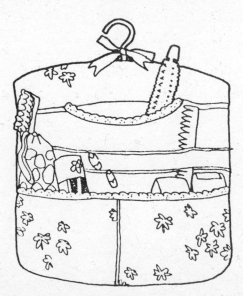

For trimmings, you can hang tassels or bells from the bottom of the orange; add beads or sequins with the cloves, holding them in place with pins; pin paper flowers to the top and bottom of the orange; or use an extra length of ribbon to tie a bow.

To vary

You can also cover the whole fruit with cloves first and then mix 1 tbsp. each of ground cinnamon and mixed spices and 15g (½ oz) of ground orris root (you can buy this from your local chemist) in a bag. Pop your cloved orange into the bag with the spices and shake well. Remove the fruit from the bag and dry in an airing cupboard for about 15 days. Then decorate with ribbons as above.

JUST FOR FUN

These three characters, made from household items, are ideal gifts to sell at Christmas bazaars, but price them sensibly as they cost quite a bit to make.

SUZY SPONGE

Time involved: 15 minutes.

Materials: sponge; mug; flannel; ribbon; coloured paper; nailbrush; toothbrush; glue; sticky tape.

To make: push sponge into mug. Fold flannel diagonally to make a headscarf and glue to sponge. Trim with ribbon

bows. Cut eyes and mouth from coloured paper; glue to sponge. Hook nailbrush over mug and tape toothbrush to other side.

DAISY DISHMOP

Time involved: 15 minutes.

Materials: dishmop; wooden spoon; elastic bands; dishcloth; tea-towel; one round and one flat pan scourer; ribbon; glue.

To make: bind the dishmop and wooden spoon together with an elastic band. Draw face on spoon with felt-tipped pens. Roll dishcloth into sausage shape; wind it twice round spoon and mop to form top and arms. Fold and pleat tea-towel to form skirt. Secure both with elastic bands. Stick the round scourer to head and flat one to end of arm; tie ribbon round waist.

CARLOS CARWASH
Time involved: 15 minutes.
Materials: coloured paper; glue; sponge; duster; large elastic band; ice-scraper;

sticky tape; two sachets car shampoo; ribbon.
To make: cut features from coloured paper; glue to sponge. Roll up duster and secure round sponge with elastic band. Tape ice-scraper to back; tuck shampoo sachets under duster. Finish with ribbon bow.

BRASS RUBBINGS
Time involved: 30 minutes–1 hour.
Note: Consult your local vicar or rector before starting on a project like this. He will be able to advise you on any suitable brasses in his parish, and may know of others in neighbouring districts. In the past, some brasses have been destroyed by using the wrong materials, so always ask permission before taking rubbings.
Materials: wall lining paper; black or coloured brass-rubbing wax; masking tape.
To make: cut a length of paper about 10 cm larger all round than the brass. Stick over the brass with masking tape. Rub the wax evenly and gently over the brass, so that the details are transferred to the paper. For a neat finish, cut out the rubbing round the edge of the brass plate. Mount on card, make a note of the date the brass plaque was laid and who it commemorated.

BOOK MARKS
Quick and inexpensive to make, so you can produce lots and sell them cheaply.

Ribbon book marks: use heavy ribbon or webbing, embroider with leaves or flowers.

Card and ribbon: take a length of ribbon, 15 cm x 1.5 cm wide. Cut 1.5 cm wide slits in a piece of coloured card 13 cm x 2.5 cm. Thread ribbon through slits, glue in place at each end. Fray 1 cm at each end of ribbon.

Parchment: cut parchment strips, 5 cm wide and 20 cm long. Write extracts from poems or plays in neat copperplate handwriting.

5
Check list

Whatever event you are holding, you should always make a check list of what has to be done, when and by whom. Use ours as a guideline.

1. Your committee: have you a written list of committee members, their addresses and telephone numbers, and their duties?
2. Has your Treasurer drawn up a proper set of books?
3. Has your Treasurer opened a current account at a bank or building society with drawing facilities for a second person?
4. Has your Treasurer opened a deposit account for monies taken?
5. Has your Secretary drawn up a mailing list of possible sponsors and donors of cash, prizes etc., and a system for seeing at a glance who has been contacted, when and with what response?
6. Is your Secretary compiling a mailing list of people who have been to your events and would like to be informed of the next one?
7. Are your organisers sure about what their duties are and the time they have available?
8. Should you think again, now you've actually started working as a team, about replacing any member? Do you have enough helpers?
9. Have you appointed a publicity person or is your Secretary going to handle it?
10. Have you contacted the local TV and radio stations/newspaper? (Even before you hold an event, pre-publicity can bring offers of help.)
11. Have you decided on your event?
12. Are you agreed on date(s)?
13. Have you arranged to have your leaflets printed.
14. Do you have a list of venues and the dates they are free?
15. Do you know what licences you need, the safety regulations involved, the insurance you need?
16. Has your Secretary written any necessary letters of booking confirmation?
17. Have you given your helpers a

complete list of what they're doing and are responsible for supplying? (And a list of what everyone else is doing!)

18. Have you obtained a Cash and Carry card?

19. Have you given all those involved with food a list of the rules they must observe?

20. Have you circulated as many people as you can asking for material contributions for prizes?

21. Have you handed out as many leaflets advertising the event as you could? And have you mailed details to the people on your mailing list?

22. Have you got enough sponsor forms?

23. Do you have somewhere to store goods before and, if necessary, after the event?

24. Have you arranged to have the venue cleaned afterwards?

25. Is there anything you need to hire?

26. If there is, do you know where to get it?

27. Do you have collecting tins, cash boxes?

28. Have you arranged night safe facilities for takings?

29. Do you have enough small change for your cash floats?

30. Will first aid facilities be necessary?

31. If children are involved, do you have enough adults in charge?

32. Has your Secretary written letters of thanks where necessary?

33. HAVE YOU WRITTEN DOWN A LIST OF EVERYTHING THAT HAS TO BE DONE?

34. Have you checked it?

Useful addresses

GENERAL

British Association of Insurers,
Aldermay House,
Queen Street,
London EC4.
(01 248 4477)

British Parachute Association,
Kimberley House,
47 Vaughan Way,
Leicester LE1 4SG.
(0533 59635)

Charity Commission,
14 Ryder Street,
London SW1.
(01 214 6000)

Charity Projects,
(non-profit making professional fund raisers)
21 D'Arblay Street,
London W1V 3FN.
(01 734 0220)

The Gaming Board for Great Britain,
Berkshire House,
High Holborn,
London WC1.
(01 240 0821)

National Council for Voluntary Organisations,
26 Bedford Square,
London WC1.
(01 636 4066)

Performing Rights Society Ltd.,
29 Berners Street,
London W1.
(01 580 5544)

Postal Finance Department,
(FA3.2),
Cashier's Sub Group,
Chetwynd House,
Chesterfield, S49 1PS.

(Unused stamps)

PUBLICATIONS

Charity Trustees' Guide,
Adrian Longley,
Martin Dockray and Jacqueline Sallon,
Bedford Square Press, 1982.
Gives brief coverage to the law affecting fund raising, lotteries and gaming, and the tax relief available to charities.

Lotteries and Gaming: Voluntary Organisations and the Law.
Bedford Square Press (2), 1983. A reasonably comprehensive guide to the laws controlling four methods of fund raising, lotteries, gaming, amusements with prizes and competitions with prizes.

HIRING

For any kind of hiring, *always* check your local newspaper and Yellow Pages first before trying outside your area.

BARBECUES

Multi-Hire Entertainment Services Ltd.,
Bishops Meadow,
Loughborough,
Leics. LE11 0RO.
(0509 216120)
They hire out bottled gas barbecues.

CHILDREN'S AMUSEMENTS

Donmar Hire,
39 Earlham Street,
London WC2.
(01 836 3221)
Has mail order available for strobe lights, electric bubble machines, snow machines, smoke machines. All weekly.

The Kensington Carnival Company Ltd.,
123 Ifield Road,
London SW10.
(01 370 4358)
Hire out slides, seesaws, trampolines.

CHINA, CUTLERY AND TABLE LINEN

Most caterers and marquee/flooring hire companies will hire out china, cutlery and table linen. See under the relevant heading in this section. Check with local off-licences, too.

Rickards,
Kingston House North,
Princes Gate,
London SW7.
(01 286 5343)
Also have bar accessories and a full range of equipment.

FANCY DRESS

Check Yellow Pages under Theatrical Costumes or Costumiers, but here are some to try. And you could also see if your local theatre or amateur drama group were interested in hiring out costumes not in use.

B & J Costumes,
65 St Helier Avenue,
Morden,
Surrey.
(01 648 2790)
For children's period and fancy dress costumes.

Barnum's Carnival Novelties Ltd.,
67 Hammersmith Road,
London W14 8UY.

(01 602 1211)
For carnival heads – Donald Duck, Minnie Mouse and many others.

Bermans & Nathans Ltd.,
18 Irving Street,
London WC2.
(01 839 1651)
For traditional costumes by the week. Fee depends on the costume.

Betsy Trotwood's Incredible Costume Emporium,
22a Ewell Road,
Cheam,
Surrey.
(01 643 4866)
Open on Sundays.

Escapade,
150 Camden High Street,
London NW1.
(01 485 7384)
Wierd and wonderful costumes, including bananas and flower pots.

Fête and Fair Enterprises Ltd.,
12 The Parade,
Beyon Road,
Carshalton,
Surrey SM5 3RL.
(01 647 2964)
For a Father Christmas outfit.

Peeks of Bournemouth,
Riverside Lane,
Tuckton,
Bournemouth,
Dorset.
(0202 429404)
For complete outfits of clothes, wig and even make-up.

The Theatre Zoo Ltd.,
21 Earlham Street,
London WC2.
(01 836 3150)
For animal costumes.

Wig Creations,
12 Old Burlington Street,
London W1.

(01 734 7381)
For outrageous wigs!

FOR FÊTES AND FAIRS

You can hire everything you need, wherever you are. Check the Yellow Pages and the Showman's Directory, available at your local library or on order, direct from the publishers:

The Showman's Directory,
Stephen & Jean Lance Publications,
Brook House, Mint Street,
Godalming,
Surrey GU7 1HE
(04868 22184)

The Showman's Guild,
Guild House,
Clarence Street,
Staines,
Middlesex.
(0784 6185)
Can supply details of how to hire a complete fair and fair equipment.

The World's Fair,
A newspaper for showmen, available through newsagents – you'll probably have to order it.

Barriers
Fête & Fayre Enterprises Ltd.,
12 The Parade,
Beyon Road,
Carshalton,
Surrey SM5 3RL.
(01 647 2964)
Hire ropes and poles.

Bunting and Flags
Check the Yellow Pages under Flags and Banners.

Black & Edington Hire,
29 Queen Elizabeth Street,
London SE1 2LU.
(01 407 3734)
One week hire of national flags, bunting, pennants and flags to carry.

Candy Floss Machine
Available countrywide. Many catering companies will hire you one, so check the Yellow Pages under Caterers.

Any Event Rental Centre,
Mercia Road,
Gloucester.
(0452 416668)
Hires a machine complete with stall and a pack of 500 sticks and colouring.

The Samson Novelty Company,
Westfield Works,
Charles Street,
White Hart Lane,
London SW13.
(01 876 2267)
Hires out machines.

Car Parking
Ask the local police for advice on security and where to have a car park which will not result in a public nuisance.

National Car Parks Ltd.,
21 Bryanston Street,
London W1A 4NH.
(01 499 7050)
Will hire out space or organise car parking.

Donkey Derbies
T.B. Phillips (Glos) Ltd.,
The Outdoor People,
Boundary House,
74 Bathurst Road,
Gloucester GL1 4RJ.
(0452 22807)
Will act as agents or deliver the necessary requirements for you to run a derby. They will also arrange other outdoor displays. NB. Check your local stables in the Yellow Pages as they may be able to arrange a derby as a donation to the cause.

First Aid Post
British Red Cross Society or *St. John's Ambulance* can be contacted locally through the telephone directory. Check whether or not they'll bring their own tent and cot or want you to supply.

Hot Air Balloons
The Hot Air Balloon Company,

13 Imperial Studios,
Imperial Road,
London SW6 2AG.
(01 731 6151)
Will arrange hot air displays.

Inflatables
Any Event Rental Centre,
Mercia Road,
Gloucester.
(0452 416668)
Can supply a bouncing dragon.

Fête & Fayre Enterprises Ltd.,
12 The Parade,
Beyon Road,
Carshalton,
Surrey.
(01 647 2964)
Hire out rocket inflatables and mini flat-bed ones.
All have electric motors and need a 13 amp
socket.

Superbounce Ltd.,
Newton Road,
Harrowbrook Industrial Estate,
Hinckley,
Leics.
(0455 636478)
Will supply the address of a local operator.

Public Address Systems
Check Yellow Pages under Audio Visual Services
for local hirers.

Essex Sound Services Ltd.,
280 Forest Road,
London E11.
(01 520 4321)
Will hire out a system, and supply a commentator
if required.

HSS Hire Shops Ltd.,
Warenne House,
31 London Road,
Reigate,
Surrey RH2 9P2.
(07372 49441)
Offer both P/A and loud hailers.

Stalls
Barnum's Carnival Novelties Ltd.,
67 Hammersmith Road,
London W14 8UY.
(01 602 1211)
Will hire out stalls with shaped or flat tops, and
also amusements such as a fat lady photograph
stand.

Fête and Fayre Enterprises Ltd.,
12 The Parade,
Beyon Road,
Carshalton,
Surrey SM5 3RL.
(01 647 2964)
They specialise in free-standing stalls with game
accessories designed to fit into an estate car.

Multi-Hire Entertainment Services Ltd.,
Bishops Meadow,
Loughborough,
Leics. LE11 0RO.
(0509 216120)
Kiosks with counters and also fête equipment like
a coconut shy.

Peeks of Bournemouth,
Riverside Lane,
Tuckton,
Bournemouth,
Dorset.
(0202 429404)
They have a mail order service for some types of
stall and accessories such as a coconut shy can
be hired from them. They will also deliver.

Steam and Vintage Vehicles
National Vintage Tractor and Engine Club,
Horton,
Bristol BS17 6OY.
(0454 313305)
Will supply details of local clubs.

Lavatories
The John Anderson Group,
Court Lane,
Iver,
Bucks.
(0753 653737)
Several types available and an attendant.

Ladder Hire Company,
Scotts Road,
Bromley North,
Kent.
(01 460 9111)
Lavatories, tents and basins, available together or separately.

Pilot Plant Hire Ltd.,
30 Dorset Avenue,
Norwood Green,
Southall,
Middx.
(01 574 3882)
Units come complete with roller towelling, soap and lavatory paper.

Rentaloo Ltd,
Crews Hill Station,
Cattlegate Road,
Enfield,
Middlesex.
(0920 830155)
Ring for a quote. They will do mains connection or a recycling type.

FLOORING

Look for addresses, under Flooring, in the Yellow Pages but most marquee companies hire out flooring, too.

Multi-Hire Entertainment Services Ltd.,
Bishops Meadow,
Loughborough,
Leics. LE11 0RO.
(0509 216120)
Hire parquet dance floors.

Stage Two Hire,
197 Watford Road,
Croxley Green,
Rickmansworth,
Herts WD3 3EH.
(0923 30789)
Have portable wooden dance floors, indoor and outdoor lighting, sound equipment and special effects.

ICE-MAKING EQUIPMENT

Knight Services,
Hoe Street,
London E17.
(01 521 4747)
Minimum rental period three months; costs include a deposit, installation fee and rental charge.

Refrigerator Rentals,
36 Hendale Avenue,
London NW4.
(01 203 5523)
Refrigerators and freezers. Delivery and collection in London area.

MARQUEES

DIY Assembly Marquees
Vincents of Martock,
North Street,
Martock,
Somerset TA12 6DJ.
(0935 824391)
Have a local service only. You'll need adequate transport.

Juliana's Party Organisers,
Unit 3a,
Farm Lane Trading Estate,
Fulham,
London SW6.
(01 937 1555)
Operate in the London area and also have a manned disco service.

Pandastand,
Wenbans Oast,
Wadhurst,
Sussex.
(089 288 2259)
Will go anywhere in the country and will also supply chairs, plus tables and other accessories.

MISCELLANEOUS ITEMS

BOC Ltd., (Head Office)
Great West House,
Great West Road,

Brentford.
(01 560 5166)
BOC sell gas for filling balloons. Check Yellow Pages or ring head office for your nearest branch.

Hire Service Shops, (Head Office)
Warenne House,
31 London Road,
Reigate,
Surrey RH2 9PZ.
(07372 49441)
Some branches specialise in catering equipment. Phone for your nearest branch.

Studio and TV Hire,
3 Ariel Way,
Wood Lane,
London W12.
(01 749 3445)
Have over 650,000 items available. Minimum hire one week.

SOUND

Check Yellow Pages under Audio and Visual or Disco Equipment, or try local music shops.

Electromusic Ltd.,
89-97 St. John's Street,
London EC1.
(01 253 9410)
Specialise in professional audio equipment.

Juke Box Junction,
90 Charlton Street,
London NW1.
(01 388 1512)
Rent out a jukebox and have 500 records in stock dating from 1950.

Juliana's Party Organisers,
Unit 3a,
Farm Lane Trading Estate,
Fulham,
London SW6.
(01 937 1555)
Operate in London area and also have a manned disco service.

The Derrington Group,
55 York Street,
Twickenham,
Middx.
(01 892 3601)
Have a wide range of audio equipment as well as disco.

STUFFED ANIMALS

Gerrard Hire Ltd.,
85 Royal College Street,
London NW1 0SE.
(01 387 2765)
Hire out stuffed animals.

TABLES AND CHAIRS

Oscar's Den,
127 Abbey Road,
London NW6 4SL.
(01 328 6683)
Have a mobile warehouse/shop for transporting their tables and chairs round London.

Party Ingredients,
1 Nine Elms,
Kirtling Street,
London SW8.
(01 627 3800)
Will deliver tables, plus accessories anywhere in the country. They also have banqueting tables.

The Kensington Carnival Company Ltd.,
123 Ifield Road,
London SW10.
(01 370 4358)
Hire low tables to seat 10 children.

TOASTMASTERS

The Institute of Toastmasters of Great Britain.
Available countrywide. Check the Yellow Pages under Toastmasters or Masters Ceremony. Fees vary but expect to pay up to £75 (at time of going to press).

TRANSPORT

Check Yellow Pages.

Glanmire Farm,
Christchurch Road,
Epsom,
Surrey.
(01 782 8432)
Operate mainly in the Surrey and London area.
Cost includes VAT and coachman/driver.

Longfield Horse Drawn Carriage Company,
Nurstead Hill Farm,
Londfield,
Kent.
(04747 2954)
Have pairs, singles, and four in hand for vehicles
that include a landau and omnibus.

Red House Stables,
Old Road,
Darley Dale,
Matlock,
Derbyshire.
(0629 733583)
Have a wide range of horsedrawn vehicles. Hiring
charge includes liveried footmen and driver.
Wagons, carts, hansom cab, landau, brougham,
sleigh and shooting brake are among the stock.

VENUES

Boats
Firms countrywide offer floating catering facilities.
Check Yellow Pages for numbers.

In London:
River Rides Ltd.,
Charing Cross Pier,
Victoria Embankment,
London WC2N 6NU
(01 930 0971)
Prices on application – you cannot use your own
catering facilities.

Tate & Lyle PLC,
Sugar Quay,
Lower Thames Street,
London EC3R 6DQ.
(01 626 6525)
Hires out the Thames sailing barge, *May*. It can
carry 46 people (including two qualified crew and
four catering staff). Total cost at the time of going
to press (excluding food and drink) £70 per hour

sailing (minimum of 5) or £65 per hour moored
(minimum 3).

Halls
Ask the local council, churches or library for a list
of halls available in your area.

Theatres
Contact your local theatre (Yellow Pages for
addresses). In London you can hire:
The Bloomsbury
15 Gordon Street,
London WC1.
(01 388 3363)
Seats 560 and full facilities are available. Cost for
a week at the time of going to press is £2,750 or
30% of the booking office, whichever is the
greater.

CRAFT SUPPLIERS

Anderson & McEuley,
(Needlework Dept.),
1-5 Donegall Place,
Belfast B I 1 5AH.
(0232 226681)

Arrowtip,
31-35 Stannery Street,
London SE11.
(01 735 8848)
Ring or write for details of polystyrene beads in
bulk – for bean bags and stuffed toys.

Christine Riley,
53 Barclay Street,
Stonehaven,
Kincardineshire,
Scotland.
(0569 63238)

Dainty Toys,
Unit 35,
Phoenix Road,
Crowther Industrial Estate,
Washington,
Tyne & Wear.
(091 4167886)
Write or phone for free price list of fur fabrics,
fillings, felt, lace and toy patterns.

Dryad Handicrafts,
PO Box 38,
Northgates,
Leicester LE1 9BU.
(0533 50405)
Spinning wheels, looms, potters' wheels, beads,
lacemaking kits, etc. Send £3 for mail order
catalogue.

Ells & Farrier Ltd,
The Bead Shop,
5 Princes Street,
London W1.
(01 629 9964)
Beads, sequins.

Equality Fur Fabrics,
20 London Road,
Hemel Hempstead,
Herts.
(0442 64854)
Fur fabrics, toy components, ribbons, etc.

Fluffy Fabrics,
26 Tribune Drive,
Trinity Trading Estate,
Sittingbourne,
Kent.
(0795 78775)
Send £1 for samples of fur fabrics, felt, fleece,
polyester fillings etc. £2 credit against first order.

Fred Aldous Ltd,
P.O. Box 137,
37 Lever Street,
Manchester M60 1UX.
(061 2362477)
Send 20p for catalogue of all handicraft supplies
including soft toy and jewellery making
equipment.

Jenners Ltd.,
(Needlework Dept.),
Princes Street,
Edinburgh.
(031 225 2442)

Mace and Nairn,
89 Crane Street,
Salisbury,
Wilts SP1 2PY.

(0722 336903)
Embroidery fabrics, designs, transfers, threads,
lace-making supplies.

Margrave,
Heathmans Road,
London SW6 4TJ.
(01 731 0300)
Toy components, such as eyes, squeakers, joints,
etc.

Norfolk Lavender Ltd.,
Caley Mill,
Heacham,
Norfolk PE31 7JE.
(0485 70384)
Send s.a.e. for catalogue of lavender based
products and loose lavender.

Ries Wools at Holborn,
242-243 High Holborn,
London WC1V 7DZ.
(01 242 7721)
Knitting yarns, patterns, needles, etc.

The Embroidery Dept,
Liberty & Co.,
Regent Street,
London W1.
(01 734 1234)
Fabrics, threads, books, kits.

The Handweavers Studio and Gallery Ltd.,
29 Haroldstone Road,
London E17 7AN.
(01 521 2281)
Fibres, fleeces, yarns, equipment, books.

The Patchwork Dog and the Calico Cat,
21 Chalk Farm Road,
London NW1 8AG.
(01 485 1239)
Materials for patchwork and quilting, books.

Richmond Art and Craft,
181 City Road,
Cardiff CF2 3JB.
(0222 490119)

The Royal School of Needlework Shop,
25 Princes Gate,

Kensington,
London SW7 1QE.
(01 589 0077)
Embroidery fabrics and threads, embroidery kits,
books, lace-making supplies.

The Silver Thimble,
33 Gay Street,
Bath.
(0225 23457)
Embroidery fabrics and threads.

SPORTS ASSOCIATIONS

Amateur Athletic Association,
Francis House,
Francis Street,
London SW1.
(01 828 9326)

Amateur Boxing Association,
Francis House,
Francis Street,
London SW1.
(01 828 8571)

Amateur Fencing Association,
Perham Road,
London W14.
(01 385 7442)

Amateur Football Alliance,
6 Langley Street,
London WC2.
(01 240 3837)

Amateur Rowing Association,
6 Lower Mall,
London W6 9DJ.
(01 748 3632)

Amateur Swimming Association,
Harold Fern House,
Derby Square,
Loughborough,
Leics. LE11 0AL.
(0509 230431)

British Amateur Dancers Association,
14 Oxford Street,

London W1.
(01 636 0851)

British Cycling Federation,
16 Upper Woburn Place,
London WC1.
(01 387 9320)

British Field Sports Society,
59 Kennington Road,
London SE1.
(01 928 4742)

British Hang Gliding School,
15 St. Mary's Green,
Biggin Hill, Kent.
(0959 73996)

British Judo Association,
16 Upper Woburn Place,
London WC1.
(01 387 9340)

British Raquetball Association,
167 Ramsden Road,
London SW12.
(01 637 0432)

British Water Ski Federation,
16 Upper Woburn Place,
London WC1.
(01 388 2546)

English Table Tennis Association,
21 Claremont,
Hastings,
East Sussex TN34 1HF.
(0424 433121)

English Volleyball Association,
128 Melton Road,
West Bridgford,
Nottingham NG2 6EP.
(0602 816324)

Grand National Archery Society,
7th Street,
NAC Stoneleigh,
Kenilworth,
Warwickshire CV8 2LG.
(0203 23907)

Index